MW01287477

This stimulating collection of essays in ethics addresses everyday moral issues, examines alternative responses to them, and explores the deeper theoretical questions which they raise. The essays focus especially on attitudes, virtues, and vices that are important to personal relationships and to how one views oneself. The primary aim is not to refine abstract theories but to understand the competing values that underlie dissatisfaction with oversimple answers produced by "applying" various theories. Among the issues are: Is it wrong to tell a lie to protect someone from a painful truth? Can one be both autonomous and compassionate? Other topics discussed are servility, weakness of will, suicide, obligations to oneself, snobbery, environmental ethics, and affirmative action. A feature of the collection is the contrast of Kantian and utilitarian answers to these problems.

"The book would be an invaluable accompaniment to Kant's own texts in a Kant's ethics course and it would make a much more interesting main text than one can usually get in a practical ethics course."

Christine Korsgaard, University of Chicago

Autonomy and self-respect

Autonomy and self-respect

THOMAS E. HILL, JR.
The University of North Carolina at Chapel Hill

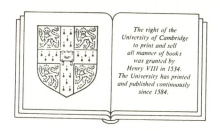

*The right of the
University of Cambridge
to print and sell
all manner of books
was granted by
Henry VIII in 1534.
The University has printed
and published continuously
since 1584.*

CAMBRIDGE UNIVERSITY PRESS

CAMBRIDGE

NEW YORK   PORT CHESTER   MELBOURNE   SYDNEY

Murray Learning Resources Center
WITHDRAWN
PA 17027

Published by the Press Syndicate of the University of Cambridge
The Pitt Building, Trumpington Street, Cambridge CB2 IRP
40 West 20th Street, New York, NY 10011-4211, USA
10 Stamford Road, Oakleigh, Victoria 3166, Australia

© Cambridge University Press 1991

First published 1991
Reprinted 1992

Printed in the United States of America

Library of Congress Cataloging-in-Publication Data

Hill, Thomas E.
Autonomy and self-respect / Thomas E. Hill, Jr.
p. cm.
Includes index.
ISBN 0-521-39464-3 (hard). – ISBN 0-521-39772-3 (pbk.)
1. Self-respect.   2. Autonomy (Philosophy) I. Title.
BJ1533.S3H55   1991   91-6990
179'.9–dc20   CIP

British Library Cataloging-in-Publication Data applied for

ISBN 0-521-39464-3 hardback
ISBN 0-521-39772-3 paperback

Contents

Sources and acknowledgments

Three of my essays included in this volume appear for the first time, and ten are reprinted, with minor editing, from prior publications. I gratefully acknowledge the following for the permission to reprint my essays.

1. "Servility and Self-Respect." Copyright 1973, *The Monist,* La Salle, Illinois 61301. Reprinted by permission.

2. "Self-Respect Reconsidered" originally appeared in *Tulane Studies in Philosophy,* vol. 31 (1983), pp. 129–37, and is reprinted here by permission of the publisher.

3. "Autonomy and Benevolent Lies" was first printed in *The Journal of Value Inquiry,* vol. 18 (1984), pp. 251–67. It is reprinted by permission of the publisher.

4. "The Importance of Autonomy" was originally published in *Women and Moral Theory.* Edited by E. F. Kittay and D. T. Meyers (Rowman and Littlefield, 1987), pp. 129–38. It is reprinted here by permission of the publisher.

5. "Symbolic Protest and Calculated Silence" was originally published by Princeton University Press in *Philosophy and Public Affairs.* It is reprinted by permission of Princeton University Press.

6. "Moral Purity and the Lesser Evil." Copyright 1983, *The Monist,* La Salle, Illinois 61301. Reprinted by permission.

7. "Self-Regarding Suicide: A Modified Kantian View" was originally published by Human Sciences Press Incorporated in *Suicide and Life-Threatening Behavior,* vol. 13, no. 4 (1983). It is reprinted by permission of the publisher.

8. "Ideals of Human Excellence and Preserving the Natural Environment" was first published in *Environmental Ethics,* vol. 5 (1983), pp. 211–24, and is reprinted here by permission of the publisher.

9. "Weakness of Will and Character" originally appeared in *Philosophical Topics,* vol. XIV, no. 2 (Fall 1986) and is reprinted by permission of the publisher.

10. "The Message of Affirmative Action" was originally published by *Philosophy and Social Policy* (1991). It is reprinted here by permission of the publisher.

The three remaining essays were not previously published: these are "Promises to Oneself," "Pains and Projects: Justifying to Oneself," and "Social Snobbery and Human Dignity." The order of presentation of these essays with the others was influenced more by topic than by the time of writing. An early version of "Promises to Oneself" in fact was the first essay written, and "Social Snobbery and Human Dignity" was the last.

During the period in which the essays selected for this volume were written I received financial and other institutional support from the University of California, Los Angeles (1968–84), the National Endowment for the Humanities (1972–73), the National Humanities Center (1982–83), and the University of North Carolina, Chapel Hill (1984–1991). This support is gratefully acknowledged.

Philosophy is, and ought to be, a cooperative venture in which one builds on others' ideas, learns from their criticisms and suggestions, and takes heart from their interest and encouragement. Over the years I have been extraordinarily fortunate in the help I have had from teachers, colleagues, students, friends, and family.

My first and deepest debt is to my mother and father who provided unfailing support in all my projects. My father first inspired my academic interests and introduced me to philosophy, and he continues to be an invaluable friend and philosophical colleague. My mother, a teacher of mathematics and physics, lived a life with grace, sensitivity, and courage, exemplifying the sort of ideals that moral philosophy at its best aspires to understand. Another early debt is to teachers at Harvard and Oxford, especially to my advisors at different periods, Raphael Demos, Roderick Firth, Gilbert Ryle, and John Rawls.

More recently I gained much from colleagues and students at the University of California, Los Angeles, especially from participants in the Moral and Political Philosophy Discussion Group started by Arnold Kaufman. Particularly helpful regarding the earlier papers in this collection were Robert Merrihew Adams, Sharon Bishop, Bernard Boxill, Jean Hampton, Gregory Kavka, Herbert Morris, Warren Quinn, and Richard Wasserstrom. I am grateful to Sharon Bishop for both personal and philosophical help. Much of my thinking about autonomy and sexism was stimulated and importantly influenced by her ideas. During my year at the National Humanities Center at the Research Triangle Park, North Carolina, I had valuable discussions with Stephen Darwall, Gerald Postema, Gregory Trianosky, Larry Thomas, Lance Stell, and Carl Wellman. My almost daily dialogues with Stell about autonomy, and other matters, were particularly helpful and have not yet been adequately acknowledged.

Discussions with my colleagues and students at the University of North Carolina at Chapel Hill have also been stimulating. I am grateful to several people, at Chapel Hill and elsewhere, for extensive comments on various drafts of later papers. These include Michael Bratman, Bernard Boxill, Christine Korsgaard,

SOURCES AND ACKNOWLEDGMENTS

William Lycan, Geoffrey Sayre McCord, Gerald Postema, Gregory Trianosky, David Schmidtz, and William Williams. Participants in discussions at the various universities and colleges where these papers were presented have also contributed usefully. Thanks are due to the participants of the Triangle Ethics Group, including colleagues at Chapel Hill, philosophers from neighboring universities and colleges, and especially David Falk, who is the host, founder, and inspiration of the group.

Geoffrey Sayre McCord first encouraged me to publish these papers as a collection, and I am grateful for his help. Thanks are also due to Claire Miller, Gucki Obler, and Kathy Sauls for staff support, to Carolyn Viola-John for her editing, and to Karánn Durland for her editing, handling permission letters, and doing the index.

Most of all I am grateful to Robin for her constant support and for giving my life new zest and meaning.

Introduction

These essays concern moral questions that virtually everyone faces in daily life, not specialized topics that arise only in the particular professions or in academic philosophical debates. Discussion typically begins with specific cases. Some are dramatic, and others quite familiar; but all of the examples raise recurring moral perplexities. Though practically important and theoretically interesting, many of these issues have been relatively neglected in recent philosophical literature.

Work on large scale moral problems such as nuclear war, famine, distributive justice, punishment, population control, and animal rights has been important and should continue, but here I focus primarily on moral attitudes, virtues, and vices that are especially important to personal relations and to how one views oneself. Philosophical works that address these last issues are not so common, and typically they start from an antecedent commitment to a particular ethical theory, such as utilitarianism or Thomism. In contrast, I raise the issues by describing concrete examples and exploring a variety of alternative perspectives, always seeking to articulate the ideals and principles that lie behind dissatisfaction with the answers generated by "applying" familiar theories. The positions that I explore are often "Kantian" in spirit, but there is no attempt here to do textual exegesis or to crank out solutions from Kant's theory.

My topics range widely, but there are common themes. The opening essays deal explicitly with the requirements of self-respect, one arguing that servility is incompatible with a certain ideal of self-respect and the other calling attention to the demands of a further conception of self-respect. Respect is often grounded in autonomy, and the next two papers attempt to clarify the idea of autonomy, how it opposes benevolent lies, and whether it is compatible with compassion. A further pair of essays raise the question whether a self-respecting person has reason to resist the pragmatic responses to evil, e.g., protesting only when protest would be effective and doing a "lesser evil" to prevent a greater one.

Other-regarding considerations often dominate discussions of suicide, but in "Self-Regarding Suicide" I ask, under what circumstances, if any, would a proper respect for oneself as an autonomous agent permit suicide? The next essay explores another way in which ideals of character may call for more than concern for the rights and welfare of other human beings. A proper humility regarding one's place in nature also seems important as we face environmental problems, though it is not easy to explain why this should be so. Because weakness of will threatens both autonomy and self-respect, I then raise the question whether the weak-willed person suffers from a psychological incapacity or defect of character. This poses the more general puzzle taken up in the subsequent essay, namely, in what sense could one have obligations *to oneself*, and what could ground such obligations? The essay on snobbery considers whether superior merit can ever warrant contempt for others. By failing to acknowledge an ideal of respect for all persons, I suggest, snobs may undervalue themselves as well as others.

The final two essays shift attention to quite different sorts of issues. In "Pains and Projects" I raise a fundamental issue of justification: how, apart from other-regarding moral concerns, can we reasonably justify to ourselves our own ultimate ends? Even in addressing this question, I suggest, we may view autonomy as a welcome freedom and self-respect as a necessary constraint. In the final essay I review several perspectives on affirmative action in public universities. Though addressing a complex social issue, my suggestion is (again) that exclusive attention to rights and welfare is not enough. The symbolic message of affirmative action is also important, and what needs to be expressed is an ideal of mutual respect more commonly understood within personal relationships.

These essays are intended for students and general readers as well as for professional philosophers. They are nontechnical in style and, for the most part, focused on specific examples of types of problems that occur in everyday life. The approach is meant to be exploratory, inviting readers to search for the principles behind their initial intuitive judgments, in contrast to the more common method of "applied ethics," which seeks to derive answers from antecedently given principles or theories.

Underlying the specific issues, however, are fundamental questions that are of interest to any moral philosopher. For example, are there viable alternatives to consequentialism outside the theory of justice? Is morality entirely other-regarding? Is there a coherent idea of "obligations to oneself"? Is it objectionable to regard the natural environment as merely a resource for human beings? Are autonomy and self-respect the ground of moral requirements? Are attitudes good or bad depending entirely upon the acts and consequences to which they lead?

Though I have little doubt that the *topics* here will be of wide interest, I also hope that my manner of approaching these issues will be found helpful. Good philosophy, I am convinced, typically starts with genuine puzzlement. In ethics a persistent source of genuine perplexity, for those who reflect with an open mind, is the conflict between strongly felt intuitive judgments about specific cases and the implications of the general moral theories that have been developed so far. Intuitions are not sacred; they need to be subjected to critical scrutiny. But moral theories are not sacred either; at best they are commendable efforts to simplify and generalize over a rich and often bewilderingly complex variety of responses to recurrent human situations. Some progress can be made by comparing existing theories and modifying them upon rational reflection on their grounds as well as their implications for concrete cases. But there is also, I think, a need to do moral philosophy "from the bottom up," i.e., from cases to theory. This is what most of my essays attempt to do in a preliminary way.

Instead of starting with an antecedently defined theory, the idea is to focus on selected examples that pose sharply a moral perplexity. The sort of perplexity most fruitful to examine is not, as in Sartre's famous case of the resistance worker, a tension generated by the conflict of two important but rather well-understood moral ideals. It is rather the perplexity that arises when obvious and familiar moral considerations, e.g., utility, conflict with strongly felt but as yet vaguely articulated ideals. The job of articulating such ideals, in my opinion, is a necessary preliminary to further useful generalization in ethical theory. My guiding principle in selecting cases for my papers, then, is not to focus on the most immediately urgent or emotionally wrenching problems, nor is it to survey all considerations morally relevant to a larger issue. Rather the aim is to isolate moral perplexities of a special kind, namely, those that may help us to clarify certain ideals that are strongly felt but still inadequately understood and too often overlooked in familiar moral theories.

I

Servility and self-respect

Several motives underlie this paper.[1] In the first place, I am curious to see if there is a legitimate source for the increasingly common feeling that servility can be as much a vice as arrogance. There seems to be something morally defective about the Uncle Tom and the submissive housewife; and yet, on the other hand, if the only interests they sacrifice are their own, it seems that we should have no right to complain. Secondly, I have some sympathy for the now unfashionable view that each person has duties to himself as well as to others. It does seem absurd to say that a person could literally violate his own rights or owe himself a debt of gratitude, but I suspect that the classic defenders of duties to oneself had something different in mind. If there are duties to oneself, it is natural to expect that a duty to avoid being servile would have a prominent place among them. Thirdly, I am interested in making sense of Kant's puzzling, but suggestive, remarks about respect for persons and respect for the moral law. On the usual reading, these remarks seem unduly moralistic; but, viewed in another way, they suggest an argument for a kind of self-respect which is incompatible with a servile attitude.

My procedure will not be to explicate Kant directly. Instead I shall try to isolate the defect of servility and sketch an argument to show why it is objectionable, noting only in passing how this relates to Kant and the controversy about duties to oneself. What I say about self-respect is far from the whole story. In particular, it is not concerned with esteem for one's special abilities and achievements or with the self-confidence which characterizes the especially autonomous person. Nor is my concern with the psychological antecedents and effects of self-respect. Nevertheless, my conclusions, if correct, should be of interest; for they imply that, given a common view of morality, there are nonutilitarian moral reasons for each person, regardless of his merits, to respect himself. To avoid servility to the extent that one can is not simply a right but a duty, not simply a duty to others but a duty to oneself.

1   An earlier version of this paper was presented at the meetings of the American Philosophical Association, Pacific Division. A number of revisions have been made as a result of the helpful comments of others, especially Norman Dahl, Sharon Hill, Herbert Morris, and Mary Mothersill.

I

Three examples may give a preliminary idea of what I mean by *servility*. Consider, first, an extremely deferential black, whom I shall call the *Uncle Tom*. He always steps aside for white men; he does not complain when less qualified whites take over his job; he gratefully accepts whatever benefits his all-white government and employers allot him, and he would not think of protesting its insufficiency. He displays the symbols of deference to whites, and of contempt towards blacks: he faces the former with bowed stance and a ready "sir" and "Ma'am"; he reserves his strongest obscenities for the latter. Imagine, too, that he is not playing a game. He is not the shrewdly prudent calculator, who knows how to make the best of a bad lot and mocks his masters behind their backs. He accepts without question the idea that, as a black, he is owed less than whites. He may believe that blacks are mentally inferior and of less social utility, but that is not the crucial point. The attitude which he displays is that what he values, aspires for, and can demand is of less importance than what whites value, aspire for, and can demand. He is far from the picture book's carefree, happy servant, but he does not feel that he has a right to expect anything better.

Another pattern of servility is illustrated by a person I shall call the *Self-Deprecator*. Like the Uncle Tom, he is reluctant to make demands. He says nothing when others take unfair advantage of him. When asked for his preferences or opinions, he tends to shrink away as if what he said should make no difference. His problem, however, is not a sense of racial inferiority but rather an acute awareness of his own inadequacies and failures as an individual. These defects are not imaginary: he has in fact done poorly by his own standards and others'. But, unlike many of us in the same situation, he acts as if his failings warrant quite unrelated maltreatment even by strangers. His sense of shame and self-contempt make him content to be the instrument of others. He feels that nothing is owed him until he has earned it and that he has earned very little. He is not simply playing a masochist's game of winning sympathy by disparaging himself. On the contrary, he assesses his individual merits with painful accuracy.

A rather different case is that of the *Deferential Wife*. This is a woman who is utterly devoted to serving her husband. She buys the clothes *he* prefers, invites the guests *he* wants to entertain, and makes love whenever *he* is in the mood. She willingly moves to a new city in order for him to have a more attractive job, counting her own friendships and geographical preferences insignificant by comparison. She loves her husband, but her conduct is not simply an expression of love. She is happy, but she does not subordinate herself as a means to happiness. She does not simply defer to her husband in certain spheres as a trade-off for his deference in other spheres. On the contrary, she tends not to form her own interests, values, and ideals; and, when she does, she counts them as less important than her husband's. She readily responds to appeals from Women's Liberation that she agrees that women are mentally and physically equal, if not superior, to men. She just believes that the proper role for a woman is to serve her family. As a matter of fact, much of her happiness derives from her belief that she fulfills this role very well. No one is trampling on her rights, she says; for she is quite glad, and proud, to serve her husband as she does.

Each one of these cases reflects the attitude which I call servility.[2] It betrays the absence of a certain kind of self-respect. What I take this attitude to be, more specifically, will become clearer later on. It is important at the outset, however, not to confuse the three cases sketched above with other, superficially similar cases. In particular, the cases I have sketched are not simply cases in which someone refuses to press his rights, speaks disparagingly of himself, or devotes himself to another. A black, for example, is not necessarily servile because he does not demand a just wage; for, seeing that such a demand would result in his being fired, he might forbear for the sake of his children. A self-critical person is not necessarily servile by virtue of bemoaning his faults in public; for his behavior may be merely a complex way of satisfying his own inner needs quite independent of a willingness to accept abuse from others. A woman need not be servile whenever she works to make her husband happy and prosperous; for she might freely and knowingly choose to do so from love or from a desire to share the rewards of his success. If the effort did not require her to submit to humiliation or maltreatment, her choice would not mark her as servile. There may, of course, be grounds for objecting to the attitudes in these cases, but the defect is not servility of the sort I want to consider. It should also be noted that my cases of servility are not simply instances of deference to superior knowledge or judgment. To defer to an expert's judgment on matters of fact is not to be servile; to defer to his every wish and whim is. Similarly, the belief that one's talents and achievements are comparatively low does not, by itself, make one servile. It is no vice to acknowledge the truth, and one may in fact have achieved less, and have less ability, than others. To be servile is not simply to hold certain empirical beliefs but to have a certain attitude concerning one's rightful place in a moral community.

II

Are there grounds for regarding the attitudes of the Uncle Tom, the Self-Deprecator, and the Deferential Wife as morally objectionable? Are there moral

2 Each of the cases is intended to represent only one possible pattern of servility. I make no claims about how often these patterns are exemplified, nor do I mean to imply that only these patterns could warrant the labels "Deferential Wife," "Uncle Tom," etc. All the more, I do not mean to imply any comparative judgments about the causes or relative magnitude of the problems of racial and sexual discrimination. One person, e.g., a self-contemptuous woman with a sense of racial inferiority, might exemplify features of several patterns at once; and, of course, a person might view her being a woman the way an Uncle Tom views his being black, etc.

arguments we could give them to show that they ought to have more self-respect? None of the more obvious replies is entirely satisfactory.

One might, in the first place, adduce utilitarian considerations. Typically the servile person will be less happy than he might be. Moreover, he may be less prone to make the best of his own socially useful abilities. He may become a nuisance to others by being overly dependent. He will, in any case, lose the special contentment that comes from standing up for one's rights. A submissive attitude encourages exploitation, and exploitation spreads misery in a variety of ways. These considerations provide a prima facie case against the attitudes of the Uncle Tom, the Deferential Wife, and the Self-Deprecator, but they are hardly conclusive. Other utilities tend to counterbalance the ones just mentioned. When people refuse to press their rights, there are usually others who profit. There are undeniable pleasures in associating with those who are devoted, understanding, and grateful for whatever we see fit to give them — as our fondness for dogs attests. Even the servile person may find his attitude a source of happiness, as the case of the Deferential Wife illustrates. There may be comfort and security in thinking that the hard choices must be made by others, that what I would say has little to do with what ought to be done. Self-condemnation may bring relief from the pangs of guilt even if it is not deliberately used for that purpose. On balance, then, utilitarian considerations may turn out to favor servility as much as they oppose it.

For those who share my moral intuitions, there is another sort of reason for not trying to rest a case against servility on utilitarian considerations. Certain utilities seem irrelevant to the issue. The utilitarian must weigh them along with others, but to do so seems morally inappropriate. Suppose, for example, that the submissive attitudes of the Uncle Tom and the Deferential Wife result in positive utilities for those who dominate and exploit them. Do we need to tabulate *these* utilities before conceding that servility is objectionable? The Uncle Tom, it seems, is making an error, a moral error, quite apart from consideration of how much others in fact profit from his attitude. The Deferential Wife may be quite happy; but if her happiness turns out to be contingent on her distorted view of her own rights and worth as a person, then it carries little moral weight against the contention that she ought to change that view. Suppose I could cause a woman to find her happiness in denying all her rights and serving my every wish. No doubt I could do so only by nonrational manipulative techniques, which I ought not to use. But is this the only objection? My efforts would be wrong, it seems, not only because of the techniques they require but also because the resultant attitude is itself objectionable. When a person's happiness stems from a morally objectionable attitude, it ought to be discounted. That a sadist gets pleasure from seeing others suffer should not count even as a partial justification for his attitude. That a servile person derives pleasure from denying her moral status, for similar reasons, cannot make her attitude acceptable. These brief intuitive remarks are not intended as a refutation of utilitarianism, with all its many varieties, but they do suggest that it is well to look elsewhere for adequate grounds for rejecting the attitudes of the Uncle Tom, the Self-Deprecator, and the Deferential Wife.

One might try to appeal to meritarian considerations. That is, one might argue that the servile person *deserves* more than he allows himself. This line of argument, however, is no more adequate than the utilitarian one. It may be wrong to deny others what they deserve, but it is not so obviously wrong to demand less for oneself than one deserves. In any case, the Self-Deprecator's problem is not that he underestimates his merits. By hypothesis, he assesses his merits quite accurately. We cannot reasonably tell him to have more respect for himself because he *deserves* more respect; he knows that he has not *earned* better treatment. His problem, in fact, is that he thinks of his moral status with regard to others as entirely dependent upon his merits. His interests and choices are important, he feels, only if he has earned the right to make demands; or if he had rights by birth, they were forfeited by his subsequent failures and misdeeds. My Self-Deprecator is no doubt an atypical person, but nevertheless he illustrates an important point. Normally when we find a self-contemptuous person, we can plausibly argue that he is not so bad as he thinks, that his self-contempt is an overreaction prompted more by inner needs than by objective assessment of his merits. Because this argument cannot work with the Self-Deprecator, his case draws attention to a distinction, applicable in other cases as well, between saying that someone deserves respect for his merits and saying that he is owed respect as a person. On meritarian grounds we can only say "You deserve better than this," but the defect of the servile person is not merely failure to recognize his merits.

Other common arguments against the Uncle Tom, et al., may have some force but seem not to strike to the heart of the problem. For example, philosophers sometimes appeal to the value of human potentialities. As a human being, it is said, one at least has a capacity for rationality, morality, excellence, or autonomy, and this capacity is worthy of respect. Although such arguments have the merit of making respect independent of a person's actual deserts, they seem quite misplaced in some cases. There comes a time when we have sufficient evidence that a person is not ever going to *be* rational, moral, excellent, or autonomous even if he still has a capacity, in some sense, for being so. As a person approaches death with an atrocious record so far, the chances of his realizing his diminishing capacities become increasingly slim. To make these capacities the basis of his self-respect is to rest it on a shifting and unstable ground. We do, of course, respect persons for capacities which they are not exercising at the moment; for example, I might respect a person as a good philosopher even though he is just now blundering into gross confusion. In these cases, however, we respect the person for an active capacity, a ready disposition, which he had displayed on many occasions. On this analogy, a person should have respect for himself only when his capacities are developed and ready, needing only to be triggered by an appropriate occasion or the removal of some temporary obstacle. The Uncle Tom and the Deferential Wife, however, may in fact have quite limited capacities of this sort, and, since the Self-Deprecator is already overly concerned with his own inadequacies, drawing attention to his capacities seems a poor way to increase his self-respect. In any case, setting aside the Kantian nonempirical capacity for autonomy, the capacities of different persons vary widely; but what the servile person seems to overlook is something by virtue of which he is equal with every other person.

III

Why, then, is servility a moral defect? There is, I think, another sort of answer which is worth exploring. The first part of this answer must be an attempt to isolate the objectionable features of the servile person; later we can ask why these features are objectionable. As a step in this direction, let us examine again our three paradigm cases. The moral defect in each case, I suggest, is a failure to understand and acknowledge one's own moral rights. I assume, without argument here, that each person has moral rights.[3] Some of these rights may be basic human rights; that is, rights for which a person needs only to be human to qualify. Other rights will be derivative and contingent upon his special commitments, institutional affiliations, etc. Most rights will be prima facie ones; some may be absolute. Most can be waived under appropriate conditions; perhaps some cannot. Many rights can be forfeited; but some, presumably, cannot. The servile person does not, strictly speaking, violate his own rights. At least in our paradigm cases he fails to acknowledge fully his own moral status because he does not fully understand what his rights are, how they can be waived, and when they can be forfeited.

The defect of the Uncle Tom, for example, is that he displays an attitude that denies his moral equality with whites. He does not realize, or apprehend in an effective way, that he has as much right to a decent wage and a share of political power as any comparable white. His gratitude is misplaced; he accepts benefits which are his by right as if they were gifts. The Self-Deprecator is servile in a more complex way. He acts as if he has forfeited many important rights which in fact he has not. He does not understand, or fully realize in his own case, that certain rights to fair and decent treatment do not have to be earned. He sees his

---

3 As will become evident, I am also presupposing some form of cognitive or "naturalistic" interpretation of rights. If, to accommodate an emotivist or prescriptivist, we set aside talk of moral knowledge and ignorance, we might construct a somewhat analogous case against servility from the point of view of those who adopt principles ascribing rights to all; but the argument, I suspect, would be more complex and less persuasive.

merits clearly enough, but he fails to see that what he can expect from others is not merely a function of his merits. The Deferential Wife *says* that she understands her rights vis-à-vis her husband, but what she fails to appreciate is that her consent to serve him is a valid waiver of her rights only under certain conditions. If her consent is coerced, say, by the lack of viable options for women in her society, then her consent is worth little. If socially fostered ignorance of her own talents and alternatives is responsible for her consent, then her consent should not count as a fully legitimate waiver of her right to equal consideration within the marriage. All the more, her consent to defer constantly to her husband is not a legitimate setting aside of her rights if it results from her mistaken belief that she has a moral duty to do so. (Recall: "The *proper* role for a woman is to serve her family.") If she believes that she has a *duty* to defer to her husband, then, whatever she may say, she cannot fully understand that she has a *right* not to defer to him. When she says that she freely gives up such a right, she is confused. Her confusion is rather like that of a person who has been persuaded by an unscrupulous lawyer that it is legally incumbent on him to refuse a jury trial but who nevertheless tells the judge that he understands that he has a right to a jury trial and freely waives it. He does not really understand what it is to have and freely give up the right if he thinks that it would be an offense for him to exercise it.

Insofar as servility results from moral ignorance or confusion, it need not be something for which a person is to blame. Even self-reproach may be inappropriate; for at the time a person is in ignorance he cannot feel guilty about his servility, and later he may conclude that his ignorance was unavoidable. In some cases, however, a person might reasonably believe that he should have known better. If, for example, the Deferential Wife's confusion about her rights resulted from a motivated resistance to drawing the implications of her own basic moral principles, then later she might find some ground for self-reproach. Whether blameworthy or not, servility could still be morally objectionable at least in the sense that it ought to be discouraged, that social conditions which nourish it should be reformed, and the like. Not all morally undesirable features of a person are ones for which he is responsible, but that does not mean that they are defects merely from an aesthetic or prudential point of view.

In our paradigm cases, I have suggested, servility is a kind of deferential attitude towards others resulting from ignorance or misunderstanding of one's moral rights. A sufficient remedy, one might think, would be moral enlightenment. Suppose, however, that our servile persons come to know their rights but do not substantially alter their behavior. Are they not still servile in an objectionable way? One might even think that reproach is more appropriate now because they know what they are doing.

The problem, unfortunately, is not as simple as it may appear. Much depends on what they tolerate and why. Let us set aside cases in which a person merely

10

refuses to *fight* for his rights, chooses not to exercise certain rights, or freely waives many rights which he might have insisted upon. Our problem concerns the previously servile person who continues to display the same marks of deference even after he fully knows his rights. Imagine, for example, that even after enlightenment our Uncle Tom persists in his old pattern of behavior, giving all the typical signs of believing that the injustices done to him are not really wrong. Suppose, too, that the newly enlightened Deferential Wife continues to defer to her husband, refusing to disturb the old way of life by introducing her new ideas. She acts as if she accepts the idea that she is merely doing her duty though actually she no longer believes it. Let us suppose, further, that the Uncle Tom and the Deferential Wife are not merely generous with their time and property; they also accept without protest, and even appear to sanction, treatment which is humiliating and degrading. That is, they do not simply consent to waive mutually acknowledged rights; they tolerate violations of their rights with apparent approval. They pretend to give their permission for subtle humiliations which they really believe no permission can make legitimate. Are such persons still servile despite their moral knowledge?

The answer, I think, should depend upon why the deferential role is played. If the motive is a morally commendable one, or a desire to avert dire consequences to oneself, or even an ambition to set an oppressor up for a later fall, then I would not count the role player as servile. The Uncle Tom, for instance, is not servile in my sense if he shuffles and bows to keep the Klan from killing his children, to save his own skin, or even to buy time while he plans the revolution. Similarly, the Deferential Wife is not servile if she tolerates an abusive husband because he is so ill that further strain would kill him, because protesting would deprive her of her only means of survival, or because she is collecting atrocity stories for her book against marriage. If there is fault in these situations, it seems inappropriate to call it *servility*. The story is quite different, however, if a person continues in his deferential role just from laziness, timidity, or a desire for some minor advantage. He shows too little concern for his moral status as a person, one is tempted to say, if he is willing to deny it for a small profit or simply because it requires some effort and courage to affirm it openly. A black who plays the Uncle Tom merely to gain an advantage over other blacks is harming them, of course; but he is also displaying disregard for his own moral position as an equal among human beings. Similarly, a woman throws away her rights too lightly if she continues to play the subservient role because she is used to it or is too timid to risk a change. A Self-Deprecator who readily accepts what he knows are violations of his rights may be indulging his peculiar need for punishment at the expense of denying something more valuable. In these cases, I suggest, we have a kind of servility independent of any ignorance or confusion about one's rights. The person who has it may or may not be blameworthy, depending on many factors; and the line between servile and nonservile role playing will often be hard to draw. Nevertheless, the objectionable feature is perhaps clear enough for present purposes: it is a willingness to disavow one's moral status, publicly and systematically, in the absence of any strong reason to do so.

My proposal, then, is that there are at least two types of servility: one resulting from misunderstanding of one's rights and the other from placing a comparatively low value on them. In either case, servility manifests the absence of a certain kind of self-respect. The respect which is missing is not respect for one's merits but respect for one's rights. The servile person displays this absence of respect not directly by acting contrary to his own rights but indirectly by acting as if his rights were nonexistent or insignificant. An arrogant person ignores the rights of others, thereby arrogating for himself a higher status than he is entitled to; a servile person denies his own rights, thereby assuming a lower position than he is entitled to. Whether rooted in ignorance or simply lack of concern for moral rights, the attitudes in both cases may be incompatible with a proper regard for morality. That this is so is obvious in the case of arrogance, but to see it in the case of servility requires some further argument.

IV

The objectionable feature of the servile person, as I have described him, is his tendency to disavow his own moral rights either because he misunderstands them or because he cares little for them. The question remains: why should anyone regard this as a moral defect? After all, the rights which he denies are his own. He may be unfortunate, foolish, or even distasteful; but why *morally* deficient? One sort of answer, quite different from those reviewed earlier, is suggested by some of Kant's remarks. Kant held that servility is contrary to a perfect non-juridical duty to oneself.[4] To say that the duty is perfect is roughly to say that it is stringent, never overridden by other considerations (e.g., beneficence). To say that the duty is nonjuridical is to say that a person cannot legitimately be coerced to comply. Although Kant did not develop an explicit argument for this view, an argument can easily be constructed from materials which reflect the spirit, if not the letter, of his moral theory. The argument which I have in mind is prompted by Kant's contention that respect for persons, strictly speaking, is respect for the moral law.[5] If taken as a claim about all sorts of respect, this

---

4 See Immanuel Kant, *The Doctrine of Virtue,* Part II of *The Metaphysics of Morals,* ed. by Mary J. Gregor (New York: Harper & Row, 1964), pp. 99–103; Prussian Academy edition, Vol. VI, pp. 434–7.

5 Immanuel Kant, *Groundwork of the Metaphysic of Morals,* ed. by H. J. Paton (New York: Harper & Row, 1964), p. 69; Prussian Academy edition, Vol. IV, p. 401; *The Critique of Practical Reason,* ed. by Lewis W. Beck (New York: Bobbs-Merrill, 1956), pp. 81, 84; Prussian Academy edition, Vol. V, pp. 78, 81. My purpose here is not to interpret what Kant meant but to give a sense to his remark.

seems quite implausible. If it means that we respect persons only for their moral character, their capacity for moral conduct, or their status as "authors" of the moral law, then it seems unduly moralistic. My strategy is to construe the remark as saying that at least one sort of respect for persons is respect for the rights which the moral law accords them. If one respects the moral law, then one must respect one's own moral rights; and this amounts to having a kind of self-respect incompatible with servility.

The premises for the Kantian argument, which are all admittedly vague, can be sketched as follows:

First, let us assume, as Kant did, that all human beings have equal basic human rights. Specific rights vary with different conditions, but all must be justified from a point of view under which all are equal. Not all rights need to be earned, and some cannot be forfeited. Many rights can be waived but only under certain conditions of knowledge and freedom. These conditions are complex and difficult to state; but they include something like the condition that a person's consent releases others from obligation only if it is autonomously given, and consent resulting from underestimation of one's moral status is not autonomously given. Rights can be objects of knowledge, but also of ignorance, misunderstanding, deception, and the like.

Second, let us assume that my account of servility is correct; or, if one prefers, we can take it as a definition. That is, in brief, a servile person is one who tends to deny or disavow his own moral rights because he does not understand them or has little concern for the status they give him.

Third, we need one formal premise concerning moral duty, namely, that each person ought, as far as possible, to respect the moral law. In less Kantian language, the point is that everyone should approximate, to the extent that he can, the ideal of a person who fully adopts the moral point of view. Roughly, this means not only that each person ought to do what is morally required and refrain from what is morally wrong but also that each person should treat all the provisions of morality as valuable – worth preserving and prizing as well as obeying. One must, so to speak, take up the spirit of morality as well as meet the letter of its requirements. To keep one's promises, avoid hurting others, and the like, is not sufficient; one should also take an attitude of respect towards the principles, ideals, and goals of morality. A respectful attitude towards a system of rights and duties consists of more than a disposition to conform to its definite rules of behavior; it also involves holding the system in esteem, being unwilling to ridicule it, and being reluctant to give up one's place in it. The essentially Kantian idea here is that morality, as a system of equal fundamental rights and duties, is worthy of respect, and hence a completely moral person would respect it in word and manner as well as in deed. And what a completely moral person would do, in Kant's view, is our duty to do so far as we can.

The assumptions here are, of course, strong ones, and I make no attempt to justify them. They are, I suspect, widely held though rarely articulated. In any case, my present purpose is not to evaluate them but to see how, if granted, they constitute a case against servility. The objection to the servile person, given our premises, is that he does not satisfy the basic requirement to respect morality. A person who fully respected a system of moral rights would be disposed to learn his proper place in it, to affirm it proudly, and not to tolerate abuses of it lightly. This is just the sort of disposition that the servile person lacks. If he does not understand the system, he is in no position to respect it adequately. This lack of respect may be no fault of his own, but it is still a way in which he falls short of a moral ideal. If, on the other hand, the servile person knowingly disavows his moral rights by pretending to approve of violations of them, then, barring special explanations, he shows an indifference to whether the provisions of morality are honored and publicly acknowledged. This avoidable display of indifference, by our Kantian premises, is contrary to the duty to respect morality. The disrespect in this second case is somewhat like the disrespect a religious believer might show towards his religion if, to avoid embarrassment, he laughed congenially while nonbelievers were mocking the beliefs which he secretly held. In any case, the servile person, as such, does not express disrespect for the system of moral rights in the obvious way by violating the rights of others. His lack of respect is more subtly manifested by his acting before others as if he did not know or care about his position of equality under that system.

The central idea here may be illustrated by an analogy. Imagine a club, say, an old German dueling fraternity. By the rules of the club, each member has certain rights and responsibilities. These are the same for each member regardless of what titles he may hold outside the club. Each has, for example, a right to be heard at meetings, a right not to be shouted down by the others. Some rights cannot be forfeited: for example, each may vote regardless of whether he has paid his dues and satisfied other rules. Some rights cannot be waived: for example, the right to be defended when attacked by several members of the rival fraternity. The members show respect for each other by respecting the status which the rules confer on each member. Now one new member is careful always to allow the others to speak at meetings; but when they shout him down, he does nothing. He just shrugs as if to say, 'Who am I to complain?' When he fails to stand up in defense of a fellow member, he feels ashamed and refuses to vote. He does not deserve to vote, he says. As the only commoner among illustrious barons, he feels that it is his place to serve them and defer to their decisions. When attackers from the rival fraternity come at him with swords drawn, he tells his companions to run and save themselves. When they defend him, he expresses immense gratitude – as if they had done him a gratuitous favor. Now one might argue that our new member fails to show respect for the fraternity and its rules. He does not actually violate any of the rules by refusing to vote, asking others not to defend him, and deferring to the barons, but he symbolically disavows the equal status which the rules confer on him. If he ought to have respect for the fraternity, he ought to change his attitude. Our servile person, then, is like the new member of the dueling fraternity in having insufficient respect for a system of rules and ideals. The difference is that everyone ought to respect morality whereas there is no comparable moral requirement to respect the fraternity.

The conclusion here is, of course, a limited one. Self-sacrifice is not always a sign of servility. It is not a duty always to press one's rights. Whether a given act is evidence of servility will depend not only on the attitude of the agent but also on the specific nature of his moral rights, a matter not considered here. Moreover, the extent to which a person is responsible, or blameworthy, for his defect remains an open question. Nevertheless, the conclusion should not be minimized. In order to avoid servility, a person who gives up his rights must do so with a full appreciation for what they are. A woman, for example, may devote herself to her husband if she is uncoerced, knows what she is doing, and does not pretend that she has no decent alternative. A self-contemptuous person may decide not to press various unforfeited rights but only if he does not take the attitude that he is too rotten to deserve them. A black may demand less than is due to him provided he is prepared to acknowledge that no one has a right to expect this of him. Sacrifices of this sort, I suspect, are extremely rare. Most people, if they fully acknowledged their rights, would not autonomously refuse to press them.

An even stronger conclusion would emerge if we could assume that some basic rights cannot be waived. That is, if there are some rights that others are bound to respect regardless of what we say, then, barring special explanation, we would be obliged not only to acknowledge these rights but also to avoid any appearance of consenting to give them up. To act as if we could release others from their obligation to grant these rights, apart from special circumstances, would be to fail to respect morality. Rousseau held, for example, that at least a minimal right to liberty cannot be waived. A man who consents to be enslaved, giving up liberty without *quid pro quo,* thereby displays a conditioned slavish mentality that renders his consent worthless. Similarly, a Kantian might argue that a person cannot release others from the obligation to refrain from killing him: consent is no defense against the charge of murder. To accept principles of this sort is to hold that rights to life and liberty are, as Kant believed, rather like a trustee's rights to preserve something valuable entrusted to him: he has not only a right but a duty to preserve it.

Even if there are no specific rights which cannot be waived, there might be at least one formal right cf this sort. This is the right to some minimum degree of respect from others. No matter how willing a person is to submit to humiliation by others, they ought to show him some respect as a person. By analogy with self-respect, as presented here, this respect owed by others would consist of a willingness to acknowledge fully, in word as well as action, the person's basically equal moral status as defined by his other rights. To the extent that a person gives even tacit consent to humiliations incompatible with this respect, he will be acting as if he waives a right which he cannot in fact give up. To do this, barring special explanations, would mark one as servile.

V

Kant held that the avoidance of servility is a duty to oneself rather than a duty to others. Recent philosophers, however, tend to discard the idea of a duty to oneself as a conceptual confusion. Although admittedly the analogy between a duty to oneself and a duty to others is not perfect, I suggest that something important is reflected in Kant's contention.

Let us consider briefly the function of saying that a duty is *to* someone. *First,* to say that a duty is *to* a given person sometimes merely indicates who is the object of that duty. That is, it tells us that the duty is concerned with how that person is to be treated, how his interests and wishes are to be taken into account, and the like. Here we might as well say that we have a duty *towards,* or *regarding* that person. Typically the person in question is the beneficiary of the fulfillment of the duty. For example, in this sense I have a duty to my children and even a duty to a distant stranger if I promised a third party that I would help that stranger. Clearly a duty to avoid servility would be a duty to oneself at least in this minimal sense, for it is a duty to avoid, so far as possible, the denial of one's own moral status. The duty is concerned with understanding and affirming one's rights, which are, at least as a rule, for one's own benefit.

Second, when we say that a duty is *to* a certain person, we often indicate thereby the person especially entitled to complain in case the duty is not fulfilled. For example, if I fail in my duty to my colleagues, then it is they who can most appropriately reproach me. Others may sometimes speak up on their behalf, but, for the most part, it is not the business of strangers to set me straight. Analogously, to say that the duty to avoid servility is a duty to oneself would indicate that, though sometimes a person may justifiably reproach himself for being servile, others are not generally in the appropriate position to complain. Outside encouragement is sometimes necessary, but, if any blame is called for, it is primarily self-recrimination and not the censure of others.

Third, mention of the person to whom a duty is owed often tells us something about the source of that duty. For example, to say that I have a duty to another person may indicate that the argument to show that I have such a duty turns upon a promise to that person, his authority over me, my having accepted special benefits from him, or, more generally, his rights. Accordingly, to say that the duty to avoid servility is a duty to oneself would at least imply that it is not entirely based upon promises to others, their authority, their beneficence, or an

16

obligation to respect their rights. More positively, the assertion might serve to indicate that the source of the duty is one's own rights rather than the rights of others, etc. That is, one ought not to be servile because, in some broad sense, one ought to respect one's own rights as a person. There is, to be sure, an asymmetry: one has certain duties to others because one ought not to violate their rights, and one has a duty to oneself because one ought to affirm one's own rights. Nevertheless, to dismiss duties to oneself out of hand is to overlook significant similarities.

Some familiar objections to duties to oneself, moreover, seem irrelevant in the case of servility. For example, some place much stock in the idea that a person would have no duties if alone on a desert island. This can be doubted, but in any case is irrelevant here. The duty to avoid servility is a duty to take a certain stance towards others and hence would be inapplicable if one were isolated on a desert island. Again, some suggest that if there were duties to oneself then one could make promises to oneself or owe oneself a debt of gratitude. Their paradigms are familiar ones. Someone remarks, "I promised myself a vacation this year" or "I have been such a good boy I owe myself a treat." Concentration on these facetious cases tends to confuse the issue. In any case the duty to avoid servility, as presented here, does not presuppose promises to oneself or debts of gratitude to oneself. Other objections stem from the intuition that a person has no duty to promote his own happiness. A duty to oneself, it is sometimes assumed, must be a duty to promote one's own happiness. From a utilitarian point of view, in fact, this is what a duty to oneself would most likely be. The problems with such alleged duties, however, are irrelevant to the duty to avoid servility. This is a duty to understand and affirm one's rights, not to promote one's own welfare. While it is usually in the interest of a person to affirm his rights, our Kantian argument against servility was not based upon this premise. Finally, a more subtle line of objection turns on the idea that, given that rights and duties are correlative, a person who acted contrary to a duty to oneself would have to be violating his own rights, which seems absurd.[6] This objection raises issues too complex to examine here. One should note, however, that I have tried to give a sense to saying that servility is contrary to a duty to oneself without presupposing that the servile person violates his own rights. If acts contrary to duties to others are always violations of their rights, then duties to oneself are not parallel with duties to others to that extent. But this does not mean that it is empty or pointless to say that a duty is to oneself.

My argument against servility may prompt some to say that the duty is "to morality" rather than "to oneself." All this means, however, is that the duty is derived from a basic requirement to respect the provisions of morality; and in

6 This, I take it, is part of M. G. Singer's objection to duties to oneself in *Generalization in Ethics* (New York: Alfred A. Knopf, 1961), pp. 311–18. Singer's objections are discussed in the essay "Promises to Oneself," in this volume.

this sense every duty is a duty "to morality." My duties to my children are also derivative from a general requirement to respect moral principles, but they are still duties *to* them.

Kant suggests that duties to oneself are a precondition of duties to others. On our account of servility, there is at least one sense in which this is so. Insofar as the servile person is ignorant of his own rights, he is not in an adequate position to appreciate the rights of others. Misunderstanding the moral basis for his equal status with others, he is necessarily liable to underestimate the rights of those with whom he classifies himself. On the other hand, if he plays the servile role knowingly, then, barring special explanation, he displays a lack of concern to see the principles of morality acknowledged and respected and thus the absence of one motive which can move a moral person to respect the rights of others. In either case, the servile person's lack of self-respect necessarily puts him in a less than ideal position to respect others. Failure to fulfill one's duty to oneself, then, renders a person liable to violate duties to others. This, however, is a consequence of our argument against servility, not a presupposition of it.

2

Self-respect reconsidered

When thinking about the servility of an Uncle Tom, an overly deferential wife, and an extremely self-deprecating person, I once suggested that one way persons can lack self-respect is to fail to appreciate their equal basic rights as human beings.[1] The failure, I thought, could stem either from unawareness of one's status as an equal or from valuing that status less than one should. The servile person, it seemed, let others violate his rights at will or too readily declined to exercise his rights.

One appealing feature of this idea was that it corresponded with the intuitive feeling that everyone ought to be respected in some ways, regardless of talent, social position, accomplishment, etc. Basic respect as a human being, one feels, does not need to be earned; and if respect is having proper regard for rights, then at least some respect is due each person without his needing to earn it. A person may lack self-respect not merely by underestimating his merits and achievements but also by misunderstanding and undervaluing his equal rights as a human being.

Although this account may still explain the instances of servility I considered, it does not fit all cases in which a person fails to respect himself. Just as one may respect others for their special merits and achievements, one may respect oneself for exceptional qualities. One who lacks this sort of respect for himself, perhaps because he does not have any special merit, does not necessarily misunderstand or undervalue his *rights*. More importantly, there are ways in which we feel everyone should respect himself which have little to do with either acknowledging one's merits or appreciating one's rights.

Consider some examples.

Suppose an artist of genius and originality paints a masterwork unappreciated by his contemporaries. Cynically, for money and social status, he alters the painting to please the tasteless public and then turns out copies in machine-like fashion. He does it deliberately, with full awareness of his reasons, but not without some sense of disgust at himself.[2]

Again, consider the talented, aspiring actress who has been supporting herself largely by waiting on tables. After comparing the hourly wages and other costs

1 "Servility and Self-Respect," in this volume.
2 This example, I think, comes from Daniel Wikler, whose correspondence has especially stimulated my second thoughts on this subject.

and benefits, she decides to take up prostitution as an interim means of support. This decision is not impulsive or from dire need, nor is it the only means to her desired career. Sometimes, she says, she hates herself for what she is doing, but at least she has some pride that she never puts up with any abuse from her patrons.

Another example comes from the classic film, "The Blue Angel." Here a respected schoolmaster gives up his position to follow a burlesque dancer and ends up playing the clown before his former students. His choices, it seems, were not impulsive, and no one forced him to do anything.

In each case a person seems not to respect himself as he should. This is not to say, however, that what they did (self-respect aside) was immoral. It is at least arguable that altering one's own painting, selling sexual services, and changing jobs from schoolmaster to clown were within their rights;[3] and, unlike my servile persons, they are not obviously guilty of letting others ignore their own rights. (The prostitute, recall, refused to accept abuse from her customers; the schoolmaster voluntarily gave up his right to be treated as a teacher instead of a clown, etc.) Their problem is also not that they have a low opinion of their merits and achievements: each may in fact give himself high marks in this regard. They may suspect and fear the low opinion of others, and so feel ashamed, but their lack of *self*-respect is more than this. Although each, in a sense, acts contrary to his values, the problem is not really weakness of will.[4] They knew what they were doing, and they made a deliberate decision, involving a change of life-plan, not a momentary aberration. It was not that their wills were weak, for they willed to do just what they did. The sign that they fail to respect themselves fully is in how they feel (self-disgust, self-hate, etc.); but the feeling is a sign, not the whole story.

These points seem confirmed when we imagine what a friend might say when he saw them and wished that they had more respect for themselves. The appropriate response is hardly, "You should not feel that way because, after all, you are within your rights." Nor would it be, "You are doing something immoral; reform your ways." It seems beside the point to say, "You have many talents and achievements, and others acknowledge them." And it would show lack of understanding to call for more strength against impulse: "You are too weak; stick to your decisions." The question is, what more could one say?

---

3   Many, I know, will argue that prostitution is wrong aside any question of self-respect; but it
    should be sufficient for the point if they will agree that the particular prostitute in our example
    shows inadequate self-respect quite aside from how one resolves the controversy about the morality
    of prostitution in general.

4   Here I realize that I am taking a position contrary to the usual view of weakness of will; but I
    would argue that it is a mistake to see weakness of will, in general, as failure to do what one
    believes right or best. One can, I think, quite deliberately will a plan which one believes base
    and even immoral, and then when one carries it out with firm resolution one is not suffering
    from weakness of will.

A clue may be found by considering ways in which we respect others. Sometimes we respect a person as an office holder (the President, one's father, etc.), but this seems largely a matter of acknowledging their special rights. We also respect people as human beings, which again seems to be respect for rights. We respect extraordinary people for their exceptional abilities and achievements: e.g., I respect Isaac Stern as a violinist, my colleagues as philosophers, etc. But none of these examples provides the sort of analogue we want. What is needed is a case of respecting someone independently of rights and special merits.

Suppose I have two neighbors who are quite ordinary in their abilities and aspirations. I respect both the human and special rights of each, and yet, in another sense, I respect one much more than the other. Neither is doing anything illegal or morally wrong, but one, unlike the other, has a clear sense of what he values and counts important and he lives accordingly. It is not that he has exceptionally high ideals. Rather he has a sense, quite aside from matters of moral right and wrong, that certain ways of behaving are beneath him, and his acts, both deliberate and impulsive, never go past this line. He will not, for example, let his house fall into disarray or his debts increase beyond a certain point; he refuses to hide or apologize for his unpopular political opinions, and he will not see films he regards tasteless or obscene even though he admits that they arouse his interest. He is not, however, a person of extraordinary strength of will; for he overeats and overdrinks even after he decides not to. Moderation and willpower in such matters are not among his fundamental values. Though he holds them deeply, he does not universalize his basic nonmoral standards (except in a trivial sense.)[5] That is, apart from certain moral principles (respect for life, honesty, some contribution to charity, etc.), he feels that others may live as they choose. He does not criticize others for their debts, their housekeeping or their preference in films. He says that he just has certain standards for himself and would lower himself in his own eyes if he did not stick by them. Even those who disagree with him, I imagine, tend to respect him.

The other neighbor, let us say, lives equally well within the bounds of the law and basic moral requirements (respect for life, etc.) but otherwise seems to have no personal standards. Not only does he lack high ideals of self-improvement, style, aesthetic taste, etc., he also lacks a sense of a minimum nonmoral standard. So long as he satisfies basic moral requirements, he does whatever he feels like doing without ever looking down on himself for it. He generally avoids what is against his interest and often does good things for others, but this is never a

---

5 It is no doubt true that one who says "I would be better if I did X" is committed to something like "Anyone in exactly similar or relevantly similar circumstances would be better if he did X"; but unless "relevantly similar" is specified broadly enough to be, for practical purposes, applicable to others, the speaker may still be without any commitment to judgments about the people he knows or is likely to meet. My first neighbor either professes to know too little of others to judge them or else construes the "relevantly similar" circumstances to include such special features about himself that his judgment about himself does not extend to them.

matter of pride or principle with him. He would feel *regret* if he acted, impulsively or deliberately, in ways that failed to have the consequences he wanted; but he would never feel *self-contempt*. Basic morality aside, he does not put his sense of self-worth on the line. He is, so to speak, tolerant and nonjudgmental about himself in the way the other neighbor is about others. Even those who find what he actually does quite agreeable, do not respect him as they do the other neighbor.[6]

These examples suggest a way in which a person can respect himself quite aside from acknowledging his merits and appreciating his rights. This form of self-respect would require that one develop and live by a set of personal standards by which one is prepared to judge oneself even if they are not extended to others. The standards might be ideals for which one strives or merely a minimum below which one cannot go without losing face with oneself.[7] The sort of standards I have in mind need not be moral ones; but they are also not identical with what one most wants. A person might find that what he most wants, all considered, is a life that conflicts with much of what he really values, sees as admirable for himself, or at least ensures his good opinion of himself. Weighing the pain of self-contempt against potential pleasures of another sort, he might quite reflectively choose what he regards as a lower way of life for himself. The peace of mind that comes from congruence between one's values and one's behavior is doubtless always seen as desirable; but one can deliberately sacrifice it for other things one wants more. Though a person need not believe that his values for himself are "objective" or irrational to deny, he cannot simply make anything, arbitrarily, one of his values. One who claimed it as his ideal, or minimum value, to get as fat as he could, or avoid exerting himself, or to tear bits of paper all day, would hardly be convincing, barring very peculiar background beliefs. The sort of personal standards and ideals on which one's self-respect depends are typically seen as inescapably a part of oneself. Whether one sees them as objective

---

6   An exception might be a person who lived the same sort of life as my second neighbor *on principle*. That is, he sees it as a defect to be "judgmental" about himself (basic morality aside), admires and strives to emulate those who seem free from liability to self-contempt. Such a person has, as it were, a second-order ideal to live without the sort of personal standards the first neighbor subjects himself to. For simplicity, let us imagine that the second neighbor lacks this sophisticated second-order ideal. He is not *proud* of living without personal standards, as one might be who has struggled his way out of neurotic attachments to such standards; he simply lacks them.

7   The standards in question need not be to do what is morally ideal or supererogatory, for two reasons. First, they need not be standards which everyone morally ought to pursue or even ones which anyone would be morally admirable for pursuing. They might, include, for example, artistic achievement, stylish dress, a comic personality, etc. Second, they need not be remote stars for which one reaches or goals one would be pleased to achieve but which one does not see as required. Some of the personal standards may be seen as (nonmorally) "required"; one is not particularly pleased, merely satisfied, to meet the standards, but failure to live up to them lowers oneself in one's own eyes. Of course, many, perhaps most, people make it a personal standard to live by moral principles and to do what is morally supererogatory; but then, I think, their lack of self-respect when they act immorally is due, not simply to violating moral standards, but to violating personal standards which they happen to believe morally required.

or not, one genuinely takes the attitude that one is, in one's own view, better or worse according to how one measures up to them.

Returning to our initial examples, we can see how the artist, the prostitute, and the schoolmaster failed to respect themselves. Unlike my second neighbor, they had personal standards but they did not live by them. The artist's self-disgust reveals that he regards altering his masterpiece for money and popularity as contrary to his own ideals. In admitting that she sometimes hates herself, the actress/prostitute shows that she feels that, at least for her, prostitution is a lower way of life. The schoolmaster's self-contempt drives him insane, leaving no doubt that, rightly or wrongly, he felt he had cheapened himself. Had each lacked standards for themselves, they would not feel self-contempt; but, assuming the absence was complete, they would also have no way to treat themselves with respect. As it was, they had ideals but chose instead to pursue other wants. What they failed to respect was not their rights or merits but their own personal standards. What they lacked was not simply a certain feeling but behavior in accord with a self-imposed standard.

Those who have self-respect are often said to have a "sense of their own worth." While often moving and doubtless important, this idea is also puzzling. What sort of worth, one wonders, is in question? Not simply worth *to* others; for a person who is useful to others, is loved by others, and knows it, can lack this sense of self-worth. Also a person who is neither useful nor loved sometimes has a strong sense of self-worth. This sense is also not identical with a belief that one has, despite others' opinion, an equal status in a system of moral rights; for unfortunately not everyone who appreciates his *moral* equality feels that self-worth which parents, and then psychotherapists, try to foster in their children. One can be aware that he is morally equal to others but still feel depressed and worthless in another way. It is as if one's interests, projects, and plans seem worthless even *to oneself*. Though often couched in objectivist language, the attitude is hardly to be explained as belief that one lacks an objective, inexplicable, intuitable property, "worthiness." Though the topic remains a difficult one, one conjecture emerges from our examples: at least part of a sense of one's own worth is having, and living by, personal standards or ideals that one sees, whether objective or not, as an important part of oneself.

In the paper mentioned earlier, I tried to isolate a type of self-respect which it seemed plausible to say everyone should, morally, try to have. *That* self-respect, however, involved appreciating one's own *moral* rights. Since the form of self-respect discussed above is not respect for any moral standard, the question naturally arises whether it is any moral fault not to have such self-respect. The question is too large for more than a brief comment, but one preliminary thought may be in order. Philosophers have often thought that we have duties to ourselves as well as to others; but others have rejected the idea partly, it seems, because they find it intuitively implausible that we have a moral duty to promote our own happiness. After all (as Kant noted) we are usually all too ready to seek our own happiness. An ideal moral legislator, aware of the burden of imposing duties, would see little reason to make such pursuit a matter of duty (as with restraint from killing) even though he counted the happiness of all an ideal end. The most intuitively plausible cases, however, in which one feels a person has a duty to himself seem to be cases in which a person is not respecting himself, not cases in which he is curtailing his happiness. It is tempting to say to the artist, the actress, and the schoolmaster in our examples, "You owe it *to yourself* to change." This is not just an estimate that a change will bring greater happiness, though we may believe that too. It is as if we take a moral interest in persons' setting and living by their own values, even when the values are not required for all. We care for their having the satisfaction of a good opinion of themselves, but not just for the pleasure of it. Perhaps the moral interest is in each person living as an *autonomous* agent, where "autonomy" implies both personal integration and forming values beyond comfort, least resistance, etc.

Thinking of self-respect in the previous way (appreciation of rights), I argued that one should respect oneself as well as every other human being. And, in that sense, absence of self-respect tends to undermine respect for others. But, given the conception of self-respect I have discussed here, one cannot say the same. Perhaps we do believe that everyone should try to respect himself in this sense, but we cannot reasonably ask that everyone respect all others. For respect of the sort we have been considering requires seeing that the respected person has personal standards or ideals and believing that he lives by them. But, unfortunately, not everyone seems to have such standards, and, even more obviously, not everyone lives by the standards he has. The respect in question need not be merited by special talent, achievement, or even ambition; but one must qualify for it by setting and sticking to some personal values. Again, it is not clear that those who lack self-respect of this sort cannot respect others. But what does follow is that one who does not respect himself in this way cannot expect that others will. To ask them to respect him would be to ask them to acknowledge what he himself cannot, namely, that he has and lives by his own (morally permissible) values. As Kant remarked, perhaps too harshly, "One who makes himself a worm cannot complain if people step on him."[8]

8 *The Doctrine of Virtue* (Part II of the *Metaphysic of Morals*), ed. Mary J. Gregor (Harper Torchbooks, 1964), p. 103 (p. 437 Academy edition). Kant's remark lends itself to my point, but I do not want to argue that it is just what he meant.

3

Autonomy and benevolent lies

Often it is easy to see what is wrong with lying.[1] Many lies are vicious: they are meant to hurt, and often do. Other lies are self-serving at the expense of others: they gain something for the liar but are detrimental to those who are deceived. Even well-intentioned lies are sometimes discovered, with consequent damage to valued relationships and to trust and credibility in general. Many lies are violations of professional obligations; others are breaches of promise to particular individuals. But there are also instances in which these explanations do not seem to apply and yet the lie is still not beyond moral question. We feel that there is at least something to be said against lying even then, but it is not obvious what this is. No promises or professional commitments are at stake; no harmful consequences are intended or expected; and yet the lie still seems at least *prima facie* objectionable. We naturally wonder, "why?" To rest the matter with the intuitive remark that truth-telling is always a *prima facie* obligation is hardly satisfying. To say that killing, maiming, and causing pain are *prima facie* wrong may arouse no further questions; but why, one wonders, should truth-telling be viewed this way, especially when a lie seems likely to result in more good than harm?

At least a partial answer, I suggest, is that lies often reflect inadequate respect for the autonomy of the person who is deceived. Unfortunately, though autonomy has been an increasingly popular concept in recent years, there is no uniform understanding about what autonomy is. I hope that by tracing different conceptions of autonomy from their Kantian prototype we can see more clearly, and specifically, the various ways in which lies interfere with autonomy. But the interest in autonomy extends beyond our immediate question about lying: benevolent lies merely illustrate one of many ways in which narrow utilitarian thinking can foster unwarranted interference in others' lives.

My remarks will be divided as follows: *First,* I characterize a special class of benevolent lies which pose the main issue sharply; *second,* I distinguish several conceptions of autonomy with associated moral principles; *third,* I try to explain how, in different ways, these principles oppose benevolent lies; and *finally,* I

1 I have had the benefit of helpful comments and criticisms from a number of students and colleagues, most notably Robert M. Adams, Gregory Kavka, Warren Quinn, a U.C.L.A. Law and Philosophy discussion group, and colloquium participants at the University of Utah and the University of California, Santa Barbara.

25

comment briefly on how a believer in autonomy might respond to the hedonist contention that it is irrational not to lie if a lie will result in the most favorable pleasure/pain ratio.

My aim is not to find a precise rule or decision procedure for deciding hard cases. In fact I suspect that the search for one would be misguided. Many different considerations oppose most lies, and in difficult situations there are arguments for and against. My object is not to rank these competing factors in importance but rather to articulate one type of consideration that is too often overshadowed. Malice, harm, and breaches of trust are so obvious and so often objections to lies that subtler sorts of objection, though usually present at the same time, may be overlooked. The point of isolating very special examples of benevolent lies is to focus attention on such objections; it is not to deny the importance of other arguments or to articulate considerations that apply only in rare circumstances.

I

A former teacher related to me the following true story (which I have modified slightly). He had a student who showed in tutorial conversations signs of deep, suicidal depression. The student was later found dead, and the circumstances were such that others could easily have seen his death as accidental. The professor helped to gather up the boy's belongings to return to his mother, and no suicide note was found. But the mother, a devout Roman Catholic, was deeply worried about her son's soul, and she asked the professor point blank whether he had any reason to suspect suicide. The professor, an atheist, wanted to comfort her and so, by a quite deliberate lie, assured her that, as far as he knew, the boy had been in good spirits.

Another true story concerns a doctor who discovered that his mother, a very elderly but happy woman, had extremely advanced atherosclerosis. Her doctor had apparently chosen to treat the problem as best he could without informing the woman how near death she was. The son had no objection to the medical treatment or her doctor's decision to withhold information. Though he thought his mother psychologically and physically capable of handling the truth, he believed that her last days would be happier if she did not know. The problem arose when she asked her son directly, "Do you think the doctor is telling me everything?" The son lied; but since the question concerned his opinion and he had learned of her condition in ways she did not suspect and without anyone else knowing that he knew, he felt confident that she would never discover his lie. He lied to make her more comfortable, and she was in fact happy until her death.

Consider, lastly, a dilemma which could occur even if it has not. Mary has made a painful break from her ex-lover, John, and though pulled towards him, is on the mend. Her roommate is pleased for her, as she knows that John and

Mary were, and will remain, painfully incompatible. She is fearful, though, that John and Mary will get together again, causing both unnecessary misery before the inevitable final separation. Overhearing John talking with a friend, she learns that John is ready to "start over" if only he receives an encouraging sign; and she expects that Mary, ever the optimist, would give the sign. Later Mary asks the roommate, "Do you think he would want to try again if I asked him?" As an act of kindness, the roommate replies, "No, I am sure he knows it would never work."

These examples illustrate the special sort of benevolent lies I want to consider. The lies are benevolent because they are intended to benefit the person deceived, for no ulterior motives, and they actually succeed in giving comfort without causing pain. Despite the benevolent motives, there is no denying that deliberate lies were told. We are not dealing with examples of mere silence, evasion, ambiguous response, and the like. The lies, moreover, are not designed to protect incompetents from truths beyond their capacities to handle sanely and responsibly. In our sample cases a lie will protect someone from avoidable pain, but it is not needed to prevent serious physical or psychological damage, violent outbursts, gross misperception of reality, and so on.

Our examples also fall outside a range of special problem situations. Some lies, for example, are told in a context where the liar has rather little chance of being believed; but in our cases there is sufficient credibility to make the deception effective. Other lies concern matters which are, intuitively, "none of the business" of the questioner: for example, a lie told to a curious student who asked his teacher about his private sex life. But the questions in our examples are clearly not "out of bounds" in this way. What is asked for is information or opinion about what deeply concerns the questioner's own life. Also the lies in our stories cannot be deemed trivial. Unlike "little white lies," they are about matters of the utmost importance to the deceived: heaven or hell, life or death, reunion or separation from a loved one. Further, our examples concern lies between individuals, not lies from public officials or to institutions, and so certain questions of public responsibility are left aside. Finally, let us imagine that the deceived has not forfeited a right to know, for example, by his own repeated lying or by having a plain intent to misuse the truth.

Lies are often wrong at least in part because they are breaches of a promise to be truthful, but, to simplify matters, let us suppose that there were no such promises in our examples. It is easy to imagine that the professor, the dying woman's son, and the roommate never made an *explicit* promise to tell the truth as, for example, one is required to do before testifying in court. The more difficult matter is to remove the suspicion that they made a tacit or implicit promise to be truthful. W. D. Ross maintained that we make such an implicit promise every time we make an assertion, and so he viewed all lies as breaches of promise. But this position, surely, is implausible. Suppose, for example, two enemies distrust each other, have no desire to be honest with each other, and both know this. As seems to be common in international relations, they tell the truth to each other only when they expect that lying will not give them an advantage. In this situation when one asserts to the other, say, that he has documents damaging to the other's political ambitions, we cannot reasonably interpret this as a promise. Neither person believes that the speaker intends to put himself under obligation. Given their mutual understanding, the speaker cannot seriously intend to lead the other to believe that he is making it a matter of conscience to convey the truth. Furthermore if every assertion amounted to a promise to say what is true, we would not think, as in fact we do, that a lie preceded by an explicit promise to be truthful is usually worse than a lie not preceded by such a promise. There are, of course, implicit promises but it requires more than mere assertion to make one. Suppose, for example, Mary and her roommate had often discussed how they valued each other's honesty and frankness, and each had on other occasions insisted that the other tell the truth, however painful, and neither gave any hint of reservations about giving and counting on complete truthfulness between them. With this special background we might want to say that they had made implicit promises to tell each other the truth. However, to focus attention away from promises, let us suppose that in our examples there were no such special conditions to create implicit promises to be truthful.

Our examples are also meant to minimize the force of utilitarian considerations that so often tell against lying. Most importantly, the lies in our stories are extremely unlikely to be discovered. It is a moralist's fiction that lies can never remain hidden: perhaps a useful fiction, but untrue nonetheless. In each of our examples a person is asked about what he knows or believes, and if he is determined to stand by his response there is no practical way others can find out that he is lying. Even if the student's mother learns that her son committed suicide, she cannot know that the professor lied; the elderly woman can find out that she is seriously ill, but not that her son lied about his opinion; Mary may learn that John is still available, but she has no way of discovering that her roommate knew. There is, of course, always *some* chance, however remote, that those who lie will give themselves away; for example, they may talk in their sleep. If the discovery of the lie would be an utter disaster, then from a utilitarian point of view even this very small risk might not be warranted. But to simplify, let us suppose that in our cases discovery would not be disastrous. The persons deceived, let us say, have an unusually forgiving and trusting nature. If they realized the special circumstances and benevolent intent, they would forgive the lie; and, though disappointed, they would not become unreasonably suspicious and distrustful. Again, typical lies tend to multiply, one lie calling for another and each lie making successive ones easier; but we can imagine this not to be so in our example. Our professor, doctor/son, and roommate, let us suppose, are of firm character and would lie only in the special circumstances we have defined, and they do not need an entangled web of further deception to hide the first.

Lies of the sort pictured here are no doubt rare; but, by minimizing the usual considerations of utility and promises, they enable us to focus on other relevant considerations, which may be important in more typical cases as well. In particular, we can reflect on how lies can fail to respect persons' autonomy.

II

What does it mean to respect the autonomy of a person? Autonomy has been conceived in quite different ways, and there are, accordingly, different principles and ideals associated with autonomy. Since most, if not all, recent conceptions of autonomy have roots in Kant's writing, a useful procedure may be to review Kant's theory of autonomy and then trace out several other conceptions of autonomy to which one is naturally led when one sets aside some of Kant's metaphysical and moral presuppositions.

Kantian autonomy. Kant held that autonomy is a property of the *will* of rational beings.[2] To have a will is to be able to cause events in accord with principles. That is, a rational being has a will insofar as he can "make things happen" in a way which makes appropriate explanations like, "He did (caused) it, because it is his principle to . . . (or for the reason that . . .)." To have autonomy it is also necessary that one's will be *free in a negative sense*. This implies that one is capable of causing events without being causally determined to do so. Even more radically, negative freedom implies ability to cause events without being motivated in any way by one's own desires. But since willing requires acting on principles, in order to exercise this capacity one must have some principles to which one is committed not because one desires to follow them or because the principles are expected to lead one to anything one desires (or will desire). All rational beings, Kant argued, have such principles; they are committed to them simply by virtue of being rational. The principles are self-imposed insofar as they stem from one's rational nature rather than from fear of punishment, desire for approval, blind acceptance of tradition, animal instinct, and so on. To have *autonomy* of the will is to be committed to principles in this way and to be able and disposed to follow them.

Kant argued further that the principles to which one is committed by virtue of one's autonomy are the basic principles of morality. This implies that one is under moral obligation to do something if and only if it is required by the principles one accepts for oneself as a rational being free from determining causes

---

2 What follows is a brief summary of Kant's views in the *Groundwork of the Metaphysics of Morals*, interpreted in the light of his later writings. Some points are controversial but, I believe, defensible.

and independently of all desire. Nothing else can impose moral obligation; tradition, power, ecclesiastical authority, majority opinion, and natural dispositions in themselves have no moral force. Kant believed that he could draw from these ideas more particular moral results which have also been influential in later discussions of autonomy. For example, he maintained that having autonomy is the basis for human dignity, and in particular for the idea that rational nature in every person ought to be treated as unconditionally valuable, above all "price." Other derivative principles include rights to a wide area of individual liberty and insistence on respect for all persons. Given Kant's long-standing reputation for being unduly moralistic,[3] it is somewhat surprising to find that the particular moral principles he sketches in the *Metaphysics of Morals* leave so much room for free choice. There are no ends such as pleasure or Moore's "intrinsic value" which one is morally required to maximize. Within the bounds of basic principles of liberty, respect, limited beneficence, and self-improvement, etc., one may pursue one's own pleasure or others', or whatever else one desires.

These fundamental features of Kant's theory of autonomy are notoriously embedded in a metaphysical framework and surrounded by specific moral opinions which most philosophers today, quite rightly, reject. Kant held, for example, that a person's commitment to moral principles does not take place in space or time and is incapable of empirical explanation. The uncaused decision to follow those principles in particular situations or not also belongs to the "intelligible" or noumenal world which is admitted to be beyond comprehension, even though criminals may be executed for the wrong decision. All of our desires, without distinction, are treated together as "alien" forces, not part of one's "true" self but only of oneself as appearance. Most of Kant's specific principles, such as the prohibition of lying, are held rigoristically; they cannot be overridden, they include within them no built-in exceptions, and yet they are supposed to bind all human beings, at all times and places. But despite these unacceptable features, Kant's theory suggests less encumbered ideals of autonomy which continue to have a wide appeal.

Sartrean autonomy. Suppose one is attracted by Kant's idea that one is morally bound by nothing but what one imposes on oneself and also by his denial of determinism regarding human choices, but one cannot accept Kant's noumenal/ phenomenal distinction, his moral rigorism, or his belief in principles of conduct which are necessarily rational for everyone. A natural result would be acceptance of what I shall call Sartrean autonomy.[4] To say that persons are autonomous, or

---

3 Other ways in which Kant opposed moralism I discuss in "Kant's Anti-Moralistic Strain," *Theoria*, Vol. XLIV (1978).

4 This conception is a distillation from some ideas in Sartre, but I would not argue that it fully captures the complexity and variety of Sartre's view. Variations on the theme, with significant differences, can be found in R. M. Hare, *Freedom and Reason*, and H. D. Aiken, *Reason and Conduct*.

free, in this sense has two main implications: (1) People act as they do because they choose to do so, and their choices are not causally determined; in fact nothing is to be viewed as a force even partially compelling a person to act, and this includes threats from others, one's own desires and emotions, and even so-called compulsions, addictions, and the like. (2) People are morally and rationally free to do as they choose in that there are no objective values, only self-imposed commitments. No general moral principles follow from the contention that persons are autonomous in this sense. A naturally associated principle (which, strictly, does not follow) is that one should not deny anyone's autonomy either by treating him as if he were compelled to act as he does or by moralizing to him as if he were subject to moral constraints not of his own making. Acknowledging persons' autonomy, however, would not require tolerating their behavior or even refraining from value judgments about their choices for, after all, one is free to make and express one's own values and these may prescribe opposition, even violent response.

Autonomy as a psychological capacity. Kantian and Sartrean autonomy were supposed to be features of all human beings, but autonomy is often conceived as a characteristic of only mature, reflective persons. Autonomy on this view is not freedom from causal determinism, still less an ability to act independently of desire. It is a capacity and disposition to make choices in a rational manner; and this means choosing in the absence of certain particular attitudes and inner obstacles, such as blind acceptance of tradition and authority, neurotic compulsions, and the like. The paradigms of a person who is nonautonomous in this sense include the child who accepts authority without question, the adolescent who rebels against authority with as little understanding, the traditionalist who will not consider new ways of doing things, the compulsive gambler who cannot stop gambling even though he wants to, and the masochist and the sadist who impulsively hurt themselves or others without any idea why. This conception, like Kant's, treats autonomy as a capacity and disposition to make rational choices free from certain "alien" factors, but now the factors are more narrowly circumscribed. To be autonomous one need not act independently of all causes and desires but only from certain causes and desires which interfere with rational choice. The ideals naturally associated with this conception of autonomy are the development of rational capacities in education, the overcoming of unconscious psychological disabilities through psychotherapy, and the *use* of one's rational capacities in making important choices.

Autonomy as a right. Sometimes the assertion that persons are autonomous is an attribution of a right rather than a psychological capacity. To say that persons have autonomy in this sense is not a descriptive statement that they are in fact free from certain influences (such as inner compulsions and slavery to convention) but instead a claim that they ought to be free from certain influences (inappropriate interference by others). Insofar as the idea has roots in Kant, it stems more from his principles of liberty and respect for persons than his metaphysical doctrines. Though other rights have been associated with autonomy, the right I have in mind is a moral right against individuals (not the state)[5] (a) to make one's own decisions about matters deeply affecting one's life, (b) without certain sorts of interference by others, (c) provided certain conditions obtain. The right presupposes a background of other moral rights and legal rights within a just system, which define an area of permissible conduct.

Consider first (a) the area of choice to be protected. In some sense one's "freedom" is limited when others prevent one from beating up children, entering others' houses at will, etc.; but the right of autonomy concerns decisions within an area of morally and legally permissible conduct. Fair competition, when successful, can also "interfere" with what one can choose to do, as when someone else wins a desired spot on a team or buys the last copy of a rare book. But, again autonomy is not a right to be successful in such competitive situations. My "freedom" is also limited when I cannot control others in matters which primarily affect them, e.g., my son's choice of college major, his hair style, and his dating partners. But autonomy is usually thought to be freedom to make one's own decisions about matters which most deeply affect one's own life, not to control others in matters which more seriously affect them.[6] Common examples would be choices about what jobs to take (among those for which one is qualified), what people to associate with (among those willing to reciprocate), what books to read, where to live, etc.

Even within this circumscribed area, the right of autonomy is only a right to make one's choices (b) free from certain interferences by others. Among these interferences are illegitimate threats, manipulations, and blocking or distorting the perception of options. The most obvious sorts of threats which violate a person's right to make his own decisions are threats to do things which would be wrong to do quite aside from considerations of autonomy: for example, threats to kill, maim, spread false rumors, deliberately ruin a career, or disown a child. When a person uses such a threat to control another's decisions, say, about whom to marry or whether to apply for a certain job, then the threat seems especially wrong (more wrong, for example, than if the threats were used to make someone keep a secret not pertaining to his own life). Even threats to do what one has a

5   For some purposes one may well want to claim a right of autonomy against undue interferences by the state, but, while not denied here, this is not especially pertinent to the issue at hand.

6   Two comments may help to prevent misunderstanding. *First,* while the line between matters which deeply affect one's own life and other matters is admittedly imprecise, the principle uses this notion only to characterize roughly the range of cases in question, not to distinguish in general permissible from impermissible interferences. Thus, unlike Mill's liberty principle, the principle does not try to mark off a private sphere in which one's choices do not significantly affect others. What deeply affects my life may deeply affect another's as well. Second, the fact that the principle is restricted to matters deeply affecting one's own life does not preclude there being *other* principles opposed to interference in other matters: the right of autonomy is not conceived here as a comprehensive right against all undue interference.

right to do would be undue interferences with autonomy if they had no other point than to control another's basic life choices. Consider, for example, the classic threat, "If you don't marry me (go to bed with me, etc.), I will marry the first woman who will have me (jump off a cliff, join a monastery, etc.)." Such a threat is obviously designed to control another's decision, not merely to explain one's contingency plans. It would be quite a different situation, and not an illegitimate threat, if at some point in a long relationship a person expressed a genuine conditional intention for which he (or she) had good reasons independently of a desire to control another's choice: for example, "If you do not marry me (go to bed with me, etc.), I intend to look for a new partner."

Manipulation, broadly conceived, can perhaps be understood as intentionally causing or encouraging people to make the decisions one wants them to make by actively promoting their making the decisions in ways that rational persons would not want to make their decisions. Obvious examples would be subliminal advertising, posthypnotic suggestions made to nonconsenting subjects, "brainwashing," getting someone drunk or drugged before a major decision, bribes appealing to a person's weaknesses, playing on a person's neurotic guilt feeling, coloring certain options black by insinuation, and so on. But fully rational persons not only want to make their important decisions free from these subversions of the deliberative process; they also want to have the opportunity to know their options and to reflect on any relevant considerations for and against each option. In short, a rational decision maker wants not only to have a clear head and ability to respond wisely to the choice problems presented to him; he wants also to see the problems and the important facts that bear on them realistically and in perspective. Thus one can also manipulate a person by feeding him information selectively, by covering up pertinent evidence, and by planting false clues in order to give a distorted picture of the problem situation.

Manipulation implies an actual intent to control another person by getting him to make decisions we want him to make; but one can also fail to honor persons' right to make their own decisions when one knowingly and actively interferes with their opportunity to see the significant choices that the circumstances offer, even if such interference is only a foreseen, unintended consequence of what one primarily intends to do. Suppose I liked very much the picture on a poster announcing a scholarship competition for study abroad and so, not caring at all whether anyone might apply for the scholarship or not, I took the poster to decorate my office. Though my intention was not to manipulate anyone's choices, I still knowingly and effectively prevented others from making choices that might significantly affect their lives. Or, again, suppose a father explained to his angry, newly feminist daughter: "When I taught you to be 'feminine,' I never meant to keep you from choosing to be a pilot (jockey, surgeon); I only wanted you to be popular and fit in well." By this he might avoid the charge of *manipulating* her career choice, but not the more general charge that he had failed to honor her right to make such choices without undue interference; at least this is so, if the means by which she was taught to be "feminine" were predictably ones which kept her from realizing that she had choices other than being a housewife, model, etc.

Most of us, surely, believe in a moral right of autonomy only (c) provided certain conditions obtain. Most obviously, the right makes sense only when its possessor has at least a minimum capacity for rational choice. But perfect rationality is not a prerequisite. We do not hold that persons have a right to make their own decisions only so long as they will decide in a perfectly rational way, and that therefore we may interfere with *any* predictably irrational decision. The attitude here is akin to the way many believe we should view autonomous states. At least if they are functioning political/legal systems (not, for example, in anarchy or violent revolution) and they are operating within some minimum standards of justice, it is generally thought inappropriate for other countries to interfere with their "internal decisions," even if likely to be imperfect or stupid. Other nations should not, for example, try to control the outcome of their elections or legislative process by threats, propaganda, or circulating false rumors. This idea of the autonomy of nations is often disregarded, of course, just as the autonomy of individuals is often ignored; but it is still an ideal which many profess.

The right of autonomy of individuals is also commonly understood to be qualified by a *proviso* that interference is not required to avert a major disaster or to prevent the violation of other, more stringent rights. If, for example, the only way to persuade someone to make a decision that will prevent a riot or a series of murders were to make an otherwise impermissible threat or a nonrational appeal to his weaknesses, then surely most would grant that such interference would be justified. Though important, autonomy need not be considered an absolute right.

Autonomy as capacity for distinctly human values. A central feature of Kant's theory of autonomy was his belief that human beings can and do value some things in ways that animals do not. Human beings have dignity, Kant thought, because they have distinctively human concerns which elevate them in our estimation above animals. Most of us, no doubt, will disagree with Kant's tendency to identify these special concerns with respect for purely rational moral principles, accepted independently of all desire; but a residue of his view may have wider appeal. Let us say that persons have autonomy in this residual sense if and only if (a) at least some of their values are not simply instinctual responses to an immediate environment, and (b) they value and are disposed to bring about some states of affairs without expecting that these states of affairs will bring them pleasure (or other "good experiences") or prevent pain (or other "bad experiences") for them, or at least they do not value those states of affairs *for the sake of* the pleasure (avoidance of pain, etc.) which they expect will result. To say that human beings are autonomous in this sense implies the denial of several forms of psychological hedonism; for autonomous persons not only value and aim for more than their *most* favorable pleasure/pain ratio, they also have some values and aims which are not for the sake of *any* anticipated pleasure (or prevention of pain). What is not denied, however, is the theory that early pleasant and painful experiences are among the causes of our developing the values we have.

That human beings are autonomous in the residual sense just defined seems quite obvious, once this is properly understood. Even setting aside moral values, surely people can and do sometimes care that their children survive and thrive after they, the parents, are dead and incapable of enjoying anything. They also want that people not laugh at them behind their backs, even though they will never know. Not all such values are altruistic, of course; for I might want my enemies to suffer horribly after I am dead. To say that the concerns in these cases are "really" desires *for* one's own good experiences (or avoidance of bad experiences) is surely a mistake. My desire that my children thrive and my enemies suffer after my death is not a desire to have the pleasure of *thinking* that the children will thrive and the enemies suffer. You would not fulfill my desire if, after my death, you tortured my children and rewarded my enemies but had earlier given me the false pleasure of believing that you would do the reverse. What one does not know, perhaps, does not *hurt* one; but sometimes we *want* states of affairs about which we will never know.

What ideals and principles are associated with this conception of autonomy? Much of what we respect and cherish in human beings, which is lacking in (most?) animals, is at least dependent on this human capacity to value more than what is immediately before them and more than agreeable experiences for themselves. More importantly, I believe that many of us at least implicitly accept the following principle: *First,* in dealing with competent human beings who are not violating anyone's rights, one should not presume that they prefer their own comfort (optimal experiences) over other values (such as the welfare of others, the completion of a project, self-awareness, etc.); and, *second,* when one aims to do something *for* others (say, from gratitude, charity, or love), one should not count their comfort (optimal experiences) as more important than values which they sincerely declare to be more important to them, provided at least the declared value is not a violation of others' rights, not the result of momentary impulse, manipulation, obviously false belief, etc. One would violate this principle, for example, if one treated elderly but competent people like small children or pets, caring scrupulously for their comfort and physical well-being but ignoring any desire they might express about what happens in the world outside the confined area which they can experience or check on.

Autonomy as an ideal rational life. A person could have autonomy in some of the preceding senses but lack autonomy in other senses. One could, for example, have rational decision-making capacities but still be manipulated by those who control one's information, or the opposite. One could have a right to make one's own decisions but be incapable of caring for anything but maximizing one's pleasures; alternatively, one could have all manner of distinctively human values but lack both the right and the psychological capacities to pursue these values in the ways a rational person would want. These possibilities suggest a final conception of autonomy, which combines several others and adds one further feature.

Let us say that persons have autonomy, or live autonomously, in a final sense if the following is true: (1) They have the psychological capacities for rational decision making which are associated with autonomy; (2) they actually use these capacities when they face important choice situations; (3) they have the right of autonomy discussed previously, i.e., a right to make morally and legally permissible decisions about matters deeply affecting their own lives free from threats and manipulation by others; (4) other people actually respect this right as well as their other rights; (5) they are able and disposed to have distinctly human values; (6) others respect this capacity by not presuming that they value only good experiences for themselves and by not counting their comfort as more important than their declared values; and, finally, (7) they have ample opportunities to make use of these conditions in living a life over which they have a high degree of control.

This last point requires special explanation. One might at first think it sufficient for an ideal rational life to have the capacities, rights, and good treatment from others indicated in (1)–(6); but further reflection quickly shows otherwise. Even if (1)–(6) were true, people could still find themselves unable to make use of these favorable conditions for any of several reasons. For example, though rationally disposed to make the best of their situation and unhindered by threats and manipulation by others, they might be severely confined in the choices they could make by widespread poverty, disease, overpopulation, and absence of technology and culture. Even if it is no one's fault, when one has to labor in the fields all day to survive, one has little opportunity to live *as* a rational person controlling his life. The choice to labor may be perfectly rational, of course; but it may be almost the only rational choice one has a chance to make. Harsh conditions also restrict the range of morally permissible choices: one cannot do philosophy if one must mine coal to feed one's children. Opportunities to live an ideally rational life may be further restricted by pointless role-expectations, conformist attitudes, and the lack of what Mill called "experiments in living." And even though one may be able to select from many brands of soup and cosmetics, if communal values are lost in a capitalistic society then more significant options are effectively closed. Finally, and significantly for present purposes, opportunities for rational, self-controlled living are restricted when one does not know the realities of one's choice situations. I could be able and eager to seek information, to reflect critically, to be on guard against manipulation and neurotic patterns, and to decide rationally on the basis of my beliefs, but still I would not really be in rational control of my life if my beliefs about my situation were drastically mistaken. Opportunities to learn the relevant facts are also needed.

III

How might the principles and ideals of autonomy we have considered help to explain the intuitive feeling that, even in our special cases, benevolent lies are to some degree objectionable? I will pass over Kant's conception of autonomy as a respected ancestor of later conceptions but not itself a viable option. I also cannot accept the Sartrean conception, and in any case it offers little help with our problem. The only relevant principle suggested by the Sartrean conception is that one should not lie in "bad faith," that is, pretending to oneself, when one "really" knows better, that a lie is necessary because the truth would *make* someone do something undesirable or because comforting someone when it causes no harm is an *objective* duty. The ideal of developing the psychological capacities associated with autonomy may give some reason to hesitate to tell lies to protect people from painful realities, but not a reason that applies in all cases. Probably, as a rule, having to face unpleasant truths about matters deeply affecting one's life helps one to develop the capacity for mature, reflective decision making. If so, there would be a general presumption against benevolent lies, even if it would not always be persuasive as, for example, when we are dealing with the very elderly whose capacities have presumably already been developed as much as they will be.

If we believe in the *right* of autonomy, however, we have more reason to object to benevolent lies. This is most obvious in our example of the roommate lying to keep her friend from reuniting with her ex-lover. The roommate manipulates her friend's decision (to call or not to call her "ex") by actively concealing pertinent information. If we accept the right of autonomy, this could only be justified if the reunion would have been so great a disaster that the right is overridden. In other cases the right of autonomy may be violated but in a less obvious way. The professor and the doctor/son, for example, did not lie in order to control the decisions of the people they deceived; they only wanted to spare them avoidable pain. Nevertheless, there were important, life-altering decisions which the deceived might have made if they had not been deprived of relevant information; and surely the professor and the doctor/son knew this. They knowingly prevented certain options presented by the real situation from ever being faced by the people they deceived: to pray or not, and, if so, how; to continue life as usual or to reorder one's priorities; to face death and tragedy stoically or to be open in a new way with friends.

Someone may object as follows: "Sometimes benevolent lies interfere with life-altering decisions, but not always; often benevolent lies merely keep people from suffering unnecessarily because of something which they can do nothing about. When, for example, a widow demands to know whether her husband suffered when he was killed in the war, there is little she can *do* if she is told truthfully that he died in horrible agony. And similarly, if the suicide's mother had been bedridden and terminally ill, the professor's lie would not have interfered with any important decisions."

The appropriate response, I think, is this: Benevolent lies do not necessarily or always violate the right of autonomy, but we should not be hasty in concluding that a particular lie does not concern any significant decisions. Good novelists and biographers know what philosophers too easily forget, namely, that the most important decisions in life are not always about external behavior, about what to *do* in the public world. How we face death, family tragedy, our own successes and failures, and the way others treat us, is partly a matter of decision, as Sartreans knew but exaggerated. Even *whether* to see a situation as success or failure, tragic or routine, is not simply a matter of perception of fact. We can also interfere with these life-altering decisions, or prevent a person from facing them, by keeping certain truths from him – even if he is immobile for the rest of his life.[7]

Consider next the principles associated with autonomy as a capacity for distinctly human values. Their implications for benevolent lies depend upon what we know about the preferences of the person to be deceived. Suppose, first, that we have no reason to doubt that the questioner wants an honest answer. His question is in effect an expression of a desire to know the truth. To give him less because we want to spare him pain would be to count his comfort more important than what he himself professes to value more and so would be contrary to our principles.

Sometimes, of course, people ask questions wanting to be reassured rather than to learn the truth. What should we do if we have indirect evidence that the questioner does not really want to know? Much depends, I think, on the nature and strength of the evidence. Suppose, for example, the evidence is rather evenly mixed: the person often shrinks from painful realities but, on the other hand, he asked in a serious tone, he never said in advance not to reveal the sort of fact in question, and the truth is not outside the range of answers he could anticipate. Often when we are in doubt whether a person really prefers what he professes, we can remove the uncertainty by asking further questions; but the peculiarity

---

7 Several have suggested to me that opposition to lying in these cases stems from the judgment that knowing the truth, or facing tragic realities, is intrinsically valuable regardless of the pain it causes; but I suspect that theories (such as G. E. Moore's) which make it a duty to promote an objective intrinsic value will repeatedly call for interference with autonomy. Robert Adams suggested that an ideal of autonomy might include *"living"* one's own life," e.g., experiencing the tragic realities actually surrounding one, quite aside from opportunities to make *decisions*, rational or otherwise; but I think that autonomy is so closely associated with the idea of "self-governing" that his ideal is probably better classified under some other conception.

of the dilemma of the would-be benevolent liar is that he cannot resolve the uncertainty this way. To ask, "Would you *really* prefer the truth even though it will hurt?" is in effect to give away the answer. When faced with such mixed evidence and unresolvable uncertainty, one guided by our principles of autonomy would, I believe, again be disposed to tell the truth; for respecting a person's capacity for distinctly human values implies that, other things equal, it is worse to presume that someone prefers comfort to some other declared value than to presume the opposite.[8]

If there were definitive evidence that the questioner preferred not to learn the painful truth, then autonomy as a capacity for distinctly human values would not be relevant. This would be the case if, for example, the questioner had explicitly requested in advance not to be told the truth in specified circumstances, and then, later, those circumstances arose and ample evidence indicated that he had not changed his mind.

Such cases, however, are probably rare. Normally even if a person has previously asked not to be told the truth, his subsequent question raises legitimate doubts about his current preferences. Suppose the earlier request was not made in anticipation of a period of incompetence – like Ulysses' request to his crew before facing the Sirens ("Don't listen to what I say later"). Then the would-be liar is apparently faced with two conflicting requests: an earlier request for deception, and a later request for truth. Unless there are independent reasons for discounting the latter, or for not treating the later question as a request for truth, then one might argue that respect for autonomy gives precedence to the more recent request. Other things equal, we respect a person's autonomy more by allowing changes of mind, honoring what he *does* profess to value over what he *did* profess to value.

The many-sided *ideal* of autonomous living will usually give further reason for hesitating to tell benevolent lies. Even if benevolent lies do not violate a *right,* they still deprive people of a realistic picture of their situation. Insofar as having such a realistic picture is needed for genuine rational control over one's life, to that extent the benevolent liar fails to promote an ideal end.[9]

It may be objected that this argument supports the desirability of volunteering the truth just as much as it supports the desirability of not actively depriving

---

8   This may seem strange if one supposes (mistakenly) that we should give people what they want – truth or comfort, whichever they prefer. But the principle in question was in fact rooted in a different idea, namely, that persons are to be respected for their distinctly human (e.g., non-hedonistic) values. From this point of view, given uncertainty, it is worse to err in supposing that they prefer comfort to truth than to err in the opposite direction.

9   It may be argued, rightly, that sometimes benevolent lies may promote the ideal of autonomous living in other respects. This might be so if, for example, coping with a painful truth, about which little could be done, would so preoccupy a person that other important aspects of life would be comparatively neglected. Sometimes, perhaps, too much information can also interfere with rational decision making.

someone of the truth; and yet, it might be said, it is counterintuitive to suppose that we have as much reason to volunteer painful truths as to tell them when directly asked. The ideal does give reason to volunteer the truth, I think, but there are also reasons why lying in response to a direct question is worse than merely not volunteering the truth. There is a general presumption that one should not cause avoidable pain to others, but this presumption is at least partially set aside when the person requests the painful treatment for the sake of something he wants: e.g., painful medical tests. Thus, although there is a general presumption against expressing truths which cause pain, this presumption is at least partially set aside when a competent person asks for truth; but the presumption is not set aside when one simply volunteers the truth without being asked. Thus, though the ideal of autonomy gives some reason for volunteering painful information about someone's life, the case for volunteering is not as strong as the case for telling the truth when asked.

Another objection might be this: "Sometimes we need to lie in order to increase the chances that a person will make his own decisions (and so live autonomously). For example, when my son asked me where I wanted him to go to college, I lied, telling him that I did not care. Actually I wanted very much for him to go where I went; but I figured that he could make up his own mind better if I kept my preference to myself."

The objection points to a practical problem difficult to resolve in real cases, but it does not, I think, show that the ideal of autonomy unequivocally recommends lying even in the example just presented. *One* aspect of the ideal, to be sure, was encouraging people to make their important decisions in a rational way free from inner psychological obstacles such as neurotic need for a father's approval. Thus, if the son in our example was so dominated by his father's opinions that he could not make a rational choice once his father expressed his desires, then one aspect of the ideal of autonomy would urge the father to hide his opinion. But let us suppose, as in our previous examples, the person deceived is rationally competent with respect to his choice problem and so is not a slave to his father's wishes. In this case another aspect of the ideal of autonomy would urge the father to express his wishes: he should make clear both that he prefers his son to go to his old college and also that he wants his son to decide on the basis of what he, the son, most wants. This puts the pertinent facts on the table, giving the son an opportunity he would have otherwise lacked, namely, to choose whether to give weight to his father's wishes or not and, if so, which wish to count more important. By lying, the father would have helped the son make a self-interested choice; but, as we have seen, one's autonomous choice is not always self-interested. To "make up one's own mind" is not necessarily to decide without regard for others' wishes but to decide maturely in the light of the facts about the situation.

So far we have considered ways in which principles and ideals of autonomy help to explain why we view even benevolent lies as to some degree objectionable; but we also have intuitive opinions about which sort of lies (or deceptions) are worse than others. Let us consider, then, whether considerations of autonomy help to explain these intuitions as well.

To consider several factors together, I suppose it is commonly accepted that deceptive responses to questions are worse, other things equal, when (a) the response is a direct lie rather than a merely evasive, misleading, or deceptively ambiguous response, (b) the person deceived trusts the deceiver and was encouraged to do so, and (c) the lie concerns the life of the deceived rather than matters only remotely touching him. The lies of the roommate and the doctor/son described earlier exemplify the first sort. An example of the second, less significant sort of deception might be this: A person asks me, simply from curiosity, "Do you know whether so-and-so is gay?" and, though I know, I answer, "How would I know?"

Now utilitarians will have familiar explanations why the first sort of lie is regarded as more serious than the second; but it is worth noting that our principles and ideals of autonomy provide an alternative, or additional, explanation. In brief, one's opportunity to live in rational control of one's life is increased when there are people one can unmistakenly identify as prepared to give straight, honest answers to direct pointed questions. If one does not want to know, one can refrain from asking; if the first answer is evasive or ambiguous, suggesting a reluctance on the other's part to reveal the truth, then one can choose to put the question again more pointedly or to back off; and if one does insist ("I want a straight, honest answer!"), then, while allowing for honest errors, one can make important decisions with more confidence that one understands the real situation. To live in a world without people we can rely on in this way would be to live in a world in which we have less control over our lives. Utilitarians often stress the unpleasantness that results when lies which violate trust become discovered, and for this reason our examples were designed to minimize the risk of discovery. But now it emerges that ideals of autonomy not only oppose undiscoverable benevolent lies; they also oppose lies which risk discovery of a breach of trust, for discovery of such lies encourages us to be distrustful and suspicious and so less able to make use of even the honest answers trustworthy persons give us; and this limits our opportunities for rational control over our lives.

IV

These conclusions, of course, are both hypothetical and intuitive: that is, the argument has been that if one accepts certain principles of autonomy, then one has reasons to refrain from benevolent lies. But imagine now an objection from a normative hedonist unwilling to rest the issue on intuitive principles. He argues that, intuitions aside, it is *irrational* to prefer truth to comfort, unless having the truth would maximize one's pleasure in the long run. Thus, he continues, when one aims to be benevolent towards another, it is *irrational* to give him the truth if a lie will contribute more to his total satisfaction.

The objection rests on the common, but mistaken, assumption that, at least when free from moral constraints, a fully rational person would always aim for his most favorable pleasure/pain ratio. But why so? As we have seen, people do in fact have (nonmoral) concerns independent of any anticipated good experiences. Some, perhaps, make maximum pleasure their goal; and others do not. What determines whether one is rational is not, by itself, the content of one's aims, but how they are arrived at, how they fit into one's life plan, etc. More plausible than the hedonist's conception of rationality, I think, is that of John Rawls, who defines ideal rationality, roughly, as satisfying certain "counting principles" (means-end efficiency, inclusion, etc.) and then deciding in light of full information about one's desires, circumstances, etc. Given this conception and the falsity of *psychological* hedonism (i.e., that all seek only to maximize their pleasure), then the rational life will be different for different people. For some, maybe, it will be predominantly pursuit of pleasure; but, unless we suppose that all non-hedonistic desires would extinguish when exposed to more information, for many the rational life will include pursuit of other values, such as truth, independently of their payoff in personal satisfaction.

The principles of autonomy which we have considered, though still un-unified in a general theory, point toward a conception of morality quite different in spirit from familiar forms of utilitarianism, hedonistic and otherwise. The latter start with views about what is intrinsically valuable as an end, and then define morality, in one way or another, as what promotes this end. A theory of autonomy, following Kant, Rawls, and others, would first define principles for moral institutions and personal interactions, leaving each person, within these constraints, the freedom to choose and pursue whatever ends they will. Such a theory would not oppose benevolent lies on the ground that truth-telling will maximize some intrinsic value other than pleasure (e.g., self-awareness); rather, it would encourage truthfulness as, in general, a way of respecting people as free to choose their own ends.

4

The importance of autonomy

For many years we have been hearing that *autonomy* is important.[1] Immanual Kant held that autonomy is the foundation of human dignity and the source of all morality; and contemporary philosophers dissatisfied with utilitarianism are developing a variety of new theories that, they often say, are inspired by Kant. Autonomy has been heralded as an essential aim of education; and feminist philosophers have championed women's rights under the name of autonomy.[2] Oppressive political regimes are opposed on the grounds that they deny individual autonomy; and respect for the autonomy of patients is a recurrent theme in the rapidly expanding literature on medical ethics. Autonomy is a byword for those who oppose conventional and authoritative ethics; and for some existentialists, recognition of individual autonomy is apparently a reason for denying that there are objective moral standards. Both new rights theorists and the modern social contract theorists maintain that their theories best affirm autonomy.[3] Finally, and not least in their esteem for autonomy, well known psychologists speak of autonomy as the highest stage of moral development.

Recently, however, the importance of autonomy has been questioned from a variety of sources. Utilitarian critics have struck back at the neo-Kantians, and a group of moral philosophers, sometimes labeled "personalists," have challenged the Kantian ideal that we should be moved by regard for impartial principles rather than concern for particular individuals.[4] A "different voice" is being heard, emphasizing aspects of morality too often ignored in the persistent praise of autonomy. Some suggest that, far from being the source and highest development of morality, autonomy may be the special ideal of a particular dominant group, and in fact an ideal which serves to reinforce old patterns of oppression.[5] If so,

1 This paper was written for presentation to students and faculty at Ripon College as a part of a colloquium on "Autonomy and Caring," which was inspired by Carol Gilligan's *In A Different Voice*. Thanks are due to the participants at that conference, and especially to Robert Hannaford, for their comments.

2 A noteworthy example of the latter is Sharon Bishop Hill's "Self-determination and Autonomy" in Richard Wasserstrom's *Today's Moral Problems* (New York: Macmillan, Third Edition, 1985).

3 See, for example, John Rawls's *A Theory of Justice* (Cambridge: Harvard University Press, 1971) and Robert Nozick's *Anarchy, State and Utopia* (New York: Basic Books, Inc., 1974).

4 Notably among these are Lawrence Blum, whose *Friendship, Altruism and Morality* (London, Boston and Henley: Routledge & Kegan Paul, 1980) has stimulated much useful discussion.

5 This remark applies only to those who try to draw certain moral and political conclusions from Carol Gilligan's research. In her book, Gilligan herself claims only to have uncovered tendencies in male and female populations and not to have established any ideological generalizations.

43

feminists who appeal to autonomy may be unwittingly adopting a dominant male ideology and ignoring the best in a feminine outlook on morals. Animal liberationists join the new feminists, personalists, and utilitarian critics in calling for a reemphasis on the role of compassion in a moral life; for, as they point out, classic theories of autonomy attach no intrinsic importance to the suffering of animals.[6]

Out of this confusing morass of claims and counterclaims, I want to isolate three ways in which I believe that autonomy is important; or better, since "autonomy" means different things to different people, I should say that what I want to do is focus upon three *senses,* or ideas, of autonomy and explain why, despite recent critics, I still believe each of these ideas has an important place in an ideal conception of morality. Exaggerated reactions to extravagant praise of autonomy, I fear, have put us in danger of overlooking some elementary points embedded in the autonomy-glorifying tradition. These points should be rather obvious and nonthreatening once they are disentangled from certain unnecessary accompaniments; and they are fully compatible with recognition of the moral importance of compassion.

My point of view is that of moral philosophy, not that of developmental psychology; and so I will have little to say about the stages of moral development and whether autonomy represents a peculiarly masculine point of view, as Carol Gilligan's work seems to suggest. My aim, instead, will be to explain three modest theses about autonomy, unencumbered with some of the more extreme Kantian baggage that usually travels with them. My hope is that, once properly understood, these points will be recognized as an important part of any complete conception of morality.

I

"Autonomy," like many philosophers' favorite words, is not the name of one single thing; it means quite different things to different people. None of these ideas is simple, and the relations among the different senses of autonomy are staggeringly complex. Little progress can be made in debates about autonomy until these different ideas are sorted out.[7] To begin this effort, let me consider first a classic idea of autonomy introduced by Immanuel Kant and followed, with modifications, by John Rawls and others.

Autonomy, Kant held, is a property of the wills of all adult human beings insofar as they are viewed as ideal moral legislators, prescribing general principles to themselves rationally, free from causal determinism, and not motivated by sensuous desires. For present purposes, two points in this conception are crucial.

6 See, for example, Peter Singer's *Animal Liberation* (New York: Avon Books, 1977).
7 For some discussion of these distinctions, see my "Autonomy and Benevolent Lies," in this volume.

First, having autonomy means considering principles from a point of view that requires temporary detachment from the particular desires and aversions, loves and hates, that one happens to have; *second,* autonomy is an ideal feature of a person conceived in the *role* of a moral legislator, i.e., a person *reviewing* various suggested moral principles and values, *reflecting* on how they may conflict and how they might be reconciled, and finally *deciding* which principles are most acceptable, and whether and how they should be qualified.

To elaborate the first point, the autonomy of a moral legislator means that, in debating basic moral principles and values, a person ideally should not be moved by blind adherence to tradition or authority, by outside threats or bribes, by unreflective impulse, or unquestioned habits of thought. More significantly, an autonomous moral legislator must try not to give *special* weight to his or her particular preferences and personal attachments. In debating the standards of arbitration between sheep herders and cattlemen, for example, one must try to discount one's particular aversion, or attraction, to sheep. In searching for the appropriate values regarding the relations between the sexes, one must try not to tailor the decision to the advantage of the sex one happens to be. Kant called this "abstracting from personal differences,"[8] and Rawls refers to it as choosing "behind a veil of ignorance."[9] The central point for both is that, for purposes of trying to adjudicate fairly and reasonably among competing principles and values, certain considerations must be ruled out of court. For example, the fact that a principle would benefit *me, my* family, and *my* country instead of someone else, someone else's family and country, is not *in itself* a reason for anyone, as a moral legislator, to favor that principle. In other words, at the level of deliberation about basic principles, morality requires impartial regard for all persons.

The second point, however, states an extremely important qualification. Autonomy, as impartiality, is part of an ideal for moral legislation, or general debate about moral principles and values; it is not a recommended way of life. Unfortunately, some philosophers, including Kant, seem at times to conflate this legislative ideal with another idea, which does not really follow; namely, the idea that in facing the moral choices of daily life we should constantly strive to act on impartial principles, to free ourselves of particular attachments, and to ignore the distinguishing features of individuals. In fact, far from being a consequence of autonomy in legislation, this idea that we should live with our eyes fixed on abstract, impartial principles seems quite the opposite of what autonomous moral legislators would recommend. Even from an impartial perspective, which gives no special advantage to interests just because they are one's *own,* one can see good reasons for moral principles such as "Be compassionate," "Take responsibility, within limits, for your family, your country, and yourself," "Don't

8 See *The Groundwork of the Metaphysic of Morals* translated by H. J. Paton (Harper), p. 101.
9 See John Rawls, *A Theory of Justice,* pp. 136–42.

face concrete moral problems as if they were mathematical puzzles, but restructure them with sensitivity and find a 'caring' solution."

Now one might well wonder why impartiality in the review of basic principles has been called *autonomy,* especially since such impartiality seems to have little to do with the right of self-governance and other things that nowadays pass for autonomy. The explanation, I think, is rooted in Kant's idea that one's "true self," in a sense, is the way one is when free as possible from transitory concerns, personal eccentricities, and the particular attachments one is caused to have by nature and circumstance. In this conception, one is most fully oneself, expressing one's true nature, when one "rises above" the particular natural and conditioned desires that distinguish one from others; and one does this by adopting principles from an impartial point of view and acting from respect for these principles. In this way, it is thought, one is self-governing, or autonomous, i.e., governed by one's true (impartial) self.

While this seems to be the historical origin of the use of the word "autonomy" for the idea of impartiality in the review of basic principles, these originating associations are not an essential part of that idea. In other words, one can perfectly well reject the notion that a person is truly self-governing only when making and acting from impartial principles and yet still agree with the main point, namely, that autonomy as impartiality is a crucial aspect of the ideal perspective from which moral principles are to be reviewed and defended.

Once this point is seen clearly for what it is, who would want to deny it? Only those extreme relativists who believe that reasonable debate about basic moral principles is either impossible or presupposes a prior arbitrary personal commitment that cannot be rationally defended to anyone who happens to feel differently.[10] For all the impartiality thesis says is that, if and when one raises questions regarding fundamental moral standards, the court of appeal that one addresses is a court in which no particular individual, group, or country has *special* standing. Before that court, declaring "I like it," "It serves *my* country," and the like, is not decisive; principles must be defensible to anyone looking at the matter apart from his or her special attachments, from a larger, human perspective.

Is not this, in fact, just what most of us, men and women, believe? Of course, when faced with a concrete moral problem, we are guided by thoughts such as, "He is, after all, my friend," and "I have a responsibility to my family – and myself." But if the philosophical question is raised, "Why does one have such responsibilities and what are their limits?," do we really think we could get a satisfactory answer *solely* by reference to our own needs and wants or to the needs and wants of others (e.g., family), identified essentially by relation to ourselves?

---

10 Examples might be Nietzche, early emotivists, and more recently Andrew Oldenquist in his provocative paper "Loyalties" in the *Journal of Philosophy* 79 (1982), 173–93.

At this stage, when the moral grounds and limits of personal responsibility are called into question, the discussion moves to a more abstract level in which impartiality plays an important role. At this point if one says, "I don't care what impartial people would say," then one has simply given up the effort to find a reasonable moral adjudication and defense of one's beliefs.

To avoid misunderstanding, it is worth emphasizing again that the impartiality thesis we have been considering is not the same as its more controversial cousins. For example, it does not assert, with Kant, that basic moral principles are grounded in pure reason, independent of all contingent features of human nature, that they admit no exceptions, or that they command only our wills and not our feelings. Our thesis does not imply that self-sufficiency is better than dependence, or that the emotional detachment of a judge is better than the compassion of a lover. No one is urged to live with his or her eyes fixed on abstract moral principles, still less with concentration on their justification from an impartial perspective. Nothing is implied about which motives make acts morally commendable. Impartiality has its important place, but its place is not that of a model for moral sainthood.

A footnote here may be helpful. Modern philosophers sometimes talk rather loosely about "the moral point of view." It is frequently said that the moral point of view is an impartial point of view, detached from one's individual loves and hates.[11] But, in fact, there is not a single "moral point of view;" what point of view is morally appropriate depends upon what is being viewed and what the question about it is. When a conscientious mother faces the question of how to respond to her daughter's unwanted pregnancy, compassion and sensitivity to individual needs are crucial to a moral perspective. When, later, awareness of cultural differences leads her to question the nature and grounds of the moral values she has relied on, then her compassion and sensitivity alone will not settle the issue. Another point of view is called for, a perspective from which she could discuss these matters reasonably with others who have different particular attachments. It is here that impartiality becomes important. To talk as if there is a single "moral point of view" only confuses the issue.

II

Often we hear the complaint that someone has violated the autonomy of another, for example, by trying to manipulate the other person with lies or improper threats. The idea here is quite different from the previous, philosophers' notion of autonomy. The autonomy in question here is not a feature of ideal moral legislators but a *right* that every responsible person has, a right to make certain decisions for himself or herself without undue interference from others. To respect

11 For example, Kurt Baier, *The Moral Point of View* (Ithaca: Cornell University Press, 1958).

someone as an autonomous person in this sense is to acknowledge that certain decisions are up to him or her and thus to refrain from efforts to control those decisions. To say that a person is autonomous, in this view, is not to *describe* the person (e.g., as mature, reflective, or independent); it is to *grant* the person a *right* to control certain matters for himself or herself. The operative analogy here is with autonomous nations. They may not be especially wise or well governed, but they have a right to determine their internal affairs without outside interference of various sorts.

Exactly what these rights of autonomy are is, of course, a matter of controversy. But, to focus discussion, let us think of a right of individual autonomy as follows: it is a right to make otherwise morally permissible decisions about matters deeply affecting one's own life without interference by controlling threats and bribes, manipulations, and willful distortion of relevant information. Like most rights, this right of autonomy may be defeasible – or overridden in special circumstances; but it is nonetheless important.

The right of autonomy is a right to freedom of a certain sort, but, of course, it is not an unlimited right to do as one pleases. It is limited, for example, by principles of justice, noninjury, contract, and responsibility to others. Autonomous persons are not free to cheat on their taxes, beat their children, or renege on their promises. Nor is autonomy a freedom to win in situations of fair competition: you do not violate my autonomy if you prevent me from having a place on a team by performing better than I do in the tryouts. Again, autonomy is not freedom to control others' lives in matters that mainly affect them, for example, a friend's choice of companions, jobs, and hairstyle. On the contrary, a person's right of autonomy protects certain decisions that deeply affect that person's own life so long as they are consistent with other basic moral principles, including recognition of comparable liberties for others.

When we say that a person has a right of autonomy, however, we are not simply saying that he or she is morally *permitted* to make his or her own decisions within the appropriate area of choice; we are also saying that others should not interfere in certain ways. What sorts of interferences are ruled out? Most obviously, physical coercion and threats that would be wrong to carry out in any case: e.g., threatening to slander someone if he or she does not vote as one wishes. But other interference can be illegitimate too. Consider, for example, the manipulative parent's threat, "If you move away, I will commit suicide." If designed solely to control another's choice rather than merely explaining one's "contingency plans," the threat represents an undue interference with that person's autonomy. Generally, when we try to manipulate others' choices of partner, career, or legitimate lifestyle by nonrational techniques, we unduly interfere with choices that are rightfully their own. Respecting individuals' autonomy means granting them at least the *opportunity* to make their crucial life-affecting choices in a rational manner. Concealing or distorting information relevant to such decisions can also be a way of depriving them of this opportunity, even if one's aim is not primarily to influence their choices. For example, a father, however well intentioned, might unduly interfere with his shy daughter's important life choices if, to comfort her, he tried to persuade her that women in law and other competitive professions are always unattractive.

The right of autonomy, as I see it, is not rooted in any idea that rational decision making is intrinsically valuable, or in the optimistic faith that people will use their opportunity to make the best possible choices. All the more, I would not want to say that people have a right of autonomy only to the extent that we expect they will make rational choices. Within limits, people should be allowed to make their own choices even if the choices are likely to be foolish. Questions about the justification and limits of the right of autonomy are difficult; but I hope that, on reflection, most would agree that we are not entitled to interfere with others' crucial life choices just because we believe they are likely to be nonrational or unwise.

Accepting this right of autonomy does not mean that we must accept more extreme views that are sometimes associated with the word "autonomy." For example, we can acknowledge the right without in any way implying that self-sufficiency, independence, and separation from others are goals worth pursuing. Respecting people's autonomy requires resisting the temptation to "take charge" of their lives without their consent, but it does not deny anyone the choice to share with others, to acknowledge one's dependency, to accept advice, or even to sacrifice for the interests of others. The right of autonomy allows people some room to make their own choices; it does not dictate what those choices should be.

Also acknowledging a right of autonomy does not mean that people are morally better, or at a higher stage of development, if they constantly think of moral problems as conflicts of individual rights rather than as occasions for sensitivity and compassion. Rights are just one aspect of complex moral problems, and fixation on this aspect to the exclusion of others can be as much a moral fault as overlooking rights altogether. To say that we should respect a right of autonomy is not to say that we should ignore everything else.

But, one may wonder, does not the right of autonomy often conflict with the compassionate response to a moral problem? Suppose, for example, that by a benevolent lie I can manipulate a friend away from a potentially disastrous choice, say, to reunite with an unworthy and incompatible ex-lover. Would not compassion advise me to tell the lie despite the invasion of my friend's autonomy? Or, again, would not the right of autonomy prevent a kindhearted doctor from compassionately distorting the truth regarding the progress of a patient's terminal illness?

Such conflicts, I think, are unavoidable; the question is how should we handle them? Should we deny that there is anything here but compassion to consider?

Or should we rather acknowledge such conflicts as tragic choices between two competing values each important in its own right – the prevention of unnecessary suffering and the individual's opportunity to make his or her own crucial life choices? The latter, surely, would be the answer of a balanced moral conception which encompasses both the male and female perspectives described by Gilligan. This would mean that concern for rights at times constrains what a compassionate person may do, but in no way does it deny the moral importance of compassion.

III

Neither of the previous ideas of autonomy implies that in general, being an autonomous person, or living autonomously, is a morally desirable goal. But many have felt that, in some sense, autonomy is such a goal. Some, for example, may think of autonomy as constantly being motivated by pure respect for impartial principles rather than by compassion; but, as I have said, I find it far from obvious that this is a moral ideal. At least, it is a more controversial ideal than the two autonomy theses I have presented so far. Others seem to think of autonomy as self-sufficiency, independence, "making it on one's own"; but, though some people may prefer this way of life, it is hard to see why it should be regarded a *moral* goal. Is a person morally worse for acknowledging his or her dependency and preferring close ties with others to self-sufficiency? Surely not; and, as Gilligan suggests, any development theories that implied this would be naturally suspected of prejudice.

There is, however, a more limited idea of autonomy that might be recommended as a moral ideal; and this idea lies behind a third way I believe autonomy is important.

Suppose we focus on the situation of an ordinary person facing a real moral decision. The context is not, as before, general philosophical reflection or debate about the nature and justification of moral principles but rather an immediate need to decide what to do about an actual problem at hand. Is there any sense in which making the judgment as an autonomous person is a moral ideal, so that we should make it our goal to face such problems as autonomous persons?

Impartial detachment from particular concerns, I have suggested, is not such a goal; and the *right* of autonomy we have considered is concerned with how we affect others by our decisions rather than with how we make our moral choices. Is there, then, any other sense of autonomy in which we should strive to make particular moral decisions as autonomous agents?

A clue is provided by the very word "autonomy," which suggests "self-governance." People are not self-governing, in a sense, when their responses to problems are blind, dictated by neurotic impulses of which they are unaware, shaped by prejudices at odds with the noble sentiments they think are moving them. When we make decisions like this we are divided against ourselves. There is little profit in debating which is the "true self" — the "self" revealed in high-minded, consciously adopted principles, or the "self" of prejudice and neurotic impulse that really determines the outcome; there is no unified "self" here to govern the decision.

While it may be debated whether having a unified personality is in general a moral goal, surely we can agree that it is a morally worthy goal to try to face our important moral decisions with as few as possible of these self-fracturing obstacles. Ideally autonomous, or self-governing, moral agents would respond to the real facts of the situation they face, not to a perception distorted by morally irrelevant needs and prejudices. The principles and values they try to express in their decisions would be genuine guiding considerations and not mere epiphenomena unrelated to their real moral motivation. If compassion is the guiding value, it would be genuine compassion and not a self-deceptive mask for concern for reputation. If respect for rights is the guiding consideration, then it would be sincere respect and not fear of punishment. This is not to say that other motives are bad or inappropriate (though they may be), nor that approaching moral decisions with autonomy of this sort is sufficient for making the right decision. The point is rather that, ideally, moral agents face their moral choices with awareness of both the relevant features of the problem and effective understanding of their real values.

To say that autonomy in this sense is an ideal is not necessarily to condemn those who lack it; for it is far from the only moral ideal, and it is very hard to achieve.

Is this third idea of autonomy compatible with compassion? Of course, it is. Holding autonomy of this sort as an ideal is neutral in disputes about which is more important, compassion or respect for rights. What it tells us is merely that we should try to face moral decisions with integrity and self-awareness. Or, perhaps better, if it favors either side, the ideal of autonomy for particular moral decisions urges us to face such problems with compassion: for I suspect that without compassion one can never really become aware of the morally relevant facts in the situation one faces. The inner needs and feelings of others are virtually always relevant, and without compassion one can perhaps never fully know what these are — or give them their appropriate weight.

I conclude, then, that there are at least three modest but important ways that autonomy is needed in a complete conception of morality. None is incompatible with recognition of the importance of compassion; and, though one ideal of autonomy puts some constraints on the reliance on compassion alone, another ideal of autonomy itself seems to require compassion. If, as Carol Gilligan's work suggests, autonomy represents a male value and compassion a female value, then my conclusion is that we must get the sexes together.

5

Symbolic protest and calculated silence

The reasons for protesting a serious injustice are usually not hard to find.[1] One wants to put an end to the wrongdoing, to prevent its recurrence, or at least touch some consciences in a way that may prove beneficial in other contexts. But sometimes there seems to be no reasonable hope of achieving these ends. The perpetrators of injustice will not be moved, protest may be inconvenient or risky to oneself, and its long-range effects on others may be minimal or may include as much harm as help. To protest in these circumstances seems at best a symbolic gesture. But is it a gesture worth making? Attitudes about this diverge sharply. Some say that, despite the consequences, protest is called for: "One cannot stand silently by." To denounce injustice at a risk to oneself is morally admirable, they say, whether or not it produces a positive net utility. Others see symbolic protest as pointless and at times reprehensible. If the overall effects for others are not better and it entails harm or risk to oneself, is it not foolish? And isn't the motive simply a self-righteous desire to be, or appear, morally "pure"?

These conflicting attitudes pose a problem of understanding for moral philosophy. The point of view behind the second attitude is clear enough: acts, including speech acts, are to be evaluated by their probable consequences; no one is morally required to take risks unless the probable consequences are beneficial; what is commendable is regard for the best results, not futile gestures. If silence, even compromise, is well calculated to produce the best consequences, then that is the course one should take. This consequentialist attitude is familiar and, in the absence of cogent alternatives, very appealing. In reflecting on sample cases, however, many of us, I think, will find ourselves drawn to the first attitude, which regards symbolic protest as commendable despite the risks. But what can be said for it? Why should we feel that symbolic protest is often appropriate and admirable rather than foolish and self-righteous?

I

It may be well to begin by fixing attention on some examples. Consider first an old woman in Nazi Germany. She lives on modest savings and offers no support

---

1 I have profited from discussions on the topic of this paper with several people, most notably my colleagues, Robert Adams, Bernard Boxill, Gregory Kavka, and Richard Wasserstrom. Their protests were much appreciated even when, perhaps due to my blindness, they were ineffective.

to the Nazi regime either physically or morally. When the latest discriminatory laws against Jews are enforced, she is moved to protest. As a non-Jew she could have remained silent and thereby avoided much subsequent harassment. She is regarded as a silly eccentric and so cannot expect to make an impact on others, much less to stop the Nazi machinery. She still feels that she should speak up, but she wonders why.

Next consider a liberal businessman at a racist dinner party. Invited by business acquaintances, he is shocked to find that the conversation on all sides is openly and grossly contemptuous of certain minorities on grounds of racial bias alone. The guests try to outdo one another with tales about how they manage to circumvent equal opportunity laws. Polite opposition yields nothing but cynical laughter. The indignant liberal is convinced at last that nothing he can say will have any good effect on this company. He wonders then whether it is best to finish the dinner quietly, for the sake of his business interests, or to walk out in protest.[2]

These cases exemplify certain conditions which I shall take as paradigmatic of the problem of symbolic protest, at least of the sort I intend to discuss: (a) the protest is of a serious injustice done to others; (b) the protest cannot reasonably be expected to end the injustice, to prevent its recurrence, or to rectify it in any way; (c) the protest may cause some harm, but not disaster, to the protestor; (d) the effects of the protest on others' welfare can reasonably be expected to be minimal or to include a balance of benefit and harm. In real cases, of course, the facts may be disputed, but for present purposes let us take these conditions as given. It should be noted too that in each case the agent wonders what is the best thing to do. The issue is not whether to do what one has antecedently decided is best. Thus rhetorical appeals such as, "Do what your conscience tells you" and "Do the courageous thing," are beside the point. Conscience has not yet spoken unequivocally; and, while it is courageous to take risks for what one believes best, the decision about what is best has not been finally made.

The examples have been deliberately constructed to set aside familiar utilitarian arguments for protest. In most real situations, of course, these cannot be lightly dismissed. From a utilitarian point of view a very small chance to stop a great harm will warrant considerable risk and sacrifice. So even if protest seems very likely to be futile, the outside chance that it could work will often justify the problems it may cause. Also the indirect benefits of protest should not be underestimated in actual cases. Even the hardest heart may soften, if not melt, under moral pressure, and protest may comfort the victims and encourage others to resist injustice elsewhere.

---

2   Walking out, like refusing a handshake and turning one's back, can be means of protesting without words. So when, in the title of this paper, calculated silence is contrasted with protest, this must not be taken too literally. For the purpose of protest, symbolic actions often speak louder than words.

In setting aside utilitarian considerations, however, we do not necessarily limit our conclusions to cases in which they do not apply. For if, by focusing on the restricted cases, we can find nonutilitarian arguments for protest, these may reinforce whatever utilitarian arguments there are for protest.

II

Having set aside utilitarian considerations, it is natural to look for reasons for protest among the principles commonly held by deontologists. These would include prohibitions of promise-breaking, deliberate deception, killing of innocents, and the like. In special cases of symbolic protest these principles might be applicable. Suppose, for example, that I have made a solemn promise to a friend that I will not stand by while his good name is slandered by his enemies after his death. Then, as soon as he dies, greedy and malicious biographers try to make a quick profit by inventing scandalous stories about him. Suppose that I know that the stories are false, but I cannot prove it. Even if I cannot prevent their publication or force retractions, it seems I should protest and tell the truth as I know it. This seems so, even if the effort is inconvenient to me and the effect on others is insignificant.

There may also be times when protest is necessary to avoid deception. Suppose, for example, that a group of people is doing what I regard quite wrong, say, amusing themselves by slaughtering polar bears with rifles from helicopters. But imagine that these are wealthy, influential people, with whom for selfish reasons I want to be associated. If I let my true feelings show, they may break off the association; and I am reasonably convinced that I cannot change them. Avoiding the issue, let us say, is impossible: I must pretend to condone their activities or else let them know my objections. As they, assuming our mutual respect, come to count me as a friend, surely I should not persist in the deception.

These cases seem straightforward but atypical. Normally one does not need to make a protest to avoid breaking promises or building friendships on deception. In other special situations deontological principles come into play in a rather more complex way. Consider the judge in Nazi Germany who is ordered to sign death warrants for political prisoners whom he believes innocent. To refuse will only result in his replacement by someone else who will sign the warrants. A protest would achieve nothing but dismissal. He figures that he can bring about some good results by keeping quiet, signing the warrants, and trying to help others secretly later. But this path of calculated silence is blocked if there is an absolute, or at least quite stringent, moral principle against killing innocent people. His only remaining choices are to resign without protest or to resign (or be dismissed) with protest. The principle against killing does not itself require protest but it rules out the only appealing alternative.

There are doubtless many similar situations. Often one will want to stay within a partially corrupt institution in order to work for reform or to use its resources for some social good. The price of doing so may be suppressing the inclination to tell its leaders how much one disapproves of their corruption. But when the benefits of quiet cooperation can be purchased only by participating oneself in the spreading of false rumors, granting unjust favors, misappropriating funds, and the like, then the morally acceptable options seem more limited: one can get out quietly or go out protesting. Since one's effectiveness within the group is lost either way, the main rationale for silence has dissolved.

Sometimes the relevant deontological principle may be, not a direct prohibition of deception, killing, slandering, and the like, but a more indefinite proscription of complicity in such activities. Although rhetoric often treats any association with corrupt people or institutions as complicity, I have in mind a narrower sense of the term. The paradigm is a direct and substantial contribution to wrongdoing, made freely with acceptable options available and with the knowledge that one is so contributing. Aside from being a willing and known contribution to a wrong, the act in question may not itself be wrong. For example, a butler's selling detailed drawings of his employer's estate may not be wrong if the buyer is an art dealer, but quite otherwise if he is a notorious burglar. How direct and substantial the contribution must be is hard to say (for example, selling the burglar a flashlight), and there may, of course, be overriding considerations (for example, tending his wounds). But at least it seems clear that complicity is not in general avoided by the claims: "If I had not helped, someone else would have," and, "Though I knew, my intent was not to aid in the wrongdoing but just to make money (keep my job, and so on)."

Like the previous principles, a principle against moral complicity can undermine the rationale for suppressing a protest even though it provides no direct reason to protest. Consider the worker in a factory recently converted from automobile-making to the production of tanks for use in an unjust war. He knows that if he resigns, he will be replaced easily; and if he protests the war, he will be fired. Losing the job would be a personal hardship, and, because he is of an unpopular and suspect race, he believes that no one would be influenced by his protest. Sabotage is out of the question, as it has been repeatedly detected and suppressed. To hold back his objections to the war and quietly continue to build the tanks seems to involve him in moral complicity. The only remaining options are to resign without giving reasons or to protest. The prohibition of complicity does not demand protest, but it blocks off as illegitimate a choice to reap the maximum benefits of remaining silent.

III

Familiar deontological principles, it seems, provide an argument for symbolic protest only in special circumstances; and even when they are pertinent, they often leave a permissible choice between protest and silent resignation. What other reasons, one wonders, could favor making a symbolic protest? Several initially tempting arguments, I believe, prove to be unsatisfying.

First, a symbolic protest is sometimes explained as if the reason for it is simply the personal satisfaction of the protestor. One hears: "I just could not bear to remain silent," and, "I would hate myself if I did not speak up." Now these remarks could be a way of saying that not protesting would cause pangs of conscience, but, if so, this is hardly a reason for believing that one should protest. On the contrary, to say that one's conscience will hurt if one does not do something *presupposes* that one believes it to be wrong. On the other hand, the remarks could be saying, more generally, that to stifle a protest would be painful, frustrating, and a cause of unhappiness about oneself. While the liability to such unhappiness may well be a sign of some morally admirable impulses, to make a protest simply to avoid experiencing the pain does not seem especially commendable from a moral point of view. To avoid pain and frustration for oneself may be a good reason for doing something, but not in general a reason for regarding it a morally good thing to do. Unless there is some further reason to express one's moral outrage, doing so seems no more admirable than giving vent to nonmoral anger, and it may often be more imprudent. To feel moral indignation is perhaps a good thing, but it remains to be seen why it is commendable to express it in protest which is not expected to be effective.

Second, one might think of symbolic protest as a minimum form of retribution. It is often thought that those who are guilty of deliberate and gross injustice deserve to suffer, or at least that they ought not to prosper unbothered while they cause others to suffer. When a person cannot stop an injustice, he is usually in a poor position to punish the perpetrators in any direct way. However, by protesting their deeds he may to some degree disturb their comfort. Most people like to have the good opinion of others, and even tyrants are apt to want at least submissive acceptance. By protesting a person gives notice that his approval is withheld and that, though he must live with injustice, he does not accept it. Instead of passively submitting, he openly encourages others to opposition in spirit – the only punishment circumstances allow. Unlike a shot in the dark, this may be thought a particularly appropriate form of retribution; for it hurts, if at all, by means of drawing attention to the moral wrongs for which punishment is deserved.

This line of argument also has its limits. The value of retribution is controversial at best, and even those who advocate it rarely offer the desire for retribution as an especially *commendable* motive. To punish the guilty may be just, but do we really admire those who, for no other benefits, undergo hardships to see that the prosperity of the guilty is disturbed? Besides, as punishments go, protest seems rather mild and ineffective.[3] The Nazi leaders may care little for the good opinion

3 It may be suspected that the argument considered here, and some subsequent ones, are really

of the old woman who denounces them, and the racial bigots may be delighted to demonstrate the ineffectiveness of the liberal's opposition. The worse the offender, and so the more deserving of punishment, the less likely is he to care about the objections of the moralist. One hopes that there is more than retribution behind the intuitions in favor of symbolic protest.

IV

If the purpose of symbolic protest is not to satisfy familiar deontological principles, to avoid complicity, to relieve personal discomfort, or to make retribution, what is the point? One conception worth exploring is that the point, at least the immediate point, is to disassociate oneself from evil. That one should do this is uncontroversial if what is meant is simply that one should refuse to do, or to help others to do, what is evil; but I have in mind something more. While committing no injustice himself, a person can nevertheless associate himself with those who do by condoning their activities; and a person can disassociate himself from a corrupt group both by acting to prevent their unjust acts and also, in appropriate contexts, by protesting, denouncing what they do, and taking a symbolic stand with the victims. "Who one is" for moral purposes – e.g., a Nazi, a racist, a Christian, a humanist – is determined not simply by substantive contributions to various good or evil causes but to some extent by what and whom one associates oneself with, and in some contexts this depends importantly on the symbolic gestures one is prepared to make.

Attempts to disassociate oneself from evil can take several different forms, and the extent to which we regard this as commendable will depend on many factors: for example, whether the attempt is to disassociate from groups, individuals, or principles and policies; how serious the wrong or corruption is; what hope there is of reform; the nature of one's previous association with a group or individual; how much good can be achieved by continued association; the means of disassociation; and what further motives underlie it. Moral opinion about these matters is complex and doubtless varies considerably, but to further discussion let us consider three sorts of disassociation which, I believe, would be widely accepted and which can sometimes be achieved through symbolic protest.

First consider disassociation from organizations or groups that are deeply involved in injustice and prove to be beyond reform. To refuse all commerce and communication with corrupt groups would be foolish and dangerous; and to proclaim repeatedly, "I am not one of them!" seems self-righteous and unnecessary. But a more limited disassociation in special contexts is often regarded as morally appropriate and even commendable. Suppose, for example, that a person

consequentialist arguments of the sort which I have tried to set aside. However, the issue is not whether protest causes more long-range benefit than harm but whether it is effective in satisfying a deontological principle, such as to reward and punish in accord with desert.

finds himself a member of an organization that has just become, or is just discovered to be, thoroughly corrupt, reaping profits from all manner of harmful and unjust practices. The organization might be a social club, an athletic team, a political party, a business firm, or any voluntary group capable of joint action, incurring obligations, and having common interests and principles. Often, we hope, corrupt organizations can be effectively reformed and their injustices rectified; but not always. Often the offensive part of the organization can be isolated and opposed without complete withdrawal; but sometimes not. The corruption may be so severe and so deeply entrenched that to remain a member, especially a nonprotesting member, seems morally intolerable. Given that one cannot effectively combat the corruption and provided that there are not overiding moral reasons for continuing in the group, it seems that one should disassociate oneself. To deplore the corruption inwardly seems insufficient. Even if one does not personally contribute to the wrongdoing, and so avoids the charge of complicity considered earlier, still it seems that one should break off the association.

Sometimes, of course, a person can disassociate himself from a group without making a protest. If the group is highly structured, there may be formal procedures for severing the connection: resigning, refusing to pay dues, getting rid of one's stock holdings, and so on. Sometimes, however, the group is so loosely bound by ties of sentiment, mutual expectations, common aims, and the like, that there are no official procedures for getting out. One must make one's objections explicit or be counted a continuing member. The membership conditions may even be so vague that without an overt act of disassociation one will still *be* a member. Suppose, for example, you have deliberately but informally associated yourself with "whites" in a racially polarized community, with a certain social set, with an unstructured group of fans of a team or a politician, or with a revolutionary movement. As there are no dues, membership lists, and the like, there can be no formal resignation. In time, perhaps, you can disassociate yourself by neglect and refusal to give continued support. But to dissociate at once you may have to say something or do something to express your new attitude of opposition.

Disassociation of the sort intended here presupposes that one has associated oneself with an organization. It is not simply a refusal to associate with a group, or a public declaration that one is not a member. Thus the relevant principle of disassociation does not require the ordinary citizen to "disassociate" from the Mafia, assuming he never had anything to do with it; the principle is addressed instead to the Mafia members and those who associate themselves with it by supporting it, dealing with it, condoning it, and the like. Also disassociation is not simply an inward disapproval or secret resolve to oppose; these amount to only a wish or plan to disassociate. Again, disassociation is not simply a matter of words or symbolic gestures; for the person who *says* that he disassociates himself, even turns in a formal resignation, is not always convincing. If he continues to favor the group and secretly gives it aid, then he has only pretended to disassociate himself or has done so only in form. To disassociate, one needs both an appropriate attitude, including a disposition to refuse support, and some outward manifestation of that attitude, for example, opposition or refusal of support when the occasion allows or, at least, tokens of one's intention to oppose or refuse support if nothing more is possible.

The principle that one should disassociate from irreparably corrupt groups, if accepted, would favor symbolic protest in many cases. If, to alter my previous examples, the woman in Nazi Germany had voted for the Nazis, or was a party member or government employee, she might reasonably regard herself as associated with the leadership even though she came to disapprove of their policies. Lacking an opportunity for effective opposition, she might well think that a symbolic protest was necessary to disassociate her, so far as possible, from them. Again, if my liberal businessman was in partnership with other guests and if their racist attitudes affected joint policy, he would naturally feel that a symbolic protest was the least he could do. But the examples as originally described were not so clear-cut. The old woman was a German but not otherwise associated with the Nazis, and the liberal was acquainted with the other guests but not in partnership with them. These associations lie at best on the border of the class of voluntary groups we have considered; and so the argument for symbolic protest as a way of disassociating from evil groups is blurred in these cases. Moreover, a slight shift in the cases would make this rationale for symbolic protest even more dubious. Suppose, for example, that the old woman was not even a German but a foreigner just passing through Nazi Germany. As she is not associated with the Nazis, she has no need to disassociate herself in the sense we have been considering. Similarly, if the liberal businessman had overheard racist talk from strangers on a bus, rather than from partners or fellow guests, he had no need to break off an association. The principle that one ought to disassociate from irreparably corrupt organizations is also of limited application for another reason, noted earlier: one can often disassociate without protesting. For example, one can resign from a company without giving reasons, divest oneself of stock in a morally dubious enterprise without explaining why, and run away from military induction without stating one's moral objections to it or the war it supports.

Another principle which, I suspect, is widely held in some form or other is that one should refuse to associate oneself with individuals who are thoroughly corrupt. This would apply in contexts where one had no previous association with the individuals, such as friendship or membership in the same clubs. The idea is that when a person reaches an extreme point of corruption, and seems to offer no hope of reform, one should not merely deplore what he does but deny him much of what is normally extended to those with whom one associates oneself: for example, loyalty, trust, respect as an individual, social amenities, readiness to cooperate and compromise, and the various signs of being pleased to share in mutual projects. The principle, no doubt, is acceptable to most only if suitably qualified. There may be overriding reasons of state which require some association with the worst of leaders. Some would say that everyone is owed respect as a human being, and others might add that all should be loved. Organizations can be abandoned as worthless and beyond repair without anyone necessarily being the worse for it, but when the same attitude is generally taken towards a person it seems inevitable that at least one person will be hurt. Refusal to associate with someone can easily be hypocritical; people in glass houses should hesitate to throw stones, and most of our houses are to some extent brittle. Nevertheless, if these matters are taken into account, many would still say that there are times when one should refuse to associate with corrupt people and morally appropriate ways to do it. A European prince was widely applauded, for example, when he literally turned his back on a notorious African tyrant, and a late presidential candidate was roundly condemned by many for posing for photographs with his arm around the man who had come to symbolize hostility to civil rights.

The principle that one should refuse to associate oneself with extraordinarily corrupt people would favor symbolic protest in situations where silence creates a presumption of normal social relations, giving the impression that what is really outrageous is in fact overlooked or condoned. The businessman, for example, would give an impression of being ready to associate himself with the racists if he finished his dinner quietly listening to their stream of bigotry. And even a visitor in Nazi Germany would seem ready to associate with the Nazis if she went through the motions of the happy tourist while Jews were being rounded up for deportation. In these circumstances a person who wanted not to associate himself with extreme racists would naturally see vigorous protest as at least a partial way of expressing this and of preventing association from developing.

The principles just considered favor symbolic protest only in extreme cases, in which the protestor wants to get out of a corrupt group altogether or avoid becoming associated with extraordinarily corrupt individuals. There are many other situations, however, in which the symbolic protest may seem appropriate: for example, when one belongs to a basically good organization which is seriously unjust in some limited aspect, or when one has important overriding moral reasons to remain a part of a basically bad organization, or when for good reasons one does not wish to shun an unjust individual but only deplore what he does. In these cases too symbolic a protest might be motivated by a desire to disassociate oneself, in a sense, from evil. The idea would be not to break or avoid an association with an individual or group but to put oneself on record as opposed to the sort of acts and policies that are protested. One protests not to shun the unjust group or person but to express openly one's unwillingness to condone, support, or imitate unjust practices. Only a busybody would feel a need to denounce every wrong act and policy he encounters, but there are times when taking a symbolic stand seems called for. This is especially so when the acts or policies are very seriously unjust, when they are acts or policies of groups to which we belong, and when the circumstances make silence a token of consent. Thus the old German woman may have no special reason to protest an injustice in a Chicago Kiwanis Club which she reads about in the foreign press, but a protest would be more clearly called for if the injustice was done by her own local church and everyone talked to her about it as if she approved.

V

Even if these principles are intuitively appealing, we still naturally wonder *why* we should disassociate ourselves from evil in the various ways we have considered. By hypothesis, protest will not put an end to the injustice or have, on balance, beneficial consequences. One familiar response, suggested by both critics and advocates of symbolic protest, is that the purpose is "to keep one's hands clean." This view can take many forms, most of which do little to support our initial intuitive feelings for symbolic protest.

It is sometimes said, for example, that by his silence the nonprotestor shares the guilt of the wrongdoer or, more dramatically, that the blood of the victims will stain his hands as well as the oppressor's. But this requires interpretation. On one reading, the contention reflects a confused idea of moral guilt. It treats guilt as something which can pass from one person to another by contact, like the stains of fresh blood or dye, or by social intercourse, like reputation and stigma. This notion has its roots in the old idea that guilt, not just responsibility or liability to sin, can be passed on from generation to generation by inheritance. But on any standard view of guilt which implies a wrong on the part of the guilty, guilt cannot be transferred in these ways. If the nonprotestor is guilty, it is for something he himself has done (or omitted), not for what others have done (or omitted). If there are stains of guilt on his hands, only he can have put them there.

Now it may be that the nonprotestor has done something wrong by refusing to disassociate himself from unjust groups, individuals, or policies; and, if so, one could express this without confusion by saying that he shares in the guilt of the oppressors, meaning thereby that he and they are both wrong for their (distinct) parts in the continuing injustice. But, if this is what is meant, we still need a reason for saying that his refusal to disassociate himself was wrong. To say that his refusal makes him share the guilt, in this sense, expresses the *conclusion* that his refusal was wrong but it does not explain why.

Another sense that can be given to the contention that the nonprotestor's hands will be stained is that by refusing to set himself publicly against the wrongdoers, or their unjust acts, the nonprotestor will in time become corrupt like them. This would be an assertion of cause and effect: continued association with corrupt people and silence in face of injustice tend to lead one into corruption. We are imitators by nature, and when we do not protest a corrupt regime we are more likely to be invited to take a full part in it. But, like most predictions, such contentions are fallible and not always convincing. Our old woman in Nazi Germany might be reasonably convinced that, even if she does not protest, she will never herself join in racial or religious discrimination. And our liberal businessman will hardly be persuaded to risk his business interests by protest if the argument is simply that if he does not, he himself will become a bigot.

Another version of the "clean hands" argument would say that disassociation is required to avoid sharing *responsibility* for the injustices done by a group. But responsibility in what sense? We have already ruled out cases in which the nonprotestor is *causally* responsible for wrong acts: his silence does not contribute to the wrong, and there is nothing he can do to stop it. Further, we cannot say without begging the question at issue that the nonprotestor's refusal to disassociate makes him responsible in the sense of being *at fault* or guilty. What remains, it seems, is only shared responsibility to make amends, to pay compensation, and the like. Members of groups often have this responsibility even though they themselves did not contribute to an injury done by the group and are in no way guilty because of it. In becoming members, one might argue, they took on some responsibility to help the group discharge its obligations, including whatever reparations or compensation is owed to the victims of wrongs done by the group.

This notion of shared responsibility might well give a person a self-interested reason to disassociate from a corrupt group – or to refuse to form associations with corrupt individuals. However, it is hard to see how it can provide a moral reason. To get out of a group in order to avoid having to pay for its debts, or compensate for its injustices, may be sensible but it is not especially commendable from a moral point of view.

There is, I think, a more charitable reading of the "clean hands" rationale for symbolic protest. On this interpretation, the protestor's attempts to disassociate himself are not so much efforts to avoid responsibility as expressions of the high value he places on justice. Normally one who cares for justice can show it not only by refraining from unjust acts but also by constructive efforts to reform unjust institutions, and the like. But in the contexts under discussion there are no opportunities for such constructive activity. One is faced with gross injustice and is powerless to stop it. Deploring it intensely, one would naturally prefer not to be surrounded by it, to live amiably with those who perpetuate it, and to suppress one's feelings about it. Those who care deeply about aesthetic standards will similarly want to disassociate themselves in various ways from groups and individuals who perpetuate ugliness, even when they cannot effect a change, and they will naturally want to speak out when confronted with the most blatant offenses against taste. Civility requires more restraint in this case, but the feelings can be similar. What makes symbolic protest commendable on this view is not intended results but the underlying values expressed. The protestor is not viewed here as being proud of his moral commitment, wanting to show it off, and using symbolic protest as a means. Rather, caring deeply and genuinely for justice, frustrated at his powerlessness to combat it, he wants at least to have as little to do with it as possible. It is not that he values comfort above all and so speaks out to avoid discomfort; on the contrary, he values justice deeply, aside from the effect on him, and this is what moves him to feel discomfort at associating with the unjust and to risk other sorts of discomfort by disassociating himself.

While this may help to explain why those who make symbolic protests are sometimes admired and commended, it does not offer much of an argument to a person who is wondering whether or not he should make a symbolic protest. Should we say to him, "Disassociate yourself because you will thereby give natural expression to your deep concern for justice, which is something commendable to have"? If he lacks the deep concern, protest would only fool others and make him no better. But if he has it and knows that this is what makes him *want* to disassociate himself from corrupt groups or individuals, he may wonder why he would be more commendable if he decides to act on this desire. To express a commendable desire just to show others that one has it is not an especially worthy motive. Why not suppress the desire if possible?

The idea that one should disassociate oneself from evil in order to "keep one's hands clean" focuses attention on what disassociation is supposed to do for the protestor: for example, absolve him of guilt, prevent his corruption, remove from him the responsibility to compensate, and give vent to his outrage at injustices he cannot prevent. An alternative conception, suggested by Kant, would turn attention in another direction. The point, on this view, is not so much to keep one's own hands clean as to avoid white-washing the bloody deeds of others. In answer to the question of whether or not one is permitted to associate with the wicked, Kant says:

> But where the vice is a scandal, i.e., a public display of contempt for a strict law of duty that, accordingly, carries infamy with it, one's existing association must be broken off or avoided as much as possible, even though the law of the land does not punish the offense. It must be broken off, since continued association with such a person deprives virtue of all honor, and puts it up for sale to anyone rich enough to corrupt a parasite with the pleasures of luxury.[4]

The underlying idea is that any decent self-respecting person has more to offer individuals (and groups, causes, and so on) than whatever effective action he can take on their behalf. He can also give it "honor," credit, and acclaim; and he does this not just by explicit praise but by identifying himself publicly with

---

4 *The Metaphysical Principles of Virtue*, trans. James Ellington (Indianapolis: Bobbs-Merrill, 1964), pp. 140–141.

those individuals (groups, causes, and so on). That such intangibles are regarded important is evident in all sorts of contexts where morality is not at issue. For example, in friendships, families, well-knit teams, and social clubs, we value not only the time, money, and other substantive support that our associates give us; we also care about their good opinion and the honor they do us by identifying with us. But a person who is indiscriminate about whom and what he associates himself with debases his currency, so to speak, and so makes his choice to associate no honor at all. And those who associate themselves with the flagrantly unjust cannot then adequately bestow honor and acclaim in the ways that the ideally moral person would want to do. The point of disassociation, on this view, is not so much to gain benefits for oneself or to punish the corrupt but to enable one to honor the persons, groups, and causes that, from a moral point of view, most deserve it. One would disassociate from evil so that one could more meaningfully associate with good.

VI

Suppose that someone makes a symbolic protest in order to disassociate himself from some corrupt group, individual, or policy and so to be better able to associate himself with morally admirable groups, individuals, or policies. Might we not suspect that, rather than being commendable, the act was a sign of self-righteousness? After all, his critics might say, he seems to be moved, not by a desire to avoid doing wrong or to stop injustice, but by a desire to be in the best company and to shut out those he regards as beneath him. We naturally suspect him of being unduly moralistic, judgmental, overly concerned with reputation and status, and of having too good an opinion of himself and too little understanding of human weakness. To denounce the wrongs of others is fine, they might say, as long as there is hope of stopping them, but otherwise it is a mark of self-righteousness.

Human motivation is complex and never easy to discern, and it must be admitted that symbolic protests in the world outside of philosopher's examples may be rooted in all sorts of unsavory attitudes. It would be foolish to argue that everyone who makes a symbolic protest is commendable for doing so; the most one can hope to show is that symbolic protests genuinely made for the reasons we have discussed are not necessarily a manifestation of the various sorts of self-righteousness we naturally suspect. Philosophy can try to show that to do a certain thing for a certain reason is commendable, but it cannot say how often such acts are in fact motivated in the appropriate way.

Without attempting to give an analysis of self-righteousness, let us review some of the objectionable traits and attitudes that we might expect to find in the most extreme case of a self-righteous person. A partial list might include the following: (1) Concern for the appearance of virtue more than the substance, as shown, for example, in great efforts to build a reputation for doing what is right combined with weak efforts to do right when there are no witnesses. (2) A strong desire to be acknowledged as superior to others in whatever is thought to reflect the worth of a person, along with delight in the lower self-esteem which that acknowledgement costs others. (3) A strong desire to *be* superior to others in such matters, whether recognized as such or not, together with inner pleasure at being able to look down on others as less worthy. (4) An unrealistic, inflated idea of the excellence of one's own character, nurtured with self-deception and protected by avoidance of morally challenging situations. (5) A distorted sense of moral values, with excessive pride in rigid performance of minor duties and little appreciation of love and the need to alleviate misery. (6) A tendency to search for faults in others, to interfere with their lives, and to make them conform to unnecessarily rigorous standards from an underlying desire to dominate them. (7) An unforgiving and intolerant attitude toward the wrongdoing of others, with absence of sympathy and without understanding how much of one's own good record is due to one's good fortune in having few pressures and only minor temptations. (8) A desire to disassociate from corruption that is so great that, rather than have a compromising part in one relatively minor wrong, one would choose to let a hundred more serious wrongs be done by others.[5]

None of these traits is necessarily behind symbolic protest even when the purpose is to disassociate from evil. The protestor, for example, may care nothing for the appearance of virtue when disconnected with the substance (1). He may not wish to be acknowledged as superior, or even to be superior, but instead sincerely want for all to live by moral principles, just as a person with high intellectual or aesthetic standards might want that everyone equally satisfy them (2), (3). In disassociating from a group or a policy, he does not necessarily look with contempt on the individuals involved (3); and even if he decides not to associate himself with the corrupt individuals, he need not fail to understand them or lack sympathy for them (7). By disassociating oneself from the most extreme forms of corruption, one does not claim to be perfect; in principle one could protest with humility based on a realistic awareness of one's own short-comings (4). When a protest is directed against a serious injustice, is not a substitute for effective action, and does not harm others, there is no special reason to suppose that the protestor values minor dutifulness over more important matters such as the alleviation of misery (5). The protestor's life may prove him not to be a busybody who repeatedly moralizes on minor matters; he may in fact only speak up against the most outrageous injustices (6). Finally, though he

---

5 "Having a part in a wrong," as I mean it, does not simply mean "doing what is, *all things considered*, wrong to do." Obviously one should not do what is wrong, all things considered, even if it would prevent a hundred wrongs by others. What is meant, instead, is doing or helping others to do what is prima facie and normally wrong, for example, suppressing evidence in a trial, using public funds in unauthorized ways, and the like.

wishes to disassociate himself from irreparably corrupt organizations, this desire need not be so unrestrained that he would refuse all compromises which could effectively prevent others from perpetuating an injustice; in symbolic protest he disassociates himself only when there is nothing more he can do (8).

Supposing that my reflections have isolated some common intuitive beliefs about symbolic protest, important questions remain. *First,* do the intuitive principles we have considered have a rational basis in a critical, reflective moral theory? If so, will the ultimate justification turn out to be indirectly consequentialist after all? The fact that an intuitive principle directs us to act without foreseeing a desirable outcome does not foreclose the possibility that at some theoretical level the rationale will hinge upon the effect of different forms of life on human happiness and misery. *Second,* if there is an adequate rationale for symbolic protest of the sort considered here, where only the protestor himself may be harmed, do similar considerations favor symbolic protest in some situations where the harm may fall on others? For example, when a protest is made by a leader of a nation on behalf of the citizens of his country and their interests are jeopardized as well as his, is there still something to be said for it?

6

Moral purity and the lesser evil

In a morally perfect world we would not face many of the hard choices which confront us in the real world. If everyone were fully conscientious, moral dilemmas might still be posed by natural circumstances; but many of our most difficult and tragic choices would not arise. In particular, we would never need to decide whether we should ourselves do a lesser evil in order to prevent someone else from doing a greater one. Unfortunately we do not live in such a perfect world. Through greed, malice, jealousy, false pride, or whatever, people are prepared to commit the most heinous crimes against innocent victims; and sometimes, it seems, they can be prevented only by means which no one would consider in the morally perfect world. One must choose among evils; doing a lesser evil oneself or allowing others to do an even greater evil.

Harry Truman apparently saw his decision to drop atomic bombs on Hiroshima and Nagasaki in this way. To do so was clearly an evil, a wrong to many innocent people. On the other hand, the Japanese leadership, Truman thought, would otherwise refuse to surrender, causing the deaths of far more people than would be killed by the bombs. The problem, in his view, was set up by the Japanese leaders: they were wrong to bomb Pearl Harbor and would be wrong to continue the war at great cost in 1945. By forcing an immediate surrender, dropping the bombs seemed to him a justified "lesser evil."

Many have seen themselves as faced with a similar choice on a smaller scale. Men who abhor war have chosen to fight to repel unjust aggression or to put an end to slavery, genocide, and even war itself. Politicians often vote for bills they regard unjust, thinking that the likely alternative would be worse. Double-talk, lies, and burglary of private files have been defended as "lesser evils." Vigilantes regarded their lynchings as necessary deterrence of greater crimes. In *Roots* millions saw another, particularly vivid example, when a white man was forced to whip his friend, a slave, in order to keep his bosses from doing the same more cruelly.[1]

Attitudes about these situations differ sharply. At one extreme there is what I shall call the *Pragmatist*. He has no hesitation about doing the lesser evil. He is in-

---

1 Alex Haley, *Roots*, and the television series based upon this. Another striking literary example can be found in John Fowles's *The Magus*. Here a ruthless Nazi commandant orders someone to beat to death two bound prisoners; refusal, the commandant says, will result in the immediate machine-gunning of a much larger group of prisoners, all within the view of their wives and children.

terested only in results; if he can reduce the amount of harm and serious wrongdoing in the world by bending the usual rules, he will gladly do it. Moral rules, for him, are merely statements of what is *normally* and *prima facie* wrong; it is never wrong, *all things considered*, to make exceptions when doing so will prevent greater wrongs. Having done the lesser evil, the Pragmatist sees nothing to feel guilty about or ashamed of. He has fulfilled his responsibility, which was simply to do the right thing in the circumstances. Someone needed to do the lesser evil, and it would be selfish to leave the job to others just so he could maintain his "purity."

At the opposite extreme stands the *Purist*. He maintains that one should never do the "lesser evil" even to prevent a far greater evil. Moral rules for him are rigid: they do not permit us to make exceptions just because other people are not fulfilling their duties. What they do is their responsibility, not ours. If one does the lesser evil, one is right to feel guilty and ashamed. One's life is morally tainted, and one has a responsibility to make restitution to those one has wronged. If a "lesser evil" is to be done, the Purist prefers, and feels that he should prefer, that it be done by someone else. He believes that one's primary concern should be to keep one's own record clean, not to try to minimize, by any means, the quantity of wrongdoing in the world.

Most people, I expect, would find both of these positions too extreme. The contrast, however, raises three questions which deserve attention. *First,* when, if ever, should one do a lesser evil in order to prevent another from doing a greater evil? The case *for* doing the lesser evil is obvious; what is puzzling is why one should feel any hesitation about it. Even if we cannot draw a precise line showing when a lesser evil is justified, perhaps we can at least understand more clearly the moral considerations that tend to oppose our doing it.[2]

Second, how should one feel about oneself and those one harms when one does the lesser evil to prevent a greater one?[3] For the Purist and the Pragmatist the answer is easy: "guilty" or "not guilty," depending entirely on whether the lesser evil is thought to be justified. But for many of us, I believe, the question is not so simple. Even if we believe that doing a certain lesser evil is warranted, we often feel bad about having done it, not merely sympathetic with the persons harmed (as we might feel even if someone else had done the lesser evil) but somehow tainted, responsible, deeply regretful that the episode had to be a part of *our* lives. These feelings, however, are puzzling. After all, if we did the right thing in the circumstances, what more could we expect of ourselves?

---

2 My discussion, as will be evident, does not even attempt to state a principle which distinguishes justified from unjustified instances of doing the lesser evil; my focus, instead, is on reasons tending to oppose or support doing the lesser evil and on related questions about self-regarding attitudes. For a rich and stimulating discussion of how one might draw the line between justified and unjustified cases of doing the lesser evil, see Terrance C. McConnell, "Moral Blackmail," *Ethics* 91 (July 1981): 54–67.

3 My thoughts on this question, as on many others, are stimulated by discussions with Herbert Morris.

This second issue leads to a *third*, more general question: what is the proper attitude towards one's own moral record?[4] To be sure, one should want it to be "pure" in the minimal sense that one did only what, to the best of one's knowledge, was right in each circumstance. But is there any reason to want it to be "pure" in a stronger sense, i.e., free from even *justified* lies, killings, voting for unjust laws, etc.? In particular, is there reason for *preferential* concern for one's own record, for example, for caring more deeply that *I* avoid doing a justified lesser evil than that someone else avoid it? Such preferential concern looks suspiciously like selfishness or self-righteousness; and yet it may also seem to be merely a proper regard for one's own integrity.

My comments on these difficult issues will be divided as follows. First, I review and set aside several arguments which might tempt us to dismiss too quickly the controversy about whether doing the lesser evil is justified. There may be merit in some of these arguments, but they are far from settling the issue. Second, in a search for clues towards a more adequate response to the first question, I consider the second; for reflection on the way one should view oneself and others when doing the lesser evil, even when doing so is justified, suggests reasons why we should be reluctant to believe that the lesser evil *is* justified. Third, I try to sketch these reasons, that is, considerations which tend to oppose doing the lesser evil. Finally, I consider briefly the objection that my proposals would sanction a preferential concern for one's own purity which is selfish and self-righteous.

I

There are several ways of trying to dismiss too quickly the controversy about whether one should do the lesser evil. Perhaps the easiest to see through are plays upon words. Consider, for example, the following argument: "Of course one should never do the lesser evil; for a lesser evil is, after all, an evil; and one should never do what is evil." This argument takes too literally the initial description of the problem situation. In describing this as a case in which one must do a "lesser evil" to prevent a "greater," we do not intend to settle all moral questions in advance. What is meant is simply that to prevent someone from doing a serious wrong one must perform an act of a sort that is *normally* and *prima facie* wrong (though less so than the act that would be prevented). The "lesser evil," in other words, would not have a place in a morally perfect world, but whether it is wrong to do, *all things considered*, is still an open question.

Another sort of misunderstanding would lead us in the opposite direction. Consider this argument: "Of course one should always do the lesser evil; for it is, by hypothesis, the *lesser* evil; that is, it is less offensive morally than what it replaces; ideally one would avoid evil altogether, but when one cannot, then, by

---

4   The best of what I have to say on this issue, I think, is due to Robert M. Adams.

definition, one should choose the lesser." This argument fails to make a distinction which is important for understanding our problem. It is no doubt true, perhaps a necessary truth, that if I must choose between *my* doing X and *my* doing Y and X is a lesser moral offense ("evil") than Y, then I ought, all things considered, to do X. In short, if one cannot altogether avoid doing something morally offensive, then one should try to do what is least offensive. But note: the sort of choice envisioned here is not the sort described in our initial statement of the problem. Our problem arose when *one person* had to do something at least prima facie offensive or else *another person* would commit an even greater offense. It was not given that one person had to choose between *doing* a lesser evil and *doing* a greater. It is not at all obvious, and certainly does not follow from the truism above, that if I must choose between *my doing* X and *someone else's doing* Y and X is a lesser offense than Y, then I ought, all things considered, to do X. This last proposition is in fact just what is at issue.

This way of putting the issue may lead someone to object as follows: "The agent still has two choices open to him, doing something to prevent the greater evil or standing by and letting it happen; one cannot assume that action is worse than inaction; and so the fact that the 'lesser evil' is an act of commission rather than an omission does not imply that standing by is morally preferable." Actually nothing has been said to deny these points. The crucial distinction can be drawn in a way that shows this explicitly. It is, of course, a truism that if I must choose between my doing X and my omission Y (not taking steps to prevent another from doing Z) and if (it is given that) X is a lesser offense than Y, then I ought, all things considered, to do X. But in our cases it is not *given* that X (the action) is a lesser offense than Y (the omission); that is what is at issue. What is given is that X is a lesser offense than Z, the act of another which I could prevent. What is controversial is not the truism above but this: if I must choose between X and Y (omitting to prevent Z) and if X is a lesser offense than Z, then I ought, all things considered, to do X.

Another way of dismissing our problem too lightly is simply to deny that one is ever forced to choose among evils in the way our examples suggest. "There must be another alternative," some will say; "if you search with diligence and wisdom, you can always find a way to avert the greater evil without engaging in the lesser." In support examples might be cited. For instance, it is arguable that Truman could have forced the Japanese surrender by demonstrating his atomic bombs in unpopulated areas. The Vigilantes might have found a way to strengthen legitimate law enforcement, and so on.

This response rightly calls attention to the need to search for better alternatives when, in real life, we *seem* to be forced to choose among evils. Often, no doubt, a wise and diligent search will turn up other options and the apparent problem will disappear. But to suppose that this is *always* possible is, I think, an act of faith rather than an inference from observation. That there is always "another way out" is not what we learn from experience. To insist that it *must* be so suggests a need to believe that is independent of evidence. If, for example, one believes that one ought unconditionally to prevent the greater evil and yet also believes that one ought unconditionally to avoid the lesser evil, then one obviously wants to suppose that one can do both. But wishing will not make it so.

If we admit that the hard choices must sometimes be made, we might still try to settle the issue quickly by appeal to intuitions about responsibility. In fact Kant, defending his notorious view that one should not tell a lie even to prevent a murder, seems to argue this way: if another person does something wrong, then the responsibility for the harm that results is his, not yours; but if you do the "lesser evil" in an effort to prevent the other's wrongdoing, then you are responsible for any harm you cause; so you should not undertake the lesser evil.[5]

The argument as it stands seems incomplete. The relevant premises are:

(P1)   You are responsible for any bad consequences of the lesser evil (e.g., the lie).

(P2)   You are not responsible for the bad consequences of the greater evil you fail to prevent (e.g., the murder by someone else).

The conclusion desired is:

(C)   You would be wrong, all things considered, to do the lesser evil (e.g., the lie).

The conclusion does not follow directly. What is needed seems to be this:

(P3)   The lesser evil will have bad consequences; or it at least runs a risk of causing some harm and this risk itself can be considered a bad consequence.

(P4)   One is responsible for the bad consequences of one's acts (or omissions) *if* the acts (or omissions) were wrong, all things considered.

(P5)   One is responsible for the bad consequences of one's acts (or omissions) *only if* the acts (or omissions) were wrong, all things considered.

From (P1), (P3), and (P5) we can infer the conclusion (C) that it is wrong to do the lesser evil (e.g., lie). From (P2) and (P4) we can infer that it is not wrong to fail to prevent the greater evil (e.g., the murder).

The required premises, however, are open to question. Consider, for example, (P5), a crucial assumption if wrongdoing is to be inferred from the intuition that we are responsible for any harm that doing the lesser evil may cause. Are we not responsible sometimes for the harm that results from our acts even though what we were doing was not wrong? For example, suppose I am driving safely

---

5   See "On the Supposed Right to tell a Lie from Altrustic Purposes," in *Kant's Critique of Practical Reason and other Works on the Theory of Ethics.* Translated by T. K. Abbott (London: Longmans, Green, 1873, reprinted, 1954).

but must suddenly swerve, striking a parked car, in order to avoid hitting a child who has just run into the street. In law, I am told, we are responsible for damages in such cases (though not criminally liable); is there not a moral responsibility as well? But surely it was not wrong to swerve. Similarly, in a classic case, if one takes someone else's horse and runs it to death in an effort to escape a gang of murderers, the law says that one did not do wrong but is nevertheless responsible for the consequences.[6] Fanatical animal lovers aside, I expect that moral opinion tends to follow the law in this assessment.

It might be replied that we need to distinguish senses of "responsible." In one sense, the sense in which (P5) is false, "responsible" merely means "owes restitution," "is liable for damages"; but in another sense, the sense intended in the argument, "responsible for" means something more like "wrongfully brought about." In this sense, it might be argued, "he is responsible for the bad consequences" means roughly "his misdeeds caused the bad consequences." In this sense (P4) and (P5) are obviously true. But if the argument is to succeed, "responsible" must be understood the same way throughout; and the new reading robs (P1) and (P2) of their initial plausibility. Now they become far from obvious, in fact just as controversial as the issue they were supposed to resolve. For (P1) now says: you *wrongfully* bring about whatever bad consequences result from doing the lesser evil and (P2) now says: you do not *wrongfully* bring about the bad consequences of not preventing the greater evil. These propositions are, in effect, just what is at issue. No one who initially believed that you should sometimes do the lesser evil would accept them; for they do little more than assert the opposite.

The arguments reviewed so far leave us right where we started: the case *for* doing the lesser evil is obvious, for it reduces the amount of serious wrongdoing in the world by, in effect, trading a greater moral offense for a lesser. If the amount of harm varies with the seriousness of the offense, then doing the lesser evil will also reduce the amount of harm done. The problem is to understand what can be said *against* doing the lesser evil. Now in each case there will be *some* moral considerations against the lesser evil, namely, the considerations which lead one to call it an "evil," or prima facie wrong, in the first place. For example, if the lesser evil is a lie, then its effects on general trust can be cited; if it is a lynching, then both the dangers of the precedent and rights to lawful trial can be given as negative considerations. But these reasons specific to each offense can never by themselves show that one should not do the lesser evil; for, by hypothesis, there will be stronger reasons of this type for the nonoccurrence of the greater evil. Assuming that the lesser evil will really prevent the greater, it seems the decision will always favor the lesser evil so long as we put the question as a neutral observer might: "Weighing up the amount of serious wrong done, the

6 See Herbert Morris, "The Status of Rights," *Ethics,* 1981.

stringency of rights violated, and harm produced, are there stronger reasons for wanting the lesser evil to occur or for wanting the greater to occur?" At least this will be so unless we find some *special* reasons for thinking that each agent should regard his own avoidance of (prima facie) wrongs more important in his decisions than others' avoidance of such wrongs (the same or worse). These would need to be reasons why each person should not simply calculate how to minimize the wrongdoing in the world but should rather give a special priority to the purity of his own life.

The Purist might accept this challenge to provide *special* reasons for avoiding the lesser evil, giving the following argument: "Our duty, surely, is not to follow the example of actual conduct in this imperfect world but rather to live by the standards of a more ideal world, to march, as it were, to the tune of a more distant drummer; instead of conforming to standards we find in practice, we should follow the laws of a morally perfect world; and in a morally perfect world where all are prepared to do their duty, commitments to justice, fairness, mutual respect, truthfulness, noninjury, etc., would not be qualified and conditional; they would tell each to govern his own conduct by certain basic standards without exception, leaving others to discern and follow their duties; therefore, our duty is to abide by these unconditional principles, not worrying about the corruption of others but living for our own part as if we were in the ideal moral community."[7] Notice that the argument is not the consequentialist one that we should take whatever means will most likely bring about the ideal moral world, or our best approximation to it; for such an argument would allow, even require, compromising with corruption and doing the lesser evil whenever doing so was a more effective means to the desired end. The Purist argument says instead that we should live now *as if we* were in the ideal moral community, ignoring the fact (for purposes of moral decision at least) that not everyone is conscientious.

Though this Purist argument has appealing features and was apparently endorsed by at least one great philosopher, the present version is open to the following serious objection. The reasoning seems to be *utopian* in the pejorative sense; that is, it makes an illegitimate inference from a description of a possible ideal state of affairs to a prescription about how people in a nonideal situation ought to behave. Some inferences from ideal worlds to ideal behavior in the actual world may be legitimate; but others are not. A clear example of an illegitimate inference would be this: "In the ideal world of milk and honey in which the necessities of life are so abundant they can be had by all without effort, there would be no need for welfare programs; therefore, we ought not to have welfare programs." A possible legitimate inference might be this: "If all judges

---

7   This pattern of argument, I think, is suggested by Kant's formula of the "kingdom of ends." I discuss the problem, as I see it, in "The Kingdom of Ends," *Proceedings of the Third International Kant Congress,* ed. by L. W. Beck, D. Reidel, 1972, and also in "Kant's Utopianism," *Akten des 4. Internationalen Kant-Kongresses,* Sonderdruck, *Kant-Studien,* 1974.

in an ideal world in which judges were impartial, fully informed, sympathetic, etc., would oppose trial by fire, then we should oppose trial by fire." The Purist argument for avoiding the lesser evil, unfortunately, seems more like the former, illegitimate inference. It asks us to imagine an ideal world which lacks a certain morally important feature of our world (namely, that unless prevented, unscrupulous people will cause great harm); then it asks us to live by the rules that would be appropriate in *that* world even though, in this morally relevant respect, our world is different from it. But clearly unconditional adherence to the rules for that perfect world can result in disaster in this imperfect world; and that possibility is morally significant. As it stands, the Purist argument seems blind or indifferent to morally relevant features of the real world.

II

Most people, I suspect, take an intermediate position between the Pragmatist and the Purist on the question whether one should do the lesser evil to prevent the greater. That is, they believe that doing the lesser evil is sometimes right, sometimes not, depending on various circumstances of the particular case. Let us suppose for a moment that this view is right. We can then raise our second question: when a person does the lesser evil with justification, how should he feel about himself and those (if any) he harms? Alternatively, for those who will not grant that the lesser evil is ever justified, we can ask this relativized question: if someone does what he sincerely believes is a justified lesser evil, how, given that belief, should he feel about himself and those (if any) he harms? Reflection on answers to these questions, I think, suggests arguments relevant to the main question of the preceding section, namely, what moral considerations stand for and against regarding the lesser evil as justified?

The most obvious, but least interesting, response of an ideal moral agent towards having to do a justified lesser evil is sympathy for those (if any) who are harmed and regret that there were no better options. These are uninteresting responses for our purposes because they are responses that anyone, not just the agent, should have. When the white man in *Roots* must whip his friend, a slave, any bystander should have sympathy and regret that such a choice had to be made. But what we are looking for is some way the agent should respond differently from bystanders.

Some will say that the agent should feel *guilty*. Even those who admit that the lesser evil is justified may insist that guilt is commonly, and quite rightly, felt in such circumstances. Perhaps if the lesser evil is the sort of act (like killing) which is justified only in extreme circumstances, a conscientious person could not help feeling some "residual guilt" when the rare circumstances first confront him and he must kill. Also it is surely appropriate to feel that one has done a kind of act that one deplores, a kind that would have little or no place in a morally perfect world. One may have reason to feel guilty over one's motives and attitudes: for example, one may find that one took some pleasure in the killing. Again, the occasion may arouse displaced guilt over something else, about which one has grounds to feel guilty. One might well feel guilty, for example, if the fact that one faced a choice among evils was a result of prior negligence. But, setting aside residual guilt, displaced guilt, and the like, it seems quite inappropriate for one who does the justified lesser evil to feel guilty in the fullest, paradigmatic sense. The latter implies, I think, belief that what one did was wrong, all things considered. If it was really right to do the lesser evil, then guilt of this sort is inappropriate.

Some might say that even if a person is not guilty, strictly speaking, for doing the lesser evil, his life nevertheless becomes *tainted* when he does it. The morally pure life, on this view, is not merely free from intentional wrongdoing; it is the sort of life one would live in the morally perfect world. Oedipus' life became impure in this sense when, through no fault of his own, he killed his father and married his mother; and, according to one tradition, all human life is tainted through "original sin" so that the most conscientious effort cannot eradicate the evil in one's attitudes, thoughts, and feelings. In a similar spirit, it might be said that one who must lie, kill, and associate himself with corruption in order to prevent greater evils does not lead a "morally pure" life, even though he only does what circumstances require him to do. Thus, an appropriate response when one does the lesser evil, even with justification, is to feel that one's life is morally tainted.

To assess this view, we need to ask, as William James would say, what is the "cash value" of this idea of *moral taint?* If "moral taint" is not simply another word for guilt or the name of some mysterious metaphysical property, then there must be some practical implications of the belief that doing the lesser evil taints one's life, implications other than "it was the wrong thing to do." The idea, I think, has at least three implications: (a) that one should wish not to do the lesser evil and regret that one had to do it; (b) that it is appropriate to look down on oneself for having done it; and (c) that one should strive to avoid getting into situations where one will be required to do the lesser evil.

The second and third implications, however, seem objectionable. Consider (b). This implies that, barring extraordinary luck, the most conscientious person in the world cannot live a life he is proud of; doing nothing but what is right and having the best possible will would not allow one to feel free from shame and self-contempt. For, assuming there are situations, however rare, in which it is morally required to do the lesser evil, whether one finds oneself in such a situation will be partly a matter of luck. Being conscientious does not guarantee that one will not face hard choices. But is it not implausible, unreasonably harsh, to say that a person should look down on himself when he tried his best to avoid setting up the choice among evils and then did what was right when unavoidably the choice arose?

The third implication, (c), also raises problems. Should one, without quali-fication, seek to avoid situations where one will be morally required to choose the lesser evil? Surely everyone should try to prevent situations from arising where *someone* will be morally required to engage in one evil to prevent a greater; that is, one should try to arrange things to that *no one* faces such choices. Also, as I suggest later, a moral person may well *wish* that someone else do the lesser evil when the choice cannot be avoided and so someone ought to do it. But to say that one ought in general to try to avoid having to do a justified lesser evil implies that one should avoid many of the most morally challenging ways of life; for the surest way to avoid the hard choices is to shun positions of leadership and responsibility, to live by oneself or in a small righteous community isolated from the world. This would be one's best chance to live without "taint," but is it really what we should aim for?

If not guilty or "tainted," how should one feel about doing the lesser evil? Would we expect the best moral agents to feel any more than the Pragmatist, who says, "I am sorry that someone has to do this and sorry for those who are hurt, but otherwise I am content because the lesser evil is the right thing to do in the circumstances"? I suggest that, intuitively, the response we might expect from a morally sensitive person would go beyond this Pragmatic attitude in several respects; in particular, it would typically include the following: (1) concern about whether one correctly estimated the necessity and effectiveness of doing the lesser evil; (2) regret that one did not relate to others in the ways one wants to; (3) regret that one could not live a pure and integrated life, expressive of one's deepest values; and (4) anger or resentment towards those whose ill will forced one to make the choice. Each of these, I suggest later, points to a moral consideration against thinking that one is always, or easily, justified in doing the lesser evil.

The first point reflects the limitations of our knowledge and power concerning the wrongdoing of others. It is obviously difficult in most circumstances to be sure that doing the lesser evil *will* actually prevent the greater, and it is often even more difficult to be confident that doing the lesser is *necessary* to prevent the greater. The lesser evil is closer to home: its moral quality and consequences are usually easier to discern than the quality and consequences of others' misdeeds, and we can prevent the lesser evil simply by refusing to do it whereas others' acts are harder to control. For these reasons a conscientious person will naturally have some concern about whether he has assessed the situation correctly: he can often be confident that his act is an evil, but he may well feel some doubt about whether it is a lesser offense than what is to be prevented, whether it will effectively prevent the other evil, and whether it was necessary for that purpose.

The second point is that an ideal moral agent will want to relate to other people in certain ways, with respect, caring, support, etc. Thus he will not want to do the lying, whipping, killing, etc., involved in the lesser evil. The idea is not merely that he wants that no one do these things, that acts of this type not occur. He wants *that*, of course, but also something more: namely, not to mar his relationships with the individual victims by doing these sorts of things to them. He wants that these things not be done and especially that he does not do them. This does not mean that he would never choose, from altruism or duty, to undertake the burden of doing the lesser evil so that someone else would not have to; but he would, I think, do so reluctantly and sadly, with a regret that reflects at least some preferential concern about how he relates to those he injures. If, for example, he is convinced that someone will whip the slave and that someone humane ought to do it in preference to someone cruel, he will not shrug with indifference when he learns that he, rather than someone else, is in a position to do it humanely. What one who cares for the victim naturally wants to say is not merely, "I regret that this was done to you," not merely "I regret that it was done by a friend," but also "I regret that *I* did this to you." It is not necessary for present purposes to suppose that a person would be morally deficient if he lacked all preferential concern of this sort, wishing merely, as a neutral god might, that no one have to do the whipping; but it is hard to imagine that a *human* being who was committed to moral ends and cared for the individual victim could have only such an impartial dislike for the whipping. Some will no doubt suspect that this preferential concern is unduly self-centered; but the suspicion, I think, stems from a confusion between the preferential concern described here and other attitudes to be considered in the last section.

The third point is that doing the lesser evil would frustrate the desire of an ideal moral agent to lead a pure and integrated life, expressive of his deepest values. A *pure* life is one *free from* certain nonideal features: (a) failure to do what, to the best of one's knowledge, is right (i.e., "subjective right"); (b) failure to do what is really right (i.e., "objective right"), through accident or excusable ignorance; (c) objectionable (though perhaps unavoidable) attitudes, thoughts, and feelings; and (d) doing the sort of things that would have no place in a morally perfect world, even if justified in the real world because of the corruption of others. Most of us, unlike the Purist, regretfully admit that the pure life is impossible; for objectionable feelings, (c), and excusable errors, (b), cannot always be avoided and sometimes the right thing to do, (a) and (b), conflicts with what one would do in a morally perfect world, (d). My suggestion is not that ideal moral agents would succeed in living the morally pure life but that they would want to. Doing the lesser evil, therefore, is a source of frustration and regret, even when it is justified.

The ideal of a *pure* life is negative, for it is a life free from certain undesirable features. But a good person, I imagine, would also want something more positive, namely, "an integrated life, expressive of one's deepest values." By "integrated life" I mean a life in which various aspects are in harmony: for example, one's plans and policies cohere with one's values and ideals, one's deeds cohere with one's words, and the whole pattern of one's "inner" and "outer" choices cohere over time not only with each other but with others' in a larger moral community. By "a life expressive of one's deepest values" I mean one in which one's words and deeds announce to the world what one cherishes, not merely a life that, on balance, promotes the ends one values but a life in which one "lives out" those values. Consider, for example, a conscientious spy in a Nazi world who believes, with reason, that he must cooperate with the Nazis and use all manner of means he deplores in order to help restore peace and a more just order. He might in fact contribute to the sort of world he values, but his life would lack the integration he would want and he could not unequivocally *express* his values in what he says and does. Those who must make war to end war, vote for unjust laws to avoid worse injustice, etc., are in a similar situation. My suggestion, once again, is not that leading an integrated life, expressive of one's values, is always right; in fact, it seems morally impossible in some extreme circumstances. The point is just that an ideal moral agent would want to live such a life, and doing the lesser evil is incompatible with that desire. Someone who stood for peace, publicly and privately, all his life but then came to believe that he must go to war, as the lesser evil, would naturally feel regret at the loss of something he valued.

The final point is that even the best sort of person would naturally feel some anger or resentment at those who forced him to choose among evils. By hypothesis, the lesser evil would not be necessary if everyone was prepared to do what he should. When required to do the lesser evil, a conscientious person must change his life in ways he finds repulsive because someone else was not willing to do his part. To be forced to do what one's best instincts make one hate to do would naturally make one angry, especially when the problem could readily be avoided if only others would do what they should. The point is not that one *ought* to feel such anger but rather that this reaction is natural and understandable in those so committed to moral values that they find doing even a lesser evil repugnant. To forgive and overcome the anger may be ideal, but one cannot really forgive unless one has felt the injury.

III

These reflections about how a good person would feel about doing a *justified* lesser evil do not, of course, show that doing the lesser evil is wrong (i.e., *not justified*). The discussion has assumed that in some situations doing the lesser evil is right, regardless of how the agent feels about doing it. So the fact that a good person would feel uncertainty, aversion, and anger at the prospect of doing a lesser evil is not by itself an adequate reason for refusing to do the lesser evil. Nevertheless, the feelings point to some general considerations against thinking that the lesser evil is easily justified.

When we think of the problem (i.e., is the lesser evil justified?) from the perspective of the reluctant moral agent who is forced to choose, moral and self-interested considerations easily become confused. Even the agent himself can be unclear about whether his primary concern is duty, distaste for certain activities, or reputation. Thus it may be well to consider the problem from a more detached perspective, namely, that of an ideal moral legislature. Suppose that, as in Kant's "kingdom of ends," a group of ideal legislators met to decide what specific moral rules to adopt. Imagine that, unlike ideal rulemakers in some other models, they are not morally neutral. They share a full range of moral ends and values; for example, they want all to prosper in a community of mutual respect and support, etc. What they lack is antecedent commitment to specific rules of conduct. It is natural to suppose that they would readily favor some sort of prohibition on lying, bodily injury, killing, etc. The question now, let us say, is whether to include in these basic rules the special *proviso*, ". . . except, if ignoring this prohibition would prevent a greater offense by someone else, then ignore it." That is, the legislators must consider whether to allow, or even require, doing the lesser evil. To avoid the charge of utopianism considered earlier, we must imagine that the legislators are fully aware that not everyone will conform to the rules they adopt. Although this thought-experiment has obvious affinities with rule-utilitarianism,[8] it is also crucially different in that the legislators are not defined as exclusively concerned to maximize utility but rather as having a full range of moral ends and values. The details of these ends and values are deliberately left unspecific so that we can use the thought-experiment to appeal to the reader's intuitions.

The reflections of the previous section suggest four arguments which the ideal legislators should consider.

First, since we can know and control our own acts better than we can know and control others', even utilitarian considerations oppose an unqualified permission or requirement to do what seems the lesser evil. Ideal legislators, surely, would want to minimize harm and wrongdoing, other things equal. If it were *certain* that a lesser evil of, say, -10 utility would prevent, and was necessary to prevent, a greater evil of -20, then utilitarian reasoning would support the lesser evil. But in fact the typical situation is different: the negative utility of the lesser evil is rather certain while a substantial probability remains that it was not necessary to prevent the greater or that the greater will occur anyway. In this case utilitarian considera-

8 See, for example, Richard Brandt's "Toward a Credible Form of Utilitarianism," in *Morality and the Language of Conduct*, edited by H. Castañeda and G. Nakhnikian, Wayne State University, Press, 1963.

tions urge caution: the anticipated greater evil has to be substantially greater to off-set the greater uncertainty about its occurrence.[9] The argument here is similar to the familiar utilitarian argument that, because we each typically know our own interests better than others do and can affect them more easily, even a utilitarianism which "counts each for one" urges individuals to pursue their own interests somewhat more attentively than those of strangers.

Second, with a full range of moral values, ideal legislators will have concerns beyond the standard utilitarian ones. In particular, they would, I think, count the satisfaction of some desires more important than the satisfaction of others, quite aside from the relative degree of satisfaction or happiness that results. For example, the desire to see others suffer will have little or no weight while a desire to see others prosper would be honored and encouraged. Now both the desire to *relate* to others with mutual respect, caring, and support and the desire to lead a pure and integrated life, expressive of one's deepest moral values, seem to fall into the second category of desires to be especially honored and protected. If so, ideal moral legislators would be reluctant to require conscientious persons to do the lesser evil. The effect of such a requirement would not merely be to cause some unhappiness but to squelch a morally good desire which we want all to have, moreover to squelch it by means of something else morally desirable, namely, the agent's sense of duty. This does not mean that moral legislators would never require the lesser evil, for when the discrepancy between the lesser

9 Suppose the lesser evil is -10, the greater -20, and both have a probability of virtually 100% (i.e., it is certain that the lesser will prevent the greater and is necessary to prevent it). Then the utilitarian can reason thus: choosing the lesser = 100% × -10 = -10; choosing to avoid the lesser = 100% × -20 = -20; so we should choose the lesser evil. But now suppose the difference between the greater and the lesser evil is small (say, -12 vs. -10) and, though only choosing the lesser evil will prevent the greater, there is only a 75% chance that it will succeed. Then the calculation favors avoiding the lesser evil (as seen in A below). Suppose again the difference between the greater and lesser is small (say, -12 vs. -10) and, though the lesser will surely prevent the greater, there is only a 75% chance that it was necessary to do so; here too the calculation favors avoiding the lesser evil (see B below). When both sorts of uncertainty are present, the case against the lesser evil is obviously stronger. The simplifying assumptions needed to use quantitative measures are, of course, artificial, but the figures may help to illustrate the general point.

	Expected utility from the lesser	Expected utility from the greater	Total
A.			
Choose the lesser	100% × -10 = -10	(75% × 0) + (25% × 12) = -3	-13
Avoid the lesser	100% × 0 = 0	100% × -12 = -12	-12
B.			
Choose the lesser	100% × -10 = -10	100% × 0 = 0	-10
Avoid the lesser	100% × 0 = 0	(75% × -12) + (25% × 0) = -9	-9

and the greater is very large (e.g., a lie vs. a murder), other considerations will be overriding.[10] But a presumption against requiring the lesser evil is indicated: simple Pragmatic calculation will not be enough to justify it.

Third, I suppose that ideal legislators would place a special value on the sort of personal relations which are built upon almost unconditional commitments. Though suggested by the reluctance that a good person would feel in relating to people as he must in doing a justified lesser evil, the argument is not that the agent's distaste for the lesser evil makes it wrong. Nor is it merely the previous point that impartial moral legislators would want to protect and honor the desire not to relate to people with lies, beatings, killings, etc. The point is rather that one moral value which would guide an ideal legislator's choice of rules is the quality of relationships based on love, friendship, and mutual respect, concern, etc., even among strangers. Most of us would sacrifice much pleasure and suffer much pain to maintain such relationships. They are not merely desired but also seen as morally ideal. The possibility for such relations seems an essential condition for any moral community. Now almost invariably such ideal personal relations are damaged or hindered when someone does either the greater evil or the lesser. But the damage done by the actual moral offense may not be the worst outcome to be feared. What seems equally, or more, significant is the effect on personal relationships in general if all were prepared to do the lesser evil to someone whenever doing so would prevent a greater evil by someone else. Then even the most conscientious persons could only make conditional commitments to each other. They could only say, "I would never lie to you, beat you, kill you, etc. . . . *unless* I found that doing so would prevent a more serious offense somewhere else." The message would be, "I care for you but you are expendable in my larger project of minimizing harm and wrongdoing in the world." Though perhaps some revolutionaries have viewed other people, including their family and "friends," this way, such a policy would surely undermine quality of the relationships we want and regard as morally ideal.

The point needs to be qualified. If the lesser evil is substantially less than the greater (e.g., a lie vs. a murder), then there seem to be overriding considerations. *Refusal* to tell a lie to save a friend from murder also carries a message; it says to the victim, "I will not commit even a minor offense to save you." And if the person lied to is the would-be murderer himself (as in Kant's story), avoiding this message to the innocent seems more important than what refusal to tell the lie would say to the would-be murderer and other potential offenders. So the argument does not indicate that one should never do the lesser evil; it only establishes a presumption against it, indicating at least that our policy should not be an unqualified willingness to do the lesser evil whenever it will prevent

10   Of course, as Robert Coburn noted to me, the legislators would also want to honor and encourage the moral agents' desire to prevent the occurrence of the greater evil, and this would be to some extent a counterbalancing consideration.

someone else's greater. Unfortunately, in an imperfect world, we cannot conscientiously make *completely* unconditional personal commitments.

Fourth, the anger or resentment a conscientious person would naturally feel when forced to do a justified lesser evil suggests that somehow the value of individual autonomy may be at stake. The resentment stems from the fact that the conscientious agent was forced to abandon his preferred life and to do something he despises because someone else threatens to do something even worse. He naturally feels angry because his autonomy, in some sense, has been invaded; but in what sense? If the appeal to autonomy is to be persuasive, it must amount to more than the following arguments: (a) the agent is understandably angry about the invasion of his autonomy and so should indulge his anger by refusing to do the lesser evil; and (b) requiring the agent to do the lesser evil is a restriction on his autonomy of choice and so, for that reason alone, he should not be required to do it. The first argument presupposes the dubious idea that one should always indulge one's justified or understandable anger; the second overlooks the fact that allowing the greater evil to occur will usually mean that a third party's autonomy will be severely restricted. My freedom is limited if I must take on the burden of preventing murder; but if I do not, the victim loses his autonomy.

Let us consider then what the ideal of individual autonomy might be for a morally perfect world, and then we can ask what application this would have for legislators who must make rules for a morally imperfect world.

In a world of conscientious agents, I imagine, individuals would have autonomy of the following sorts. (1) Each would have the opportunity to govern himself within a wide area of choices. This means, among other things, that (a) each has an understood, and rather determinate set of rights and duties, well within human capacities and known in advance, so that each can plan and live out his own preferred life within a wide but circumscribed area of free choice, and also that (b) others respect the rights of each and do not interfere with choices within the circumscribed area by coercion, threats, manipulation, etc. (2) Each is respected as morally autonomous in the sense that others leave the individual to make his own moral decisions, trusting him to be conscientious and to accept responsibility for his mistakes. (This attitude contrasts, for example, with that of moral busybodies and overly anxious parents who are inclined to treat their responsible teenage sons and daughters as little children.) (3) Each is in fact morally *self-governing* in the sense that, without external pressures, he will fulfil his duties and respect the rights of others. He not only allows others their legitimate area of freedom; he also does so on his own, without needing threats, special rewards, habits of blind obedience, etc.

Now supposing that such autonomy is an ideal, how might it influence moral legislators trying to decide what to prescribe regarding doing the lesser evil? In the situations they must consider, the person threatening the greater evil refuses to be morally self-governing, (3) above, and does not seem to deserve the trust of others, (2) above. His threat is an invasion of the autonomy of his prospective victim, (1b), as well as the autonomy of anyone who would be forced to do a lesser evil to avert the threat, (1b). Clearly the ideal of autonomy cannot be satisfied in the situation.

Nevertheless, the ideal of autonomy is not irrelevant. First, if there were substantial doubt about whether the other person was really going to do the threatened greater evil, the ideal of trust, (2), would urge caution in encouraging the lesser evil. Second, more importantly, the value of having a clearly defined, understood set of responsibilities, around which one can build a life with some reliability, tends to oppose any unqualified requirement to do the lesser evil. Such a requirement would make us perpetually "on call," not just in emergencies but whenever we could stamp out a somewhat greater offense of someone else's by giving up our preferred life to do a lesser evil. We would be obliged to be moral busybodies, as much concerned with stamping out wrongdoing in others as in ourselves. The problem would not be simply the burden of the particular occasion on which one had to do the lesser evil; it would also be the unpredictability and insecurity of living perpetually "on call." We would all be "moral policemen" standing ever ready to rush in to stop our neighbors from misbehaving, not just in dire emergencies but all too often. A third consideration might be this: even though the other person's greater evil will likely interfere with his victim's legitimate area of freedom, (1b), a requirement to do the lesser evil would typically curtail the freedom of both the victim of the lesser evil and the person who has to do it. The difference between the evils would have to be great to offset this double disadvantage. This double disadvantage would be absent when the lesser evil is something done to the very person who threatens to do the greater (e.g., the would-be killer is knocked down, lied to, etc.); for here there is no interference with a person within the legitimate area of freedom defined by his rights and duties. But this exception confirms the main point, for this is just the sort of case in which doing the lesser evil is most easily justified. Moral legislators, concerned to preserve autonomy, would have less reason to oppose the lesser evil if the only victim of the lesser evil were the person who threatened the greater evil.

IV

No decision procedure emerges from the arguments sketched in the last section, but, if properly developed, they may help to explain why doing the lesser evil is not always the obviously preferred moral choice. Let us now turn to the lingering suspicion that the Pragmatist has about any reluctance to do the lesser evil to prevent the greater: is this anything more than selfishness and self-righteousness?

In any particular case, of course, a person could be moved by unduly self-concerned motives when refusing to do the lesser evil. The motive could be:

wanting to appear superior to others; wanting to *be* superior to others so that (one thinks) one is justified in looking down upon them; wanting to avoid the discomfort of doing something distasteful, from squeamishness, preferring a great harm to someone else to a relatively minor discomfort of one's own; obsessive and inflexible concern for maintaining a "pure" and simple record, even at others' expense, as a baseball player may insist on a perfect participation record to the team's disadvantage; a stubborn refusal to think through novel moral problems, based on a self-serving reliance on traditional or authoritative solutions; an arrogant presumption that even from an objective point of view, one's own soul, purity, or reputation is more important than others'; and so forth. Philosophy cannot remove the suspicion that these motives are present in any real case; but it can, I think, show that there are other, more admirable motives which might move one to refuse to do the lesser evil.

If, for example, the arguments sketched in the previous section have force, then a conscientious person might well conclude that in many, if not most, instances doing the lesser evil to prevent the greater is not the right thing to do. A desire to do what is right might be his motive in refusing. Alternatively, he might conclude that doing the lesser evil is not morally required, though permissible, and that it is in serious conflict with certain moral ideals. Then a desire to live in accord with those ideals might be the motive for refusing. In particular, the motive might be his aversion to relate to others in the ways the lesser evil demands, or to honor a prior (permissible) commitment not to treat them in those ways. If moral rules allow him the freedom to choose, this preference need not be *self*-centered even though it conflicts with another value (prevention of the greater offense). The refusal to do the lesser evil expresses the attitude, "Despite what may happen, I will not do that to him." But this does not necessarily express the *self*-preoccupation which is suggested by, "Despite the cost, *I* will not do that to him." The policy has the outcome that more weight is given to one's own avoidance of doing wrongs to others, but this does not imply that one thinks one is more important than others. The policy is not to avoid morally challenging ways of life in which the hard choices will arise, but merely reluctance, when the problem does arise, to choose the Pragmatic option. This implies some preferential concern for one's own avoidance of offensive conduct towards others, but that is what it seems even impartial moral legislators would urge.

7

Self-regarding suicide: a modified Kantian view

Moral debates about suicide typically focus on the questions of whether suicide is immoral and whether we should interfere with suicide attempts. These questions naturally turn attention to matters such as conflicting rights, social consequences, religious belief, and the difficulty of drawing a sharp line between right and wrong in complex cases. My concern will be somewhat different. I want to consider what ideals of attitude toward human life and death may lie behind the common intuition that some suicides are morally objectionable, to some degree, even though not harmful to others and not a violation of anyone's rights.

The puzzling cases arise when the suicide is not failing in his obligations to others, but lacks any overriding moral reason to take his life. He is within his rights and yet his decision still seems morally significant. The issue is not whether suicide is strictly immoral, still less how a sharp line can be drawn between the permissible and the impermissible. The question, rather, is how an ideal person would view such choices. Or, in other words, what sort of attitudes toward life and death do we, from a moral point of view, want to encourage and see present in those who are moved to consider suicide?

My suggestion will be that to explain certain common intuitive beliefs on this question we need to move beyond consideration of rights and utility to a qualified Kantian principle about the value of life as a rational autonomous agent. Though I find Kant's rigoristic opposition to suicide untenable, the spirit of his idea of humanity as an end in itself, I think, leads to a more tenable position. This idea, appropriately qualified, opposes attitudes which sometimes motivate suicide, but it does not condemn, in fact it encourages, suicide from other motives in special circumstances. The Kantian idea accords with a view which I believe is widely held in popular thought, though currently unfashionable in philosophy, namely, that moral considerations are not all other-regarding. Though Kant went too far in saying that suicide is always a violation of a duty to oneself, there is more that a moral person considering suicide needs to think about than his relations to other people.

My discussion will be divided as follows. First, I state some intuitive beliefs about the sort of cases in which suicide falls short of the morally ideal, as well as other cases in which suicide seems unobjectionable. These are the intuitions which need to be explained and which prompt us to look beyond rights and utility. Second, I sketch some main points pertinent to suicide in Kant's ethics and indicate ways in which I believe Kant's theory needs modification. Third, I propose a qualified Kantian principle and contrast its perspective on the value of life with some alternatives. Fourth, I consider the application of the principle to suicide, indicating how it would support the initial intuitive beliefs about when suicide is objectionable and when it is not. Finally, I close with brief remarks on the possibility of employing Kantian arguments to make the principle more persuasive.

I

Real life is admittedly more complex than any of our philosophical categories, but to further discussion, I want to focus attention on four specially defined types of suicide. Pure instances are at least conceivable, though real cases doubtless contain a mixture of elements.

In each case, we are to imagine that the persons contemplating suicide are free from obligations to others which would be violated or neglected if they choose suicide. For example, there are no outstanding promises to be kept, no children to care for, no institutional obligations to be met, and so on. Moreover, unlike most actual cases, there are none who will grieve or feel guilt-ridden when they learn of the suicide. As far as anyone can, the persons who choose suicide have already paid their debt of gratitude to the individuals and society who have benefited them, and they have made constructive contributions to charity and other good causes. Perhaps some will say that no one ever discharges his obligation to others, but for present purposes let us suppose that this is not so. The point of setting aside obligations to others in this way is not, of course, to deny their importance in real, typical cases, but simply to isolate other moral considerations which may be relevant.

To further simplify, let us imagine that in the cases we shall consider, there is an absence of the sort of altruistic motives which are often thought to make suicide morally commendable. For example, suicide is not a necessary means to save one's family from disastrous financial costs involved in lingering illness; it is not the only way a spy can keep from betraying his country under torture; it is not a dramatic protest against an unjust war; and so on. So far as others are concerned, there is no reason for, or against, suicide.

(1) *Impulsive suicide.* A suicide might be called impulsive if it is prompted by a temporarily intense, yet passing desire or emotion out of keeping with the more permanent character, preferences, and emotional state of the agent. We need not suppose that the agent is "driven" or "blinded" or momentarily insane, but his act is not the sort that coheres with what he most wants and values over time. In calmer, more deliberative moments he would have wished that he would not respond as he did. If he had survived, he would have come to regret his

decision. Examples might include cases of lovers who take their lives in moments of intense grief, wealthy businessmen who experience sudden financial disaster and are frightened of facing the world without money, and active, life-loving hedonists enraged at fate when first learning that they have contracted a crippling disease. Some suicides in these circumstances might be rational, but when I refer to suicides as impulsive, I have in mind only those which would have been avoided if the agent had been in full rational control of himself.

(2) *Apathetic suicide*. Sometimes a suicide might result not so much from intense desire or emotion as from apathy. The problem is not overwhelming passion, but absence of passion, lack of interest in what might be done or experienced in a continued life. One can imagine, for example, an extremely depressed person who simply does not care about the future. The causes of his emotional state may lie in personal failure, rejected love, and so on. But what he experiences is not intense shame, anger, fear, etc., but rather emptiness. He may acknowledge that after time, perhaps with psychotherapy and antidepressive drugs, he would again take joy in living. But the thought arouses no current desire to continue living. If his suicide is irrational, it is not because his mind is unclear or his reason swayed by intense emotion.

(3) *Self-abasing suicide*. I call a suicide self-abasing if it results from a sense of worthlessness or unworthiness, which expresses itself not in apathy, but rather in a desire to manifest self-contempt, to reject oneself, to "put oneself down." The motivating attitude is more than an intellectual judgment about one's merits, relative to others or absolutely, according to various standards of morality, social utility, intelligence, etc., though such judgments may be among the causes of the attitude. Particular rejections, failures, and violations of conscience might contribute to the attitude, but it need not be a merely momentary or passing feeling. One's life is seen as having a negative value, not just devoid of things to enjoy, like an empty cupboard, but contemptible, like a despised insect one wants to swat or turn away from in disgust. Such suicide carries a symbolic message, even if only expressed to oneself: "this creature is worth less than nothing." The agent does not irrationally miscalculate whether continued life will bring more joy than misery, for he is not involved in any such calculation. In effect, he denies that he deserves such consideration, even from himself. This is more than self-punishment, which can be a way of acknowledging oneself as a responsible agent and alleviating particular guilt feelings. The self-abasing attitude, on the contrary, says "punishment is too good for me – I should be discarded."

(4) *Hedonistic calculated suicide*. By this I mean suicide that is decided upon as the result of a certain sort of cost/benefit calculation. Seeing that others will be unaffected by his decision (our simplifying hypothesis), the hedonistic calculator regards his choice as determined by his best estimate of the balance of pleasures and pain he expects to receive under each option. Immediate suicide by a painless

method will result in a short, fairly predictable list of pleasures and pains. Continued life will produce a more complex series of experiences more difficult to calculate. Uncertainties cloud the picture and disparate pleasures and pains are hard to weigh against one another with anything like mathematical precision. But, in theory, the problem is seen as simple. One chooses the course that results in the best balance of expected pain and pleasure, taking into account intensity, duration, certainty, etc. More sophisticated calculators may think in terms of preferences and ordinal comparisons, rather than cardinal rankings of sensations, but the central point remains that the value of continued life is seen as a function of the joys and miseries, delights and discomforts, etc., that one is likely to experience. Long life *per se* has no value. But, as long as the pleasure/pain balance is above a certain threshold, the more life the better. When, in one's best estimate, the balance falls irretrievably below the threshold, it is time to end the game. The reason for ending it, like the reason for continuing to live, is to obtain the best balance, over time, of pleasure over pain.

Although these four types of suicide are significantly different, I think that they all reflect an attitude towards life that is less than ideal. This is not to say that suicides of these sorts are *wrong* or *immoral*. However, it is meant to imply more than that they are "unfortunate" or that benevolent people would wish that they not occur. My sense is that, though condemnation and blame seem inappropriate, a person's life story would be morally better if it did not end in one of these ways. One would not select for emulation a biography which concluded with impulsive, apathetic, self-abasing, or hedonistic calculating suicide. Insofar as one wanted to admire the principal character, one would want to rewrite the ending.

Many philosophers, no doubt, will disagree, for the intuition here seems at odds with ethical theories which decide all moral questions by reference to rights or social consequences. By hypothesis, the suicides did not violate the rights of others and it is generally agreed that no one can violate his own rights. Again, by hypothesis, only the person committing suicide is harmed (if indeed anyone is) and it is widely held that acts which only harm oneself are *morally* insignificant. Nevertheless, I suspect that many who reflect on the cases without prior theoretical commitments will share my intuitions. My project here is not to persuade those who disagree on these starting points, but rather to trace the possible source of these intuitions to a quasi-Kantian principle. A few further intuitive remarks may at least lend some interest to the enterprise by suggesting that, for better or worse, my intuitions on these matters are not uncommon.

Although I do not want to base any argument on controversial religious premises, it is worth noting that Western religion has often opposed suicide, not simply as against God's commands, but as a failure to treasure the gift of life. Many who come to reject the theological belief that life is literally a "gift" from God, or that we are mere trustees of God's property, still retain a secular analogue of this view. The spirit of Thanksgiving, for example, is felt by many who no longer believe in any superhuman person to whom they can literally express gratitude. Doubtless some will attribute this to traces of prior belief, like residual guilt feelings for blasphemy in those who no longer believe in God. Yet this may not be the whole story. Often when moral feelings, seemingly unsupported otherwise, are attributed to religion as the source, I suspect that the reverse may be so. That is, deeply rooted moral beliefs whose grounds are hard to articulate lend support to the religions that offer a story to explain them. Theology is not so much the cause as the outcome. Be that as it may, the main point for present purposes is that it is not a remote and unfamiliar thought that suicide is morally significant because of the attitude it reflects about life, independently of its social consequences and its impact on rights.

The same point may be confirmed when we consider the moral admiration often expressed towards people who refuse to take their lives in circumstances like those of our paradigm suicides. Often, of course, resistance to suicide is praised because motivated by other-regarding considerations: "He would not do that to his family," "Despite his pain, he wanted to get his message to the world," etc. But this is not always so. Sometimes, quite aside from the effect on others, we admire the person who treasures life and refuses to give it up lightly. Consider, for example, a grief-stricken person whose deep sadness at a loved one's loss of life moves him, not to throw away his own, but to appreciate all the more each moment of being alive. Again, picture the depressed person whose thoughts of the future arouse no current feeling, but whose attitude, or stance, toward his life is like what one might have toward a friend who momentarily "leaves one cold" – one who is too long a treasured associate to abandon just because, at the present, one cannot work up any warm feelings towards him. We admire him for his willingness to make himself a future, even though at the moment he finds little pleasure in contemplating it.

Again, the attitude of the self-abasing suicide contrasts unfavorably with the lover of life, at least in the eyes of many. The former has sampled the same sort of opportunities, joys, and miseries as millions who struggle to hold on to what life they can, and yet he found or created nothing worth affirming. Having suffered and failed in the past, he will give no value to his present and future existence independent of that past. Unwilling to grant himself any potential for change, he abandons hope and refuses to forgive. He cannot accept that a person's worth as a human being is not entirely earned or subject to forfeit. Almost arrogant in a backhanded way, he in effect says, "I will accept my life and fortune as worthwhile only if I came to deserve it through my own good efforts. I refuse to accept any benefits, even renewed opportunity, if this is like a gift, more than I can credit to my own achievements." Contrast the attitude of the modest life-lover, whose thought is: "I know that most of these opportunities and obstacles, joys and sufferings, fall to me through no merit, or fault, of my own. But I am glad for the good fortune to be alive and to still have a chance to make a meaningful life."

The hedonistic, calculating suicide will perhaps be the most readily acceptable to liberal, nonreligious observers. In fact, he may even be admired for his self-control or fearlessness. Even in this case, however, the underlying attitude may be regarded as less than ideal. One who really loves life would not be so ready to bail out whenever the expected pleasure/pain balance looked unfavorable. We often admire those who refuse to give up, who grasp at remote possibilities for good under conditions of uncertainty, rather than resigning hope when the best estimate of the odds is unfavorable. Refusing to calculate, trying to make the most of what is available, deemphasizing inevitable pain and probable loss are praised beyond the point recommended by a hedonistic assessment. Caring about nature, wanting to create or just to be aware for its own sake, not just for the pleasure that results, these are seen as good features of a person, even if we do not condemn anyone for their absence. In general, we often admire those who, even aside from their obligations to others, see the value of their lives not as favorably positioned consumers, but as authors, not as a function of the pleasures and pains they expect to receive, but in part as stemming from the meaning they choose to give their lives.

The intuitive beliefs we have been considering are concerned only with suicides resulting from certain attitudes and motives. Many suicides, of course, do not fall into our special categories, and about these nothing has been said. In particular, there are several sorts of suicide which I especially want to distinguish from our four previous paradigms, because the objectionable features of our paradigm cases seem absent in these other cases. Prominent among these will be heroic, self-sacrificial suicides, done for the welfare of others. For present purposes, however, we are setting aside altruistic motives. Quite aside from these other-regarding suicides, there remain at least three important sorts of cases which, except when prohibited by religion, are widely regarded as unobjectionable. For example, I expect many would agree with me that there is little or nothing objectionable about the following.

(1) *Suicide when human life is no longer possible.* Suppose that progressive disease is inevitably destroying one's capacities to function as more than a lower animal or vegetable. One's body might remain alive for some time, yet life as a human being is all but over. If one does not choose suicide while still having lucid moments with a capacity for rational choice, one's life will continue as a vegetable, since others, let us imagine, will be unwilling to terminate it. Suicide in such a case need not be from impulse, apathy, self-abasement, or pleasure/pain calculation. One may simply see that human life is over and prefer not to continue to live as a subhuman being. Different people will draw the line between human life and subhuman life at somewhat different places, no doubt. However, at some extreme point, few will deny that the line has been crossed.

(2) *Suicide to end gross irremediable pain.* Even those of us who reject hedonistic calculation as the test of the value of life may concede that there is a point at which a person's pain is so horrible, so persistent, and so irremediable that suicide is thoroughly understandable and unobjectionable. It is not that pain and pleasure in general determine the value of life, but rather that gross, unavoidable, continuous pain can override other considerations. Living as a human being is valuable, one might say, not just *because* it has pleasures and only minimal pains, but it may be valuable to the agent *on condition that* continuing pain does not exceed some tolerable threshold.

(3) *Suicides based on self-regarding moral beliefs.* The suicides probably most often accepted as justifiable are those motivated by strong moral convictions. In the most familiar and least controversial instances, the moral considerations are other-regarding, for example, saving another's life or trying to avert a war. Yet suicide can sometimes be motivated by moral convictions not concerned with one's obligations to others, the welfare of others, etc. For example, people have sometimes found themselves trapped with no apparent options but suicide or a life they regard as base, degrading, and utterly contrary to their deepest values concerning how one should live (aside from effects on others). They cannot see how, even to a minimal degree, they can be "true to themselves" and live as they would be forced to. Some have viewed prostitution this way; others, life as a beggar, an addict, a cannibal, a boot-licking slave. Hopefully, in real life, suicide is rarely, if ever, the only alternative, and everyone does not share the same view about the comparative value of death and these ways of life. But if the choice were forced and the agent felt deeply that the only possible life for him was contrary to his most basic personal ideals, then to many surely suicide would seem the more admirable course.[1]

II

Taking these intuitive reflections for now as given, let us consider what general moral principle, or principles, might underlie them, accounting for our objections to the first four sorts of cases and our acceptance of the latter three. Principles regarding human rights are unlikely candidates to account for these cases, because the intuitions we wish to explain concern attitudes falling short of an ideal, not wrongs done to others. Utilitarian considerations might be cited in several cases (for example, impulsive and apathetic suicide), but seem not to be the whole story. The self-abaser, for example, seems to have a less than ideal attitude, quite

---

1 This category could include some cases which look like self-abasing suicides but may be significantly different. For example, a man who has just killed his wife and children in a jealous rage may feel that to continue to live would be dishonorable, that only taking his own life could begin to acknowledge his remorse. If so, the suicide could be seen as a grasp for a shred of dignity, not self-abasement in my sense.

aside from whether he or others would be happier if he changed. The calculated suicide seems to miss something, just because he considers nothing but utility. Even if (as seems doubtful) utilitarian reflection would always oppose the objectionable attitudes in (1)–(4), I think it is implausible that this adequately reflects our *reasons* for opposing those attitudes; for I suspect we sense the defects in the attitudes while still uncertain about the consequences (for example, whether the depressed person will really be happier if he continues to live). Sophisticated utilitarians may yet come up with explanations,[2] but my doubts are sufficient to lead me to explore in another direction.

An obvious alternative is Kant's moral theory.[3] My suggestion will be that, though inadequate as it stands, Kant's theory points towards a principle which could ground the intuitive beliefs about suicide which we have just considered.

The tenets of Kant's moral theory which I think are particularly important to the topic of suicide can be summarized as follows:

(1) In trying to decide whether one should do something, it is extremely important to determine what one's intentions and policies would be in doing it. These, together with one's underlying motive for having those intentions and policies, are what determine the kind of moral worth one's action will have.

(2) An essential feature of our humanity is that we are rational agents with autonomy of the will. This does not mean that we always act rationally or that we always manifest our autonomy, but it does imply that we have certain capacities and predispositions. These include the following: (a) practical reason applied to the satisfaction of our desires: that is, a capacity and disposition to pursue our ends in accord with "hypothetical imperatives," to set ourselves goals and follow informed policies about the best means to achieve them; (b) negative freedom: that is, the ability to act in accord with principles or policies without being fully determined to do so by desires or any external causal factors; (c) positive freedom or autonomy: that is, setting oneself principles and values which stem purely from one's nature as a rational being uncaused and unmotivated by one's desires or any external factors; (d) a predisposition to value one's humanity, or one's nature as a rational and free being, as an "end in itself": that is, to value the preservation, development, exercise, and honoring of one's rational nature independently of benefits and costs measured in terms of pleasure and pain or desiresatisfaction.

2 Modifications in classic utilitarianism include G. E. Moore's "ideal utilitarianism" in *Principia Ethica* (1960) and *Ethics* (1967), Mill's introduction of "qualities" of pleasure in *Utilitarianism*, and rule-utilitarianism of several types.

3 Here I draw from several of Kant's works, especially the *Groundwork of the Metaphysic of Morals* (tr. H. J. Paton, Harper & Row, 1909, pp. 80–116) and *The Metaphysical Principles of Virtue: Part II of the Metaphysic of Morals* (tr. James Ellington, Bobbs Merrill, 1981, pp. 82–85). Suicide is also discussed in Kant's *Lectures on Ethics* (tr. Louis Infield, Harper & Row, 1930, pp. 147–159). My summary concerns less the details of his remarks about suicide than the aspects of his general theory that have important implications regarding suicide. I intentionally omit Kant's unpersuasive argument from the first formula of the Categorical Imperative, *Groundwork*, p. 89.

(3) All moral considerations are ultimately grounded in our nature as rational beings with autonomy. For example, we are unconditionally obligated to follow the principles and values which we set ourselves as rational and positively free (see (2) c); and nothing else, such as tradition, religious or secular authority, natural instinct, etc., can be the ultimate ground of obligation.

(4) A fundamental moral principle, one to which any rational being with autonomy would commit himself, is: always act so that you treat humanity (that is, autonomy and rationality) never simply as a means, but always as an end in itself (that is, as something with "unconditional and incomparable worth").[4] This applies to "humanity" in oneself as well as in others. The arguments for this are several, but none appeals to the ideas of social utility or maximum satisfaction for the agent.

On the basis of these claims, Kant draws a double conclusion concerning the moral character of suicide.

(5) Suicide (at least suicide for the reasons Kant imagined) is opposed to the principle of humanity as an end in itself stated in (4) above because it "throws away" and degrades humanity in oneself. Thus, suicide expresses an attitude that one's nature as a rational, autonomous person is not of "incomparable worth" and "above all price." Suicide to end pain, for example, places cessation of pain, which is a mere "relative" and "conditioned" value, above rationality and autonomy, which (Kant says) have worth that "admits no equivalent."

(6) Suicide, therefore, is always, or nearly always, wrong. In fact, it is contrary to a "perfect ethical duty to oneself." This duty is a stringent prohibition, concerned with motives and attitudes and not merely intentional "external acts," which is grounded in the value of one's own humanity rather than in regard for others.[5]

These views of Kant's — both the tenets of his moral theory and the conclusions he draws concerning suicide — have provoked much controversy. I believe that the best of his ideas can be retained after much is conceded to his critics. Some prominent objections are the following:

Re (1): Kant is often thought to have exaggerated the role of the agent's intentions and policies and underrated the role of consequences in determining

4 My understanding of this principle is explained in "Humanity as an End in Itself," *Ethics* 91 (October 1980), pp. 84–99.
5 In the *Metaphysics of Morals,* Kant leaves open "casuistical questions" about whether taking one's life is wrong in certain extreme cases (for example, anticipation of an unjust death sentence or of madness and death from the bite of a rabid dog). In the *Lectures on Ethics* (tr. Louis Infield, Harper & Row, 1930), he says only Cato's heroic suicide has given the world opportunity to defend suicide. But even that was a violation of himself and so not really noble (pp. 149, 153). In the *Lectures,* Kant also remarks that "life is not to be highly regarded for its own sake" (p. 150), which seems paradoxical. But a close reading, I think, shows that the point is that mere life (including life contrary to duty, life as a beast, etc.) is not what one should value highly. It is rather life as a rational, autonomous, and moral agent.

what a person should do. A more modest Kantian view would insist on the importance of the agent's intentions and policies, but not deny the relevance of other factors.

Re (2): Kant is also criticized for exaggerating the degree to which actual human beings have autonomy and rationality. There is more variation in rational capacities than Kant imagined, it is argued, and the most autonomy we 'can aspire to is relative freedom from determination by unthinking impulse and narrow, selfish desires, unchecked by impartial reasoning. Adoption of pure rational principles, uninfluenced by any (even impartial) human desires, is generally thought impossible. Though Kant himself would never have yielded on this point, one might argue that the value of rationality and autonomy is not wholly dependent on Kant's extreme, other-worldly interpretation of them.

Re (3): Kant's attempt to derive all moral principles from the idea of rational free will has been far from universally persuasive. Even those who doubt Kant's attempt can grant that more is needed to ground morality than tradition, authority, instinct, etc., and that at least a part of taking a moral point of view is readiness to attribute value impartially to rational, autonomous human life within the bounds of certain other principles.

Re (4): Kant's principle that humanity should be treated as an end in itself has been variously interpreted and criticized, but the objection most persuasive to me is that it places an absolutely overriding value on the rational side of human life as opposed to the feeling, experiencing side. That is, Kant's principle not only declares that our rationality and freedom have a special intrinsic value, independent of pleasure and pain; it also implies that the preservation, development, etc., of rationality and freedom *override* any consideration of pleasure and pain with which they might conflict.[6] This means, for example, not only that one must avoid taking brain-damaging drugs for pleasure, but also that one must never neglect or damage one's rational capacities to alleviate *any* amount of pain, in oneself *or* others. However, a more qualified version of Kant's principle is possible and, in fact, in line with modifications already suggested. That is, one should treat humanity (or rational, autonomous human living) as a special intrinsic value, independent of but not always overriding considerations of pleasure and pain. As such, the principle would belong to a more pluralistic ethic than Kant's, one which requires weighing and balancing competing considerations. But that, in the end, may be the only sort of theory we can conscientiously live with.[7]

Re the conclusions concerning suicide, (5) and (6): Kant's view that suicide is always, or nearly always, contrary to a perfect duty to oneself provokes objections on at least two counts. First, that suicide is often justified (for example, in

6 See my "Humanity as an End in Itself," *Ethics* 91 (October 1980).

7 This view of ethical theory is nicely expressed in Stuart Hampshire's *Two Theories of Morality* (Oxford University Press, 1977, pp. 1–55).

situations mentioned in the last section). Second, that, because a person cannot violate his own rights, duties *to* oneself, in a strict sense, are impossible. Both objections, however, would be met if we accepted a qualified position, which remains in line with (5) above yet is consonant with previous modifications of Kant's view. One might hold, for example, that suicide *from certain attitudes* is always, or nearly always, objectionable, at least a falling short of a moral ideal, and that this is not solely because it is contrary to the welfare or rights of others. This would allow that some suicides are justified and even commendable, but suicides rooted in certain attitudes (for example, undervaluation of rational, autonomous human life) would be opposed. They would be opposed, not strictly condemned as immoral; and they would be opposed as out of line with an ideal moral attitude toward one's life, not as a violation of a strict duty to oneself.

III

Suppose, then, that we accepted the spirit of Kant's theory but adopted the qualifications mentioned above. What sort of principle might remain, and how would it apply to important choices aside from matters of life and death?

The principle I propose to consider is this: *A morally ideal person will value life as a rational, autonomous agent for its own sake, at least provided that the life does not fall below a certain threshold of gross, irremediable, and uncompensated pain and suffering.*

The main task in explaining the principle is to give some sense to the idea of "life as a rational, autonomous agent," but first some preliminary comments are in order.

First, the principle expresses an ideal rather than a duty. Thus questions of blame, censure, and enforcement associated with violations of duty are not at issue here. Also the principle is not meant to be absolute or unconditional. Other moral considerations, even other ideals, might override it in some circumstances. It is intended as at least one consideration in a pluralistic ethics which admits the need for judgment in weighing considerations of quite different sorts.

(3) In the same spirit the "certain threshold" of pain and suffering is admittedly left indeterminate. At extreme points, one hopes, there will be agreement, but no precise guidelines can be given to settle borderline cases. This indeterminacy, however, should not be confused with vacuousness. Nor should it be supposed that this qualification regarding extreme circumstances implies that in normal circumstances rational, autonomous living should be valued for the sake of plea-sure (or a favorable pleasure/pain ratio). The qualification is meant to reflect the idea that although the value of rational, autonomous living is not a function of the pleasure and pain it brings, a sufficiently gross level of suffering can undermine that value, making the sufferer incapable of finding that life meaningful or even tolerable.

The principle is not meant to suggest more than it says. In particular, it does not imply that life has value *only* when rational and autonomous. Nor does the qualification strictly imply that life has *no* value when consumed with gross, irremediable, and uncompensated pain. These matters are left open.

To say that rational, autonomous living is ideally valued for its own sake is to say that, ideally, it is seen as valuable independently of various ends to which it might serve as a means or necessary condition: for example, the general welfare, the greater enjoyment of the agent, the development of culture, or the maintenance of democratic institutions. What is not implied, once again, is that rational, autonomous living is the only good, the complete good, or an unconditional good.

The principle holds that one should value all rational, autonomous life, not simply one's own. Typically, perhaps, a person comes to value his own rational, autonomous life first and foremost, but ideally identification with others and the spirit of a moral point of view will in time lead him to value for others what he has come to prize for himself. Whether an ideal person is completely impartial, valuing the lives of all rational autonomous agents to exactly the same degree, is not determined, one way or the other, by our principle. The point is that all such lives are to be valued independently of various consequences, not that they are always to be prized equally.

The more thoroughly Kantian adherents of the principle will regard it as basic, nonderivative, and morally comprehensive. But for present purposes it need not be so viewed. That is, those who want to more nearly approximate Kant's theory will hold that the principle itself is not derived from any further moral principles (such as rule-utilitarian or divine command principles). Further, they will view the principle as a guide for moral decision in all areas of life, not just for specific problems such as drug use, moral education, capital punishment, or suicide. However, the principle could also have a more modest place in an ethical theory; that is, as an important but derivative and noncomprehensive ideal.

These preliminaries aside, the more difficult task is to say what is meant by "life as a rational, autonomous agent." Here I can only sketch the beginnings of an account that obviously needs further development.

First, following Kant, I think of rationality and autonomy as capacities and dispositions which belong to virtually all adult and nearly adult, human beings. Though they may be developed and exercised to greater or lesser degrees, basic rationality and autonomy are not special characteristics of an educated elite. They are features which distinguish virtually all human beings from lower animals.

Second, rational autonomy includes some minimum capacity and disposition to see causal connections (for example, to understand what will happen if one does this or that); to be aware of a variety of wants, for both future states of affairs as well as present ones; to set oneself ends and adopt policies and plans to achieve them; to revise ends and policies in the light of new information; to form and alter goals and policies in response to one's own deepest wants and values, to some extent independent of blind adherence to tradition, authority, and the opinions of others; and to resist immediate temptation in the pursuit of adopted ends, values, and policies.

Third, in saying that an agent is autonomous, I mean in part that he can, within a wide area of life, choose what to value and what not to value without contravening any fixed, objective, preset order of values in the world. As Kant, Sartre, and others have maintained, an autonomous person is a "creator of values," not merely a discoverer of values, at least within a wide range of morally permissible choice.[8] Within that range, we may choose to value some things, and to disvalue others, for their own sakes. Contrary to Moorean intuitionists, intrinsic values do not exist as properties in the world. They are not so much perceived as chosen.

Fourth, an autonomous agent is not restricted to pleasure and pain in what he can value. This is not a point about the causes of valuing, but rather about its scope. That is, human beings, so far as they are autonomous, have the capacity and disposition to care for things other than pleasant and painful experiences. This is not simply a denial of psychological egoism, as traditionally conceived. It is also a denial of psychological hedonism, that is, the view that human beings, whether egoistic or altruistic, can attribute intrinsic value only to pleasure and intrinsic disvalue only to pain. This idea of autonomy, which is found in such diverse thinkers as Kant, Sartre, and Nietzsche, is not so much an assertion of the high-mindedness of human beings as their wide-ranging capacity to form values. It is illustrated not merely in moral commitment and single-minded pursuit of truth, but also in more mundane concerns about what others are saying behind our backs and what is happening to our favorite forest flowers when no one is there to see them. To care about such matters is not the same as caring about their possible consequences or even about the pleasure or pain we may get in contemplating them.

Finally, it should be noted that rational autonomy, as conceived here, is *not* possession of rights to control one's life, *not* Sartrean freedom from all objective moral constraints, and *not* a pure Kantian will independent of all causation and desire. What is intended is a more modest set of capacities, which contrast not with causally explainable moral choices or objective moral constraints, but rather with being governed completely by instinct, being a creature of impulse without goals or policies, having an utterly incoherent set of goals and policies, being unable to follow through on one's own policies and principles, being blindly

8   Sartre and Kant differ, of course, on the sense in which we "create values." Kant held that moral principles are self-imposed by our nature as free *rational* beings, while the value of nonmoral "relative ends," within the limits of these principles, stems from the personal preferences of individuals. Sartre sees all values as created by individual choices, free from all objective rational constraints.

obedient to the commands or expectations of others, being rigidly bound to unrevisable self-commands, being bound in all one's choices to values one sees as fixed apart from oneself, and being unable to care about anything for its own sake except pleasure and pain.

The attitude towards life expressed by our modified Kantian principle may be contrasted with two other extreme views. The first is what I call the *Consumer Perspective*. This is exemplified most dramatically in Bentham's remarks about rational prudence. Intrinsic values are fixed: pleasure on the positive side, pain on the negative. When all is taken into account, the prudent person measures the value of his life by what he expects to receive, the number, duration, intensity and probability of pleasant and painful sensations. More time is better if one is still receiving more of the good than the bad, just as longer time at a party is better, until boredom outweighs the pleasure. The value of one's life from now on does not depend essentially on anything that has gone before; unless it happens that the past comes back to haunt one (for example, with bad memories, angry bill collectors, or hangovers), the past is irrelevant to whether continued life is worthwhile. This perspective is primarily forward-looking. To evaluate a stretch of life, one pictures oneself standing at the beginning trying to imagine what it will feel like to live through it. One's existence as valuer is only derivately important. It is needed, as it were, to receive and register the goods, which are the only things valued for their own sakes.

At the opposite extreme is what I call the *Obituarist Perspective*.[9] This looks at life as one might from life's end, preparing to summarize its salient features for the world. The focus is on the record, or story line, not how it felt to experience that life. Pleasures and pains tend to diminish in importance, as we typically weigh these more heavily in anticipation than in retrospect. "Was the result worth the pain?" considered after the fact, is more likely to invoke an affirmative response than "Will the result be worth the pain?" asked before an undertaking. Like the Consumer Perspective, the Obituarist Perspective sees the value of a stretch of life as determined by its content. But the value is measured by its contribution to the whole biography, not by a summation of discrete experiences. A principle of organic unities may be invoked. The value of the whole may exceed the sum of the value of the parts. The existence of the agent as chooser and valuer is again derivative, but now it is derived from the value of the whole life that is finally created rather than from the amount of good experiences received. If it was good that someone was alive at a time, this is because it was a necessary condition for the unfolding of a life of a certain sort.

Contrast these perspectives with what I shall call the *Author Perspective*. As I

9   I take the term from Hampshire's remark (*op. cit.*, p. 95) that Aristotle leads the reader "to view a human life, and particularly his own, from the standpoint of his eventual obituarist." But I would not pretend to reduce Aristotle's theory to my oversimple model.

imagine a working novelist might, this looks both forward and backward, wondering what it would be to experience each stretch of life, but ever mindful of how this fits into a meaningful whole. To some extent what makes the life worthwhile is not seen as fixed or predetermined – by either hedonistic or aesthetic standards. Not only what the agent will do, but also what will be the salient features, good and bad, is a matter of choice, within some limits at least. The author, in part, writes the criteria of evaluation as well as the story line. The value of the life as author, when the story is one's own, is not seen as entirely derivative from the final content of the story, once finished, nor from the feelings experienced in living through it. Rather, living as the author, making the crucial choices, deciding what to count meaningful and what trivial, these are valued for their own sakes. This is not simply to say that one enjoys being the author and so values living derivatively as a necessary condition of such enjoyment; that puts the focus in the wrong place. Even if it is true that one *enjoys* living as author, one enjoys it partly because this expresses what one is and wants to be. This is quite different from wanting enjoyment and so, for this reason, valuing the prerequisite life as author.

Probably no one assumes any of these perspectives on life exclusively, nor would I suggest that one should. The point of contrasting the metaphors is simply to make more vivid the ideal we have been considering. For to value one's life as a rational autonomous agent for its own sake means to some extent shifting from the Consumer and Obituarist perspectives to that of the Author. The crucial feature of this shift is that one values oneself as a potential maker of a meaningful life. The value of living is not entirely determined by the content of the life one makes; rather, that life acquires value in part because it is the expression of one's choices as its author.[10]

IV

The modified Kantian principle we have been considering has obvious implications regarding issues in everyday life quite aside from suicide. For example, it tends to oppose drug use which seriously impairs a healthy person's capacities to think and take charge of his life. It commends the development of one's capacities for rational self-control, not simply for the results, but because this is a natural expression of valuing for their own sake one's capacities as a rational autonomous agent.[11] The principle would urge self-respect in the sense of keeping

10 In Sartrean terms, one might say that ideally one values *being-for-itself* independently of one's *being-in-itself*.

11 Sometimes we value a capacity solely because its employment produces results we like. But sometimes the results of employing a capacity are valued simply as manifestations of an admired capacity. Kant's view of rational autonomy in persons is more nearly the latter attitude, I think. We honor the capacity in all, even those who neglect it. We want all to use it, not to achieve some independently valued result, but because it is too splendid a thing to leave unused (or to misuse or abuse).

our day-to-day choices in line with the personal standards we set for ourselves,[12] for we are not fully self-governing when our actions fail to match the values we profess to ourselves. In dealing with others, we would be urged to respect their own choices within a range of morally permissible conduct. To place their comfort or happiness above their own declared values (as is often done in benevolent lies) would not be to value them as autonomous agents. There would be a strong presumption against killing human beings in most circumstances. But euthanasia for those who have lost the capacity for even minimally rational, autonomous living would not be ruled out.

Regarding suicide, the Kantian principle, I think, distinguishes cases in just the way I initially proposed. The impulsive suicide, for example, falls short of the ideal in two ways. He places comparatively little value on his continued existence as an autonomous agent, as shown by his willingness to give this up to satisfy a momentary impulse. Further, he makes his choice in an irrational manner, being guided by a passing feeling out of keeping with the more enduring features of his character and personality. He both loses self-control and destroys his potentially controlling self. The apathetic suicide may not reach his decision in an irrational manner, but he chooses to treat his continuing potential to make a life as if it were virtually worthless – he throws it away even in the absence of strong impulses and concerns about his future. The deficiency is not in his feelings (lack of a felt wish to live), but in his policies. His act says, "Others aside, I stand for nothing. My potential to author a life means nothing to me, given that I see no future states that I now feel a desire for."

The self-abasing suicide even more dramatically undervalues his capacities for rational, autonomous living, for he views his life as worth less than nothing. He takes the Obituarist Perspective that the worth of life is measured entirely by one's record and, even more, he denies the possibility that he can make the whole story meaningful by future action; he attributes no value to living as the author of his life. Given his value assumptions, his decision may be rational; but it is not a decision that counts his being rational and autonomous as valuable. For him, all personal worth must be earned, and this attitude is incompatible with valuing life as an autonomous agent for its own sake.

Finally, the hedonistic, calculating suicide is opposed to our Kantian principle because he treats life as a rational, autonomous agent as a derivative value, good only because and so long as it is needed to achieve the ultimate end of maximum pleasure/pain balance. The Consumer Perspective is operative here. The ultimate values are fixed, not chosen. The prospective content of continued life entirely determines whether it is worthwhile. The pertinent question is, "What will I get?" not "What can I make of it?"

---

12   A fuller account of this sort of self-respect is attempted in my "Self-Respect Reconsidered," in this volume.

Contrast these cases with the suicides initially mentioned as intuitively unobjectionable. Suicides to avoid living in a subhuman condition do not contravene our principle, because the life that is ended lacks the potential for rational, autonomous agency. Troublesome questions may arise about what exact point in a gradual decline marks the end of "human" life, but, though practically difficult, these present no objections to the main point of the Kantian principle, which is that ideally what is valued is life with certain human potential, not merely being alive. Suicides to end gross, irremediable pain are not opposed to the principle, if the pain is such that it renders a person incapable of making any significant use of his human capacities. To end one's life in these conditions need not express the attitude that rational, autonomous living has no value in itself. It may simply show that one does not hold this value unconditionally and above all else.

Finally, suicide as the only way to avoid a life seen as demeaning and contrary to one's personal standards does not express an attitude inconsistent with the Kantian principle. To be sure, one cuts short the time one could live as a rational, autonomous agent; but doing so can be a manifestation of autonomy, an ultimate decision of the author of a life story to conclude it with a powerful expression of ideals he autonomously chose to live by. The principle affirms a presumption in favor of continued life as long as one's capacities are intact. But we cannot consistently maintain the value of autonomous living without admitting that, under some conditions, autonomously chosen values require one to make the choice that excludes all further choices. If you value being an author and have just one story to write, you should not hurry to conclude it. But sometimes, to give it the meaning you intend, you must end it before you spoil it.

V

My aim has been to explain a certain ideal and some of its implications, not to argue for it. Some, I know, will object that moral considerations must be other-regarding. Others may object that the author-metaphor suggests elitist standards remote from the life of ordinary people. Many will demand further reasons for accepting the ideal. These are legitimate concerns which I will not pretend to answer here. Instead, I conclude with a brief mention of two Kantian lines of argument that may merit consideration.

Kant spent little effort in constructing explicit arguments for his principle that humanity is an end in itself, perhaps because he regarded this idea as so basic and immediately persuasive. Nevertheless, he suggests at least two arguments on its behalf. The first, liberally reconstructed, is this.[13] There is, contrary to Hume, one (but only one) substantive value or "end" that can be attributed to every rational being, independently of the particular desires that he, as an

---

13 This argument is reconstructed from the *Groundwork*, especially pp. 96, 115–116.

individual, may have. This is "humanity," or "rational nature," itself, that is, one's existence as a being with reason, the capacity to set ends, and the ability to make choices with at least a degree of independence from impulse and given, nonrational desire. By virtue of being a rational agent, a person necessarily values rationality in himself. The impartiality implicit in the moral point of view requires him to acknowledge *in principle* the same value in others. The practical effect of valuing rational agency is implicit commitment to preserving it, developing it, making use of it, and "honoring" it symbolically. Since each individual also has other particular desires by virtue of not being a rational agent alone, the commitment to the value of rational agency is not always honored in practice. Sometimes we choose to destroy our rational capacities in pursuit of our special individual desires. Yet, taking a moral point of view involves adopting the principles and values of rational agents when thinking independently of their individual desires, in fact placing these above all other considerations. Therefore, taking the moral point of view requires valuing "humanity," or rational, free agency, for its own sake, not merely as a means to satisfying particular individual desires. In fact, it requires placing rational, free agency above all else.

There are, of course, many points at which the argument may be challenged, but it shows, at least, how valuing rational agency for its own sake can be deeply imbedded in a basic theory about what morality is. The argument does not lose interest, I think, merely because we take a more limited view of rational free agency than Kant. Its conclusion will be more modest if we reject the view that morality requires placing the value of rational agency *above all else* in favor of the view that a moral point of view requires giving it at least some independent value. But this more modest conclusion would be in line with our modified Kantian principle. Critics may still doubt that rational beings necessarily value their rational agency for its own sake or that a moral point of view involves adopting the principles and values of rational agents. But to challenge Kant on these points is to place the controversy where it belongs, at the heart of moral theory.

The second argument is roughly this:[14] Most valuable things have value only because valued by human beings. Their value is derivative from the fact that they serve our interests and desires. Even pleasure, which we value for its own sake, has only derivative value, that is, value dependent on the contingent fact that human beings want it. Now if valuers confer derivative value on things by their preferences and choices, those valuers must themselves have value. In fact, they must have value independent of, and superior to, the derivative values which they create.

The guiding analogy is how we value *ends*. We value certain means because they serve certain intermediate ends, which in turn we value because they con-

---

14 See the *Groundwork*, pp. 95–96.

tribute finally to our ultimate ends, that is, what we value for its own sake. The value of the means and the intermediate ends is derivative from the value of the ultimate ends; unless we value the ultimate end, the means and intermediate ends would be worthless to us. So, it seems, the source of derivative value must itself be valuable for its own sake. Since the ultimate source of the value of our contingent ends, such as health, wealth, and even pleasure, is their being valued by human beings, human beings, as valuers, must be valued for their own sakes.

Now there are a number of ways of reading this argument which render it quite implausible. If Midas could make worthless objects valuable by touching them, he would be a valuable fellow to have around. But we do not necessarily value him for his own sake. Again, if I admit that a sleazy film has market value derived from the preferences of a certain class of viewers, I am not thereby committed to valuing those viewers, as valuers, for their own sakes. One can admit that persons are a source of derivative values in these ways and yet consistently refuse to value them for their own sakes.

Nevertheless, the argument suggests an idea worth considering. Suppose we grant that, at least from a moral point of view, we should value individuals' satisfactions of their particular ends (within some limits) and, further, that these ends are to be valued *because* chosen by the various individuals. For example, we should care about Peter's athletic achievement and Paul's enjoyment of art not because athletic prowess and aesthetic enjoyment are objectively good in themselves or because *we* like these things. Rather, we should care about them because Peter and Paul chose them (within moral limits). The Kantian argument would simply remind us that, in conceding this basic point, we are committed to valuing Peter, Paul, and others, as valuers, for their own sakes. That is, from a moral point of view, their value to us as choosers does not stem entirely from a prior independent value of what they, or we, choose. Valuing the valuers for their own sakes is implicit in giving weight to their ends independent of our own likes and the content of those ends.

The application of this idea to one's own life would be this: The value of one's ends and life-projects from a moral point of view does not entirely depend upon how they serve others' wants or upon any fixed, objective intrinsic values; they have value because one chooses them (within certain moral limits). This implies that one's life as a chooser, or creator of value is to be valued for its own sake. This does not mean that one may never choose to end that life, but only that to end it *because of an attitude* which denies that value, is to fail to identify fully with a moral point of view.

Some will object, I am sure, that a moral point of view is only concerned with the value of others' ends or that the reconstructed Kantian argument begins with a premise that is still controversial. These objections cannot be lightly dismissed. But, again, debate about them is at least debate at the heart of moral theory, not at the fringes.

8

Ideals of human excellence and preserving natural environments

I

A wealthy eccentric bought a house in a neighborhood I know.[1] The house was surrounded by a beautiful display of grass, plants, and flowers, and it was shaded by a huge old avocado tree. But the grass required cutting, the flowers needed tending, and the man wanted more sun. So he cut the whole lot down and covered the yard with asphalt. After all it was his property and he was not fond of plants.

It was a small operation, but it reminded me of the strip mining of large sections of the Appalachians. In both cases, of course, there were reasons for the destruction, and property rights could be cited as justification. But I could not help but wonder, "What sort of person would do a thing like that?"

Many Californians had a similar reaction when a recent governor defended the leveling of ancient redwood groves, reportedly saying, "If you have seen one redwood, you have seen them all."

Incidents like these arouse the indignation of ardent environmentalists and leave even apolitical observers with some degree of moral discomfort. The reasons for these reactions are mostly obvious. Uprooting the natural environment robs both present and future generations of much potential use and enjoyment. Animals too depend on the environment; and even if one does not value animals for their own sakes, their potential utility for us is incalculable. Plants are needed, of course, to replenish the atmosphere quite aside from their aesthetic value. These reasons for hesitating to destroy forests and gardens are not only the most obvious ones, but also the most persuasive for practical purposes. But, one wonders, is there nothing more behind our discomfort? Are we concerned solely about the potential use and enjoyment of the forests, etc., for ourselves, later generations, and perhaps animals? Is there not something else which disturbs us when we witness the destruction or even listen to those who would defend it in terms of cost/benefit analysis?

Imagine that in each of our examples those who would destroy the environment argue elaborately that, even considering future generations of human beings and

1 The author thanks Gregory Kavka, Catherine Harlow, the participants at a colloquium at the University of Utah, and the referees for *Environmental Ethics*, Dale Jamieson and Donald Scherer, for helpful comments on earlier drafts of this paper.

animals, there are benefits in "replacing" the natural environment which outweigh the negative utilities which environmentalists cite.[2] No doubt we could press the argument on the facts, trying to show that the destruction is shortsighted and that its defenders have underestimated its potential harm or ignored some pertinent rights or interests. But is this all we could say? Suppose we grant, for a moment, that the utility of destroying the redwoods, forests, and gardens is equal to their potential for use and enjoyment by nature lovers and animals. Suppose, further, that we even grant that the pertinent human rights and animal rights, if any, are evenly divided for and against destruction. Imagine that we also concede, for argument's sake, that the forests contain no potentially useful endangered species of animals and plants. Must we then conclude that there is no further cause for moral concern? Should we then feel morally indifferent when we see the natural environment uprooted?

II

Suppose we feel that the answer to these questions should be negative. Suppose, in other words, we feel that our moral discomfort when we confront the destroyers of nature is not fully explained by our belief that they have miscalculated the best use of natural resources or violated rights in exploiting them. Suppose, in particular, we sense that part of the problem is that the natural environment is being viewed exclusively as a natural *resource*. What could be the ground of such a feeling? That is, what is there in our system of normative principles and values that could account for our remaining moral dissatisfaction?[3]

Some may be tempted to seek an explanation by appeal to the interests, or even the rights, of plants. After all, they may argue, we only gradually came to acknowledge the moral importance of all human beings, and it is even more recently that consciences have been aroused to give full weight to the welfare (and rights?) of animals. The next logical step, it may be argued, is to acknowledge a moral requirement to take into account the interests (and rights?) of

2 When I use the expression "the natural environment," I have in mind the sort of examples with which I began. For some purposes it is important to distinguish cultivated gardens from forests, virgin forests from replenished ones, irreplaceable natural phenomena from the replaceable, and so on; but these distinctions, I think, do not affect my main points here. There is also a broad sense, as Hume and Mill noted, in which all that occurs, miracles aside, is "natural." In this sense, of course, strip mining is as natural as a beaver cutting trees for his dam, and, as parts of nature, we cannot destroy the "natural" environment but only alter it. As will be evident, I shall use *natural* in a narrower, more familiar sense.

3 This paper is intended as a preliminary discussion in *normative* ethical theory (as opposed to *metaethics*). The task, accordingly, is the limited, though still difficult, one of articulating the possible basis in our beliefs and values for certain particular moral judgments. Questions of ultimate justification are set aside. What makes the task difficult and challenging is not that conclusive proofs from the foundation of morality are attempted; it is rather that the particular judgments to be explained seem at first not to fall under the most familiar moral principles (e.g., utilitarianism, respect for rights).

plants. The problem with the strip miners, redwood cutters, and the like, on this view, is not just that they ignore the welfare and rights of people and animals; they also fail to give due weight to the survival and health of the plants themselves.

The temptation to make such a reply is understandable if one assumes that all moral questions are exclusively concerned with whether *acts* are right or wrong, and that this, in turn, is determined entirely by how the acts impinge on the rights and interests of those directly affected. On this assumption, if there is cause for moral concern, some right or interest has been neglected; and if the rights and interests of human beings and animals have already been taken into account, then there must be some other pertinent interests, for example, those of plants. A little reflection will show that the assumption is mistaken; but, in any case, the conclusion that plants have rights or morally relevant interests is surely untenable. We do speak of what is "good for" plants, and they can "thrive" and also be "killed." But this does not imply that they have "interests" in any morally relevant sense. Some people apparently believe that plants grow better if we talk to them, but the idea that the plants suffer and enjoy, desire and dislike, etc., is clearly outside the range of both common sense and scientific belief. The notion that the forests should be preserved to avoid *hurting* the trees or because they have a *right* to life is not part of a widely shared moral consciousness, and for good reason.[4]

Another way of trying to explain our moral discomfort is to appeal to certain religious beliefs. If one believes that all living things were created by a God who cares for them and entrusted us with the use of plants and animals only for limited purposes, then one has a reason to avoid careless destruction of the forests, etc., quite aside from their future utility. Again, if one believes that a divine force is immanent in all nature, then too one might have reason to care for more than sentient things. But such arguments require strong and controversial premises, and, I suspect, they will always have a restricted audience.

Early in this century, due largely to the influence of G. E. Moore, another point of view developed which some may find promising.[5] Moore introduced,

---

4 I assume here that having a right presupposes having interests in a sense which in turn presupposes a capacity to desire, suffer, etc. Since my main concern lies in another direction, I do not argue the point, but merely note that some regard it as debatable. See, for example, W. Murray Hunt, "Are *Mere Things* Morally Considerable?" *Environmental Ethics* 2 (1980): 59–65; Kenneth E. Goodpaster, "On Stopping at Everything," *Environmental Ethics* 2 (1980): 288–94; Joel Feinberg, "The Rights of Animals and Unborn Generations," in William Blackstone, ed., *Philosophy and Environmental Crisis* (Athens: University of Georgia Press, 1974), pp. 43–68; Tom Regan, "Feinberg on What Sorts of Beings Can Have Rights," *Southern Journal of Philosophy* (1976): 485–98; Robert Elliot, "Regan on the Sort of Beings that Can Have Rights," *Southern Journal of Philosophy* (1978): 701–05; Scott Lehmann, "Do Wildernesses Have Rights?" *Environmental Ethics* 2 (1981): 129–46.

5 G. E. Moore, *Principia Ethica* (Cambridge: Cambridge University Press, 1903); *Ethics* (London: H. Holt, 1912).

or at least made popular, the idea that certain states of affairs are intrinsically valuable – not just valued, but valuable, and not necessarily because of their effects on sentient beings. Admittedly Moore came to believe that in fact the only intrinsically valuable things were conscious experiences of various sorts, but this restriction was not inherent in the idea of intrinsic value.[6] The intrinsic goodness of something, he thought, was an objective, nonrelational property of the thing, like its texture or color, but not a property perceivable by sense perception or detectable by scientific instruments. In theory at least, a single tree thriving alone in a universe without sentient beings, and even without God, could be intrinsically valuable. Since, according to Moore, our duty is to maximize intrinsic value, his theory could obviously be used to argue that we have reason not to destroy natural environments independently of how they affect human beings and animals. The survival of a forest might have worth beyond its worth *to* sentient beings.

This approach, like the religious one, may appeal to some but is infested with problems. There are, first, the familiar objections to intuitionism, on which the theory depends. Metaphysical and epistemological doubts about nonnatural, intuited properties are hard to suppress, and many have argued that the theory rests on a misunderstanding of the words *good, valuable,* and the like.[7] Second, even if we try to set aside these objections and think in Moore's terms, it is far from obvious that everyone would agree that the existence of forests, etc., is intrinsically valuable. The test, says Moore, is what we would say when we imagine a universe with just the thing in question, without any effects or accompaniments, and then we ask, "Would its existence be better than its nonexistence?" Be careful, Moore would remind us, not to construe this question as, "Would you *prefer* the existence of that universe to its nonexistence?" The question is, "Would its existence have the objective, nonrelational property, intrinsic goodness?"

Now even among those who have no worries about whether this really makes sense, we might well get a diversity of answers. Those prone to destroy natural environments will doubtless give one answer, and nature lovers will likely give another. When an issue is as controversial as the one at hand, intuition is a poor arbiter.

The problem, then, is this. We want to understand what underlies our moral uneasiness at the destruction of the redwoods, forests, etc., even apart from the loss of these as resources for human beings and animals. But I find no adequate answer by pursuing the questions, "Are rights or interests of plants neglected?" "What is God's will on the matter?" and "What is the intrinsic value of the existence of a tree or forest?" My suggestion, which is in fact the main point of

6 G. E. Moore, "Is Goodness a Quality?" *Philosophical Papers* (London: George Allen and Unwin, 1959), pp. 95–97.
7 See, for example, P. H. Nowell-Smith, *Ethics* (New York: Penguin Books, 1954).

this paper, is that we look at the problem from a different perspective. That is, let us turn for a while from the effort to find reasons why certain *acts* destructive of natural environments are morally wrong to the ancient task of articulating our ideals of human excellence. Rather than argue directly with destroyers of the environment who say, "Show me why what I am doing is *immoral*," I want to ask, "What sort of person would want to do what they propose?" The point is not to skirt the issue with an *ad hominem*, but to raise a different moral question, for even if there is no convincing way to show that the destructive acts are wrong (independently of human and animal use and enjoyment), we may find that the willingness to indulge in them reflects the absence of human traits that we admire and regard morally important.

This strategy of shifting questions may seem more promising if one reflects on certain analogous situations. Consider, for example, the Nazi who asks, in all seriousness, "Why is it wrong for me to make lampshades out of human skin — provided, of course, I did not myself kill the victims to get the skins?" We would react more with shock and disgust than with indignation, I suspect, because it is even more evident that the question reveals a defect in the questioner than that the proposed act is itself immoral. Sometimes we may not regard an act wrong at all though we see it as reflecting something objectionable about the person who does it. Imagine, for example, one who laughs spontaneously to himself when he reads a newspaper account of a plane crash that kills hundreds. Or, again, consider an obsequious grandson who, having waited for his grandmother's inheritance with mock devotion, then secretly spits on her grave when at last she dies. Spitting on the grave may have no adverse consequences and perhaps it violates no rights. The moral uneasiness which it arouses is explained more by our view of the agent than by any conviction that what he did was immoral. Had he hestiated and asked, "Why shouldn't I spit on her grave?" it seems more fitting to ask him to reflect on the sort of person he is than to try to offer reasons why he should refrain from spitting.

III

What sort of person, then, would cover his garden with asphalt, strip mine a wooded mountain, or level an irreplaceable redwood grove? Two sorts of answers, though initially appealing, must be ruled out. The first is that persons who would destroy the environment in these ways are either shortsighted, underestimating the harm they do, or else are too little concerned for the well-being of other people. Perhaps too they have insufficient regard for animal life. But these considerations have been set aside in order to refine the controversy. Another tempting response might be that we count it a moral virtue, or at least a human ideal, to love nature. Those who value the environment only for its utility must not really love nature and so in this way fall short of an ideal. But such an answer is hardly satisfying in the present context, for what is at issue is *why* we feel moral discomfort at the activities of those who admittedly value nature only for its utility. That it is ideal to care for nonsentient nature beyond its possible use is really just another way of expressing the general point which is under controversy.

What is needed is some way of showing that this ideal is connected with other virtues, or human excellences, not in question. To do so is difficult and my suggestions, accordingly, will be tentative and subject to qualification. The main idea is that, though indifference to nonsentient nature does not *necessarily* reflect the absence of virtues, it often signals the absence of certain traits which we want to encourage because they are, in most cases, a natural basis for the development of certain virtues. It is often thought, for example, that those who would destroy the natural environment must lack a proper appreciation of their place in the natural order, and so must either be ignorant or have too little humility. Though I would argue that this is not necessarily so, I suggest that, given certain plausible empirical assumptions, their attitude may well be rooted in ignorance, a narrow perspective, inability to see things as important apart from themselves and the limited groups they associate with, or reluctance to accept themselves as natural beings. Overcoming these deficiencies will not guarantee a proper moral humility, but for most of us it is probably an important psychological preliminary. Later I suggest, more briefly, that indifference to nonsentient nature typically reveals absence of either aesthetic sensibility or a disposition to cherish what has enriched one's life and that these, though not themselves moral virtues, are a natural basis for appreciation of the good in others and gratitude.[8]

Consider first the suggestion that destroyers of the environment lack an appreciation of their place in the universe.[9] Their attention, it seems, must be focused on parochial matters, on what is, relatively speaking, close in space and time. They seem not to understand that we are a speck on the cosmic scene, a brief stage in the evolutionary process, only one among millions of species on Earth, and an episode in the course of human history. Of course, they know that

---

8   The issues I raise here, though perhaps not the details of my remarks, are in line with Aristotle's view of moral philosophy, a view revitalized recently by Philippa Foot's *Virtue and Vice* (Berkeley: University of California Press, 1979), Alasdair McIntyre's *After Virtue* (Notre Dame: Notre Dame Press, 1981), and James Wallace's *Virtues and Vices* (Ithaca and London: Cornell University Press, 1978), and other works. For other reflections on relationships between character and natural environments, see John Rodman, "The Liberation of Nature," *Inquiry* (1976): 83–131 and L. Reinhardt, "Some Gaps in Moral Space: Reflections on Forests and Feelings," in Mannison, McRobbie, and Routley, eds., *Environmental Philosophy* (Canberra: Australian National University Research School of Social Sciences, 1980).

9   Though for simplicity I focus upon those who do strip mining, etc., the argument is also applicable to those whose utilitarian calculations lead them to preserve the redwoods, mountains, etc., but who care for only sentient nature for its own sake. Similarly the phrase "indifferent to nature" is meant to encompass those who are indifferent *except* when considering its benefits to people and animals.

there are stars, fossils, insects, and ancient ruins; but do they have any idea of the complexity of the processes that led to the natural world as we find it? Are they aware how much the forces at work within their own bodies are like those which govern all living things and even how much they have in common with inanimate bodies? Admittedly scientific knowledge is limited and no one can master it all; but could one who had a broad and deep understanding of his place in nature really be indifferent to the destruction of the natural environment?

This first suggestion, however, may well provoke a protest from a sophisticated anti-environmentalist.[10] "Perhaps *some* may be indifferent to nature from ignorance," the critic may object, "but *I* have studied astronomy, geology, biology, and biochemistry, and I still unashamedly regard the nonsentient environment as simply a resource for our use. It should not be wasted, of course, but what should be preserved is decidable by weighing long-term costs and benefits." "Besides," our critic may continue, "as philosophers you should know the old Humean formula, 'You cannot derive an *ought* from an *is*.' All the facts of biology, biochemistry, etc., do not entail that I ought to love nature or want to preserve it. What one understands is one thing; what one values is something else. Just as nature lovers are not necessarily scientists, those indifferent to nature are not necessarily ignorant."

Although the environmentalist may concede the critic's logical point, he may well argue that, as a matter of fact, increased understanding of nature tends to heighten people's concern for its preservation. If so, despite the objection, the suspicion that the destroyers of the environment lack deep understanding of nature is not, in most cases, unwarranted, but the argument need not rest here.

The environmentalist might amplify his original idea as follows: "When I said that the destroyers of nature do not appreciate their place in the universe, I was not speaking of intellectual understanding alone, for, after all, a person can *know* a catalog of facts without ever putting them together and seeing vividly the whole picture which they form. To see oneself as just one part of nature is to look at oneself and the world from a certain perspective which is quite different from being able to recite detailed information from the natural sciences. What the destroyers of nature lack is this perspective, not particular information."

Again our critic may object, though only after making some concessions: "All right," he may say, "*some* who are indifferent to nature may lack the cosmic perspective of which you speak, but again there is no *necessary* connection between this failing, if it is one, and any particular evaluative attitude toward nature. In

10 For convenience I use the labels *environmentalist* and *anti-environmentalist* (or *critic*) for the opposing sides in the rather special controversy I have raised. Thus, for example, my "environmentalist" not only favors conserving the forests, etc., but finds something objectionable in wanting to destroy them even aside from the costs to human beings and animals. My "anti-environmentalist" is not simply one who wants to destroy the environment; he is a person who has no qualms about doing so independent of the adverse effects on human beings and animals.

fact, different people respond quite differently when they move to a wider perspective. When *I* try to picture myself vividly as a brief, transitory episode in the course of nature, I simply get depressed. Far from inspiring me with a love of nature, the exercise makes me sad and hostile. You romantics think only of poets like Wordsworth and artists like Turner, but you should consider how differently Omar Khayyám responded when he took your wider perspective. His reaction, when looking at his life from a cosmic viewpoint, was 'Drink up, for tomorrow we die.' Others respond in an almost opposite manner with a joyless Stoic resignation, exemplified by the poet who pictures the wise man, at the height of personal triumph, being served a magnificent banquet, and then consummating his marriage to his beloved, all the while reminding himself, 'Even this shall pass away.' "[11] In sum, the critic may object, "Even if one should try to see oneself as one small transitory part of nature, doing so does not dictate any particular normative attitude. Some may come to love nature, but others are moved to live for the moment; some sink into sad resignation; others get depressed or angry. So indifference to nature is not necessarily a sign that a person fails to look at himself from the larger perspective."

The environmentalist might respond to this objection in several ways. He might, for example, argue that even though some people who see themselves as part of the natural order remain indifferent to nonsentient nature, this is not a common reaction. Typically, it may be argued, as we become more and more aware that we are parts of the larger whole we come to value the whole independently of its effect on ourselves. Thus, despite the possibilities the critic raises, indifference to nonsentient nature is still in most cases a sign that a person fails to see himself as part of the natural order.

If someone challenges the empirical assumption here, the environmentalist might develop the argument along a quite different line. The initial idea, he may remind us, was that those who would destroy the natural environment fail to *appreciate* their place in the natural order. "Appreciating one's place" is not simply an intellectual appreciation. It is also an attitude, reflecting what one values as well as what one knows. When we say, for example, that both the servile and the arrogant person fail to *appreciate* their place in a society of equals, we do not mean simply that they are ignorant of certain empirical facts, but rather that they have certain objectionable attitudes about their importance relative to other people. Similarly, to fail to appreciate one's place in nature is not merely to lack knowledge or breadth of perspective, but to take a certain attitude about what matters. A person who *understands* his place in nature but still views nonsentient nature merely as a resource takes the attitude that nothing is *important* but human beings and animals. Despite first appearances, he is not so much like

---

11   "Even this shall pass away," by Theodore Tildon, in *The Best Loved Poems of the American People,* ed. Hazel Felleman (Garden City, N.Y.: Doubleday & Co., 1936).

the pre-Copernican astronomers who made the intellectual error of treating the Earth as the "center of the universe" when they made their calculations. He is more like the racist who, though well aware of other races, treats all races but his own as insignificant.

So construed, the argument appeals to the common idea that awareness of nature typically has, and should have, a humbling effect. The Alps, a storm at sea, the Grand Canyon, towering redwoods, and "the starry heavens above" move many a person to remark on the comparative insignificance of our daily concerns and even of our species, and this is generally taken to be a quite fitting response.[12] What seems to be missing, then, in those who understand nature but remain unmoved is a proper humility.[13] Absence of proper humility is not the same as selfishness or egoism, for one can be devoted to self-interest while still viewing one's own pleasures and projects as trivial and unimportant.[14] And one can have an exaggerated view of one's own importance while grandly sacrificing for those one views as inferior. Nor is the lack of humility identical with belief that one has power and influence, for a person can be quite puffed up about himself while believing that the foolish world will never acknowledge him. The humility we miss seems not so much a belief about one's relative effectiveness and recognition as an attitude which measures the importance of things independently of their relation to oneself or to some narrow group with which one identifies. A paradigm of a person who lacks humility is the self-important emperor who grants status to his family because it is *his,* to his subordinates because *he* appointed them, and to his country because *he* chooses to glorify it. Less extreme but still lacking proper humility is the elitist who counts events significant solely in proportion to how they affect his class. The suspicion about those who would destroy the environment, then, is that what they count important is too narrowly confined insofar as it encompasses only what affects beings who, like us, are capable of feeling.

This idea that proper humility requires recognition of the importance of non-sentient nature is similar to the thought of those who charge meat eaters with "species-ism." In both cases it is felt that people too narrowly confine their concerns to the sorts of beings that are most like them. But, however intuitively appealing, the idea will surely arouse objections from our anti-environmentalist critic. "Why," he will ask, "do you suppose that the sort of humility I *should* have requires me to acknowledge the importance of nonsentient nature aside from

---

12 An exception, apparently, was Kant, who thought "the starry heavens" sublime and compared them with "the moral law within," but did not for all that see our species as comparatively insignificant.

13 By "*proper* humility" I mean that sort and degree of humility that is a morally admirable character trait. How precisely to define this is, of course, a controversial matter; but the point for present purposes is just to set aside obsequiousness, false modesty, underestimation of one's abilities, and the like.

14 I take this point from some of Philippa Foot's remarks.

its utility? You cannot, by your own admission, argue that nonsentient nature *is* important, appealing to religious or intuitionist grounds. And simply to assert, without further argument, that an ideal humility requires us to view nonsentient nature as important for its own sake begs the question at issue. If proper humility is acknowledging the relative importance of things as one should, then to show that I must lack this you must first establish that one *should* acknowledge the importance of nonsentient nature."

Though some may wish to accept this challenge, there are other ways to pursue the connection between humility and response to nonsentient nature. For example, suppose we grant that proper humility requires only acknowledging a due status to sentient beings. We must admit, then, that it is logically possible for a person to be properly humble even though he viewed all nonsentient nature simply as a resource. But this logical possibility may be a psychological rarity. It may be that, given the sort of beings we are, we would never learn humility before persons without developing the general capacity to cherish, and regard important, many things for their own sakes. The major obstacle to humility before persons is self-importance, a tendency to measure the significance of everything by its relation to oneself and those with whom one identifies. The processes by which we overcome self-importance are doubtless many and complex, but it seems unlikely that they are exclusively concerned with how we relate to other people and animals. Learning humility requires learning to feel that something matters besides what will affect oneself and one's circle of associates. What leads a child to care about what happens to a lost hamster or a stray dog he will not see again is likely also to generate concern for a lost toy or a favorite tree where he used to live.[15] Learning to value things for their own sake, and to count what affects them important aside from their utility, is not the same as judging them to have some intuited objective property, but it is necessary to the development of humility and it seems likely to take place in experiences with nonsentient nature as well as with people and animals. If a person views all nonsentient nature merely as a resource, then it seems unlikely that he has developed the capacity needed to overcome self-importance.

IV

This last argument, unfortunately, has its limits. It presupposes an empirical connection between experiencing nature and overcoming self-importance, and this may be challenged. Even if experiencing nature promotes humility before others, there may be other ways people can develop such humility in a world of concrete, glass, and plastic. If not, perhaps all that is needed is limited experience

---

15 The causal history of this concern may well depend upon the object (tree, toy) having given the child pleasure, but this does not mean that the object is then valued only for further pleasure it may bring.

of nature in one's early, developing years; mature adults, having overcome youthful self-importance, may live well enough in artificial surroundings. More importantly, the argument does not fully capture the spirit of the intuition that an ideal person stands humbly before nature. That idea is not simply that experiencing nature tends to foster proper humility before other people; it is, in part, that natural surroundings encourage and are appropriate to an ideal sense of oneself as part of the natural world. Standing alone in the forest, after months in the city, is not merely good as a means of curbing one's arrogance before others; it reinforces and fittingly expresses one's acceptance of oneself as a natural being.

Previously we considered only one aspect of proper humility, namely, a sense of one's relative importance with respect to other human beings. Another aspect, I think, is a kind of *self-acceptance*. This involves acknowledging, in more than a merely intellectual way, that we are the sort of creatures that we are. Whether one is self-accepting is not so much a matter of how one attributes *importance* comparatively to oneself, other people, animals, plants, and other things as it is a matter of understanding, facing squarely, and responding appropriately to who and what one is, e.g., one's powers and limits, one's affinities with other beings and differences from them, one's unalterable nature and one's freedom to change. Self-acceptance is not merely intellectual awareness, for one can be intellectually aware that one is growing old and will eventually die while nevertheless behaving in a thousand foolish ways that reflect a refusal to acknowledge these facts. On the other hand, self-acceptance is not passive resignation, for refusal to pursue what one truly wants within one's limits is a failure to accept the freedom and power one has. Particular behaviors, like dying one's gray hair and dressing like those twenty years younger, do not *necessarily* imply lack of self-acceptance, for there could be reasons for acting in these ways other than the wish to hide from oneself what one really is. One fails to accept oneself when the patterns of behavior and emotion are rooted in a desire to disown and deny features of oneself, to pretend to oneself that they are not there. This is not to say that a self-accepting person makes no value judgments about himself, that he likes all facts about himself, wants equally to develop and display them; he can, and should feel remorse for his past misdeeds and strive to change his current vices. The point is that he does not disown them, pretend that they do not exist or are facts about something other than himself. Such pretense is incompatible with proper humility because it is seeing oneself as better than one is.

Self-acceptance of this sort has long been considered a human excellence, under various names, but what has it to do with preserving nature? There is, I think, the following connection. As human beings we are part of nature, living, growing, declining, and dying by natural laws similar to those governing other living beings; despite our awesomely distinctive human powers, we share many of the needs, limits, and liabilities of animals and plants. These facts are neither good nor bad in themselves, aside from personal preference and varying conventional values. To say this is to utter a truism which few will deny, but to accept these facts, as facts about oneself, is not so easy – or so common. Much of what naturalists deplore about our increasingly artificial world reflects, and encourages, a denial of these facts, an unwillingness to avow them with equanimity.

Like the Victorian lady who refuses to look at her own nude body, some would like to create a world of less transitory stuff, reminding us only of our intellectual and social nature, never calling to mind our affinities with "lower" living creatures. The "denial of death," to which psychiatrists call attention, reveals an attitude incompatible with the sort of self-acceptance which philosophers, from the ancients to Spinoza and on, have admired as a human excellence.[16] My suggestion is not merely that experiencing nature causally promotes such self-acceptance, but also that those who fully accept themselves as part of the natural world lack the common drive to disassociate themselves from nature by replacing natural environments with artificial ones. A storm in the wilds helps us to appreciate our animal vulnerability, but, equally important, the reluctance to experience it may *reflect* an unwillingness to accept this aspect of ourselves. The person who is too ready to destroy the ancient redwoods may lack humility, not so much in the sense that he exaggerates his importance relative to others, but rather in the sense that he tries to avoid seeing himself as one among many natural creatures.

V

My suggestion so far has been that, though indifference to nonsentient nature is not itself a moral vice, it is likely to reflect either ignorance, a self-importance, or a lack of self-acceptance which we must overcome to have proper humility. A similar idea might be developed connecting attitudes toward nonsentient nature with other human excellences. For example, one might argue that indifference to nature reveals a lack of either an aesthetic sense or some of the natural roots of gratitude.

When we see a hillside that has been gutted by strip miners or the garden replaced by asphalt, our first reaction is probably, "How ugly!" The scenes assault our aesthetic sensibilities. We suspect that no one with a keen sense of beauty could have left such a sight. Admittedly not everything in nature strikes us as beautiful, or even aesthetically interesting, and sometimes a natural scene is replaced with a more impressive architectural masterpiece. But this is not usually the situation in the problem cases which environmentalists are most concerned about. More often beauty is replaced with ugliness.

At this point our critic may well object that, even if he does lack a sense of

16   See, for example, Ernest Becker, *The Denial of Death* (New York: Free Press, 1973).

beauty, this is no moral vice. His cost/benefit calculations take into account the pleasure others may derive from seeing the forests, etc., and so why should he be faulted?

Some might reply that, despite contrary philosophical traditions, aesthetics and morality are not so distinct as commonly supposed. Appreciation of beauty, they may argue, is a human excellence which morally ideal persons should try to develop. But, setting aside this controversial position, there still may be cause for moral concern about those who have no aesthetic response to nature. Even if aesthetic sensibility is not itself a moral virtue, many of the capacities of mind and heart which it presupposes may be ones which are also needed for an appreciation of other people. Consider, for example, curiosity, a mind open to novelty, the ability to look at things from unfamiliar perspectives, empathetic imagination, interest in details, variety, and order, and emotional freedom from the immediate and the practical. All these, and more, seem necessary to aesthetic sensibility, but they are also traits which a person needs to be fully sensitive to people of all sorts. The point is not that a moral person must be able to distinguish beautiful from ugly people; the point is rather that unresponsiveness to what is beautiful, awesome, dainty, dumpy, and otherwise aesthetically interesting in nature probably reflects a lack of the openness of mind and spirit necessary to appreciate the best in human beings.

The anti-environmentalist, however, may refuse to accept the charge that he lacks aesthetic sensibility. If he claims to appreciate seventeenth-century miniature portraits, but to abhor natural wildernesses, he will hardly be convincing. Tastes vary, but aesthetic sense is not *that* selective. He may, instead, insist that he *does* appreciate natural beauty. He spends his vacations, let us suppose, hiking in the Sierras, photographing wildflowers, and so on. He might press his argument as follows: "I enjoy natural beauty as much as anyone, but I fail to see what this has to do with preserving the environment independently of human enjoyment and use. Nonsentient nature is a resource, but one of its best uses is to give us pleasure. I take this into account when I calculate the costs and benefits of preserving a park, planting a garden, and so on. But the problem you raised explicitly set aside the desire to preserve nature as a means to enjoyment. I say, let us enjoy nature fully while we can, but if all sentient beings were to die tomorrow, we might as well blow up all plant life as well. A redwood grove that no one can use or enjoy is utterly worthless."

The attitude expressed here, I suspect, is not a common one, but it represents a philosophical challenge. The beginnings of a reply may be found in the following. When a person takes joy in something, it is a common (and perhaps natural) response to come to cherish it. To cherish something is not simply to be happy with it at the moment, but to care for it for its own sake. This is not to say that one necessarily sees it as having feelings and so wants it to feel good; nor does it imply that one judges the thing to have Moore's intrinsic value. One simply wants the thing to survive and (when appropriate) to thrive, and not simply for its utility. We see this attitude repeatedly regarding mementos. They are not simply valued as a means to remind us of happy occasions; they come to be valued for their own sake. Thus, if someone really took joy in the natural environment, but was prepared to blow it up as soon as sentient life ended, he would lack this common human tendency to cherish what enriches our lives. While this response is not itself a moral virtue, it may be a natural basis of the virtue we call "gratitude." People who have no tendency to cherish things that give them pleasure may be poorly disposed to respond gratefully to persons who are good to them. Again the connection is not one of logical necessity, but it may nevertheless be important. A nonreligious person unable to "thank" anyone for the beauties of nature may nevertheless feel "grateful" in a sense; and I suspect that the person who feels no such "gratitude" toward nature is unlikely to show proper gratitude toward people.

Suppose these conjectures prove to be true. One may wonder what is the point of considering them. Is it to disparage all those who view nature merely as a resource? To do so, it seems, would be unfair, for, even if this attitude typically stems from deficiencies which affect one's attitudes toward sentient beings, there may be exceptions and we have not shown that their view of nonsentient nature is itself blameworthy. But when we set aside questions of blame and inquire what sorts of human traits we want to encourage, our reflections become relevant in a more positive way. The point is not to insinuate that all anti-environmentalists are defective, but to see that those who value such traits as humility, gratitude, and sensitivity to others have reason to promote the love of nature.

9

Weakness of will and character

Some people, as we all know, are weak-willed, some more than others. This weakness is commonly regarded as a defect in a person, and when someone fails to meet his obligations from weakness of will this is not usually counted as an adequate excuse. Even when the weakness is manifested in morally innocent behavior, it tends to evoke contemptuous humor from others and feelings of shame in the agent. To the moral philosopher concerned with virtues and vices these facts raise both traditional questions and special puzzles. The traditional questions regarding any putative defect of character are "What is it?," "What reasons does one have for trying to avoid it?," and "What grounds, if any, are there for regarding it as a *moral* defect?" When we turn these questions specifically to weakness of will, we encounter the special puzzles. For example, if weakness of will is really a moral vice, why is the "lack of will power" of the compulsive eater, the alcoholic, etc., so often treated as a disability, calling for sympathy, understanding, and medical intervention rather than a defect of character calling for blame? If, on the other hand, weakness of will is a disability, like physical weakness, why is it not as readily counted as an excuse? Again, how can we regard weakness of will as a moral vice if so many of its manifestations are not themselves morally wrong? And why do we not think better of the Nazi whom we suspected of being both cruel and weak-willed when we learn that after all he has the strength of will to carry out his cruel aims?

When we review the impressive contemporary literature on weakness of will, we find that these questions are not the focus of attention.[1] Instead, philosophers have concentrated on what, quite naturally, has been taken to be a prior question: How is weakness of will possible? The main problem is seen as a puzzle for action theory, stemming from certain pervasive assumptions about the concepts of

---

1 Prominent in these contemporary discussions are the following: R. M. Hare, *Freedom and Reason* (1963); G. Santas, "Plato's *Protagoras*, and Explanations of Weakness," *The Philosophical Review*, 1966; Donald Davidson, "How is Weakness of Will Possible?" in *Moral Concepts*, edited by Joel Feinberg, Oxford University Press, 1970; Gary Watson, "Scepticism About Weakness of Will," *The Philosophical Review*, 1977; and David Pears, *Motivated Irrationality*, Clarendon Press (Oxford) 1983. Some early papers are collected in *Weakness of Will*, edited by G. W. Mortimore, Macmillan, 1971. I am indebted to these as well as the comments of many people on an earlier (unpublished) paper on weakness of will, especially Michael Bratman, J.O. Urmson, John Perry, Gregory Kavka, and Robert M. Adams. Thanks are due Bernard Boxill, Geoffrey Sayre McCord, and Gregory Trianosky for helpful comments on an earlier version of this paper.

intending, wanting, and judging best to do. The focus, typically, is not on weakness of will as a character trait but rather on the particular instances in which, it seems, a person acts, with full awareness, contrary to what he judges he ought to do (or has the best reasons to do). The apparent phenomena do not seem to square with what theories of action and evaluative language allow to be possible, and the problem has been to "save the phenomena" by making subtle distinctions or modifications of the standard assumptions. Though the term "weakness of will" appears frequently in the discussions, most often references to "will" are replaced by other terms when the problem is posed most explicitly.

This concentration on the cases most puzzling for action theory has been unfortunate in some respects. Part of the problem is that doubts about the possibility of weakness of will have resulted from dubious assumptions about evaluative language (e.g., Hare's prescriptivism). Even the ingenious efforts to circumvent these doubts have so heightened our awareness of the conceptual difficulties in this area that moral philosophers have been understandably discouraged from pursuing their traditional questions about weakness of will as a defect of character. More importantly, I suspect, focus upon the problems arising within action theory has so dominated the selection of the phenomena to be considered that the resulting conceptions of weakness of will capture only a small part of what moralists have been concerned with. Eager to avoid the evils of Cartesianism in metaphysics and Descriptivism in metaethics, philosophers have too often circumscribed their questions so narrowly that the familiar problem of character is lost.

While it is tempting to wait for solutions in action theory before returning to the moralist's questions, there may be advantages in not postponing the latter. This would be so, for example, if my suspicion is correct that the moralist's questions direct us to a somewhat different range of cases and a conception of weakness of will that is less problematic than those that have so puzzled action theorists. Perhaps, too, by looking for the conception of weakness of will that best fits the common moral assessment, we can better understand why accounts which treat weakness of will as a disability strike many of us as inadequate or as at best revisionary of ordinary concepts.

In any case, I propose to approach the subject in an unconventional way: raising the moralist's questions, focusing upon a character trait rather than isolated acts, not shunning the idea of "will" in favor of intending, wanting, etc., and not assuming that one's will and intentional acts must be in accord with what one judges best to do. Although I shall make brief suggestions regarding the other questions, my focus will be primarily on the first traditional question, namely, what is weakness of will insofar as it is viewed as a defect of character? My aim, however, is not to give a definitive answer to any of these questions, much less to resolve the much debated puzzles in action theory. The aim is rather to shift or expand the subject under discussion to include more of what is at issue for those thinking about how to live and what sort of person to try to become.

My procedure will be this: First I describe an example and what I take to be a common moral assessment of a weak-willed person. Next I try to distinguish this weakness of will from being will-less, acting against one's best judgment, and lacking willpower. Then, drawing from these discussions, I try to say more generally what weakness of will would be if conceived as a character trait that corresponds to familiar examples and our typical attitudes towards them. Finally, I make some brief comments on the disadvantages of being weak-willed and the case for thinking it to be incompatible with a fully moral life. Though I will not argue at length for the possibility of weakness of will as I construe it, I hope that it will be evident that my account avoids at least the most troublesome paradoxes which have plagued this subject.

I

Consider amiable Amy, well-intentioned and eager to please but weak-willed. Her weakness shows up in a variety of ways.

(1) *Half-hearted efforts.* She often takes part in challenging activities, such as competitive sports and arguing with her opinionated husband, but she rarely tries very hard. She wants to win and makes some feeble efforts in that direction, but when the challenge becomes difficult she never exerts herself fully. She does not exactly "give up," for she continues to take minimal steps towards winning, hoping that somehow they will be enough. Usually she does not explicitly resolve to win, or even to try hard, but she undertakes the activities with winning as the end in view and she carries on without ever deciding to abandon the end. People say that she has the ability but not the strength of will to win. The problem is not simply a particular aversion to success in competition; she behaves in a similar way whenever her projects become difficult.

(2) *Weak resolves.* Sometimes she deliberates and makes resolutions about her future conduct. Each year, for example, she makes a list of New Year's resolutions about dieting, jogging, reading good books, etc. But often the resolutions are half-hearted even when they are made. She says, quite sincerely, that she intends to keep them, and by announcing them she puts herself in the position of being embarrassed and a bit ashamed if she does not. But she would not be surprised if later she "changed her mind," and she is purposefully vague about what she would count as a good reason for changing her mind. She makes charts for daily reminders and feels good about the "new direction" she is giving her life; but she knows that she could be persuaded to deviate even at that moment if the right opportunity came along. These resolves do not usually last long, sometimes giving way to considerations that seem more important at the time and sometimes simply fading into insignificant memories.

(3) *Surrendering after a struggle.* At times, however, Amy makes more whole-

hearted commitments. As she anticipates certain future situations, it is extremely important to her that she respond in one way rather than another. The reasons why this is important to her vary: for example, she made a solemn promise to others, she wants to be beautiful, or she wants to prove something to her cynical father. She is keenly aware of the temptations and pressures that will incline her to respond in the least preferred way; and in anticipation of this, she makes a solemn and explicit resolution forbidding herself to "change her mind" for such reasons. At the time of decision nothing could dissuade her, and she wishes more than anything that she could ensure that she will feel the same later. Seeing that to be impossible, she lays down the law for herself, as it were, complete with a list of punishments she intends to impose for noncompliance. But, as time passes and the anticipated temptations arise, she "feels torn" between her resolution and her immediate wants. When she reflects on her earlier perspective, she wants to carry out her resolution and she is angry that she hesitates; but when she focuses upon the situation at hand, she prefers to do something else and is annoyed that she ever made the resolution. In these situations typically she chooses to break the resolution, knowing full well her reason for doing so but soon feeling regrets and "kicking herself" for changing her mind in the very sort of situation she planned and "told herself" not to.

(4) *Fading will.* Sometimes she resolves to do something, but then her will seems simply to fade away. Though she may be determined and quite explicit at the outset, as time goes on she thinks less about her plan and when she does, it seems less important. It is not that she literally "forgets" her resolve when she deviates from it, thinking when she remembers, "Oh, yes, I planned not to do that." Nor does she reconsider in the light of a new situation and alter the plan. She does not lose an inner battle, or simply find herself, much to her surprise, acting contrary to what she now concludes she should do. She may have no opinion about which is best, the old plan or the current choice. It is as if she hears but does not bother to listen to the plans and orders she earlier left for herself.

(5) *Unstable will.* Earlier, when she was less reflective, Amy did not make explicit resolutions but was more prepared to exert herself fully in the project of the day. The trouble was that she kept changing her projects. One day she was "determined" to be a musician; but the next day she was enthusiastic about being an athlete; another time, she decided to be a great surgeon. Each time she worked hard at the project, bought instruments, running shoes, dissecting kit, etc., and gave up parties to study and practice; but, lacking a good sense of the sacrifices required, she never anticipated the temptations to give up and so never made any explicit resolutions to overcome them. For a while she had a will to do each of these things; but it was a fragile and unstable will, easily "broken" by parental ridicule and readily changed when new role models captured her imagination.

Amy is not happy about these aspects of her life, we may suppose, for she admires her strong-willed friends and feels ashamed when they remind her how weak-willed she is. Her attitude about this, however, is not quite the same as her attitude about her involuntary stuttering, about which she is also ashamed. At least in her more honest moments, she is not inclined to say, "I can't help it; no matter how I try, it just happens." In fact she feels all the worse about herself because she believes that she could behave quite differently. She is not like the heavy smoker or heroin addict who has failed at so many sincere reform efforts that he has evidence that he cannot, by himself, change the pattern even though he still feels on particular occasions that he can resist. She feels that she would act like her strong-willed friends if she really set herself to change the pattern; but so far, despite her determination in making certain particular resolves, she has not been troubled enough to undertake this as a special task.

Except for those who draw contrary conclusions from philosophical determinism or particular psychological theories, most other people who know Amy share her view of her weakness. Though they naturally hesitate to say so, they believe she has reason to feel ashamed because they see the weakness as a defect in her character which she can and should change. When her broken promises inconvenience them, they are not inclined to excuse her on the ground that she is weak, although they may credit her for initial good intentions and forgive her because of her remorse and her generally amiable nature. When no obligations are involved, the question of blame does not arise and her displays of weakness are met variously with indifference, pity, condescending humor, self-righteous contempt, and empathetic understanding. Many see her as more likeable, and less threatening, than the typical strong-willed person; but, even aside from the broken promises, they would not mention her as a model for their children.

This description of Amy and others' reactions makes liberal use of everyday concepts, many of which are metaphorical and perplexing to philosophers; but I will not attempt to "analyze" or reduce these terms to more acceptable ones. Important questions arise even at this level of description, and we should not let our philosophical scruples constrain us so early in an investigation that we lose sight of the phenomena about which we were initially concerned.

II

The common moral reaction treats Amy as defective in some way, but we need to ask, "What is she lacking?" One answer that needs to be ruled out at once is, "a will." She is weak-willed, but not will-less. Many things, we suppose, lack a will (e.g., mushrooms, earthworms, corpses, and typewriters); others are said to have wills only by colorful exaggeration (e.g., hurricanes, newborn infants, and misbehaving computers); and some may be controversial borderline cases (e.g., committees, cats, and two-year old children). Even sane adult human beings may from time to time be will-less (e.g., when utterly depressed, inde-cisive, or drunk "out of their minds"). It may be helpful towards understanding the weak-willed person to review some of the features which we believe normal human adults (with "wills") have but which are absent in the "will-less."

To begin, having a will seems to require some foresight and awareness that some events cause others. Further, one must care about or take some interest in which outcomes occur. Thus the utterly apathetic person is said to have lost his will, and, if we could imagine it, a pure intellect indifferent to everything would lack a will. Also some awareness or belief that one can oneself make things happen seems necessary. This is what seems lacking in the newborn infant who wants to be fed but has not yet a sense of his own powers. For a similar reason we think of people as having wishes, but not a will, with respect to whatever they believe they cannot influence (e.g., the weather, living 200 years, the policy of foreign countries, and, sometimes, their teenage sons and daughters).

Again, setting aside certain speculations about God, our notion of human wills seems to presuppose we are talking about beings who experience obstacles in achieving what they want. Without this, the idea of trying, exerting more or less effort, and the like, would not make sense. Also, though perhaps we can imagine beings who experience only external obstacles, we ordinarily think of someone as willing to do something (as opposed to merely doing it intentionally) only when we suppose that they can also experience internal obstacles. For example, in thinking of primitive builders and hunters as showing a will, and not merely muscle and desire, as they lift a boulder and kill a bear, we think of their having to overcome their fatigue and fear as well as the stone's weight and the bear's strength. This requires both an awareness that one's wants may conflict and a sense of priorities among them.

Another dimension is added when we realize that we can achieve some things we want only by a sequence of acts over time. Our priorities require not only that we do something now but also that we follow through with appropriate action later. This makes room for reflective planning, devising schemes of future action that will achieve what we now want despite anticipated outer and inner obstacles. But, for better or worse, we are not designed so that current planning and intending guarantees future performance; no matter how strong our desires and efforts now, what we do later will depend on our state and view of the situation later. It is not as though we can do nothing now that will influence what we do later, but one's future acts do not flow from one's present views, preferences, and efforts in quite the way (typically) one's present acts do. Plans are essentially revisable, even if one wishes it otherwise. The problem is not simply that one's earlier view of the later situation may be inaccurate; for even if one anticipates correctly the alternatives and the inner and outer obstacles, one may later change one's priorities. These facts, I think, are the background of our full-fledged notion of having a will. It encompasses not merely our ability to act from our deliberations at a moment but also our imperfect ability to make deliberation at one time appropriately influential on our decisions at a later time. The capacity to will, as I argue later, is not primarily a capacity to make effective one's best or most thoroughly reflective deliberations, nor is it merely a capacity to act on one's *current* deliberations. Accounts of weakness of will restricted to these special cases will miss an important temporal dimension.

The absence of one or more of these characteristic features of having a will seems to account for our regarding certain people as temporarily will-less or as having lost their wills with regard to particular matters. Thus when depressed persons become utterly apathetic about the future, they are said to have lost "the will to live." The addict who has become convinced that he cannot control his drug problem may wish to change but no longer has the will. A person so "blinded" by jealous rage that he is not aware of the consequences of what he does is distinguished in law from the calculating person who "willingly" takes revenge. The good-hearted benefactor, fortunately free from the usual temptations of greed and selfishness, is not thought to show strength of will in sharing his wealth; and we would not attribute to him a will to share at all if we thought he would stop sharing at any moment he found that it required effort. Similarly, I suppose, one who so thoroughly "lived in the present" that he made no plans or commitments might be said (with some exaggeration) to lack a will, unless of course he was resolved to live this way. The same might be said, with a bit more exaggeration, about the person who only formed highly flexible plans, intentions regarded as revisable at any moment, and never commitments or resolutions. These last remarks are exaggerations (at least partly) because in correctly emphasizing will as a capacity to influence one's future conduct in a certain way they neglect a more primitive aspect of will as a capacity for strenuous effort in the activities of the moment.

The special cases described above do not raise the usual questions about weakness and strength of will; for to some degree, or with regard to certain matters, the persons depicted lack a will. Admittedly this may at times be a good thing; but our question is not about the advantages and disadvantages of having a will but about the relative merits of having a strong or weak will.

III

Most contemporary writers concerned with weakness of will, incontinence, or *akrasia* focus their attention upon individual acts rather than patterns of character, and usually they identify a weak-willed (incontinent, or akratic) act as an act contrary to the agent's best judgment at the time about what would be best for him to do. The reason for concentrating upon this case, I suspect, is not that it is found to be the most common or important manifestation of weakness of will but rather that it is thought to be philosophically the most interesting case. The philosophical interest arises because experience makes it hard to deny what pervasive assumptions about action and evaluative language make it hard to understand, namely, how someone could at the same time judge that it is best to do something but yet, quite intentionally, choose not to do it. For the traditional purposes of moral philosophy, however, I think that it would be a serious mistake to identify weakness of will with acts contrary to what at the time one judges best. To do so would leave out of consideration much of what we commonly attribute to weakness of will. To be sure, people like Amy often, perhaps typically, judge it best, in some sense, to do what they aim at and resolve to do; but this is not always so, at least in the most common senses of "judging best," and weakness of will can also reveal itself in acts which *at the moment* one judges best (in some sense).

To take the last point first, let us suppose that Amy thinks that she has good and sufficient reason to engage in her competitive activities and to do what she resolves to do. When she makes only weak efforts towards success, she is not naturally described as performing an intentional act contrary to her best judgment. Her problem is not so much in what she is doing but in how she is doing it. She judges that what she is doing (e.g., playing or arguing with a view to winning) is best but she is not doing it with determination and vigor. Again, when she makes "weak resolves," she may be doing what she judges best but she is still willing weakly. The weakness here is independent of whether later she acts against her resolve and judgment; it lies in the way she resolved, leaving herself so much leeway for opting out. Resolving weakly, in this sense, is of course often the intelligent thing to do; but nonetheless to make such weak resolves repeatedly, even when circumstances call for more, is characteristic of the weak-willed person.

Suppose, however, she makes some firm resolutions in accord with her best judgment but later suddenly "changes her mind" about what is best to do. If the change was not due to new information, unforeseen circumstances, etc., but resulted from the very sort of momentary shift in priorities which she anticipated and wanted to avoid, the change itself is of a sort which, if characteristic of her, reveals her to be weak-willed. Her will-of-the-moment, we might say, is strong, for she was initially quite determined and even later she did not act against anything she willed at that time. But we also think of a person's will as something persisting over time, and one with a vacillating, ever changing will is not a strong-willed person in the ordinary sense. A weak-willed person should not be identified as one who, paradoxically, wills against her (current) will; for the more common cases involve having a will that is unstable, fluctuating, fading, or prone to surrender under pressure. A "push-over" who can be easily persuaded to give up earlier resolutions is weak-willed even if she always acts as at the moment she thinks best.

There is a further problem with identifying weakness of will with acting contrary to what one judges best. If we make this identification, we will ignore familiar cases in which one's initial resolutions were not based on what one judged it best to do. Though this may be controversial among philosophers, it seems obvious that at times we resolutely set ourselves to pursue difficult courses of action without deciding, or even taking for granted, that doing so is the best thing to do. We may fail to act on these resolutions in just the ways we fail to act on resolutions to do what we regard best; and when we do so repeatedly, we again give evidence that we are weak-willed. Consider, for example, the boxer who learns that another fight will probably cost him his eyesight but nonetheless resolves to defeat a hated opponent at all costs. Or think of the jilted lover who sets herself on a course of revenge which she knows is morally indefensible and will result in jail or execution for herself. Some will say that they "must" have thought at the time that these undertakings were best and must have been insincere if they said otherwise. But most of us, I suspect, will find this unconvincing, more likely a desperate attempt to save a philosophical theory than an honest expression of conviction. And if the boxer and the vengeful lover balk at the moment of imminent success, not from wise reconsideration but from fear or an impulsive decision to pursue an equally unsavory alternative, then surely this can be part of the pattern which constitutes their being weak-willed.

There are different views, of course, about what it means to judge a course of action best, and these have different implications about the possibility of resolving, or breaking a resolution, without judging it best at the time to do so. But if a familiar notion of "morally best" or "prudentially best" is what is at work, it is hard to deny these possibilities. The vengeful lover may grant the obvious moral and prudential objections to her project and accordingly, let us suppose, she feels some aversion to carrying it out. In resolving to take revenge despite these considerations she need not be thinking that some further esoteric reason renders her murderous project morally or prudentially best; nor need she be momentarily blind or "out of control." She may simply count it more important to her to get even.

Prescriptivist theories hold that in judging a course of action best (in their sense) one commits oneself to a self-directed imperative to act accordingly, and they construe failure to follow such an imperative, when one can, as proof that one did not genuinely and fully judge the act to be best. (Here I treat "judging best" as the same as "judging that I ought, all considered.") This sort of theory, without refinements, must deny that one can display weakness of will by acting contrary to what one judges best *at the moment*, but it is quite compatible with many of the patterns of weakness of will which we have considered (e.g., weak efforts, weak resolves, fading and unstable will, and breaking resolutions through irrational changes of judgment). Still, persistent doubts about the prescriptivist position on the remaining controversial case (acting against one's *current* judgment about what is best) are often counted as a major objection to the theory. When,

126

to allay these doubts, the prescriptivist makes action in accord with one's judgment *definitive* of judging it best in *the prescriptive sense,* then one's doubts naturally turn to whether the prescriptive sense, so defined, is what is at work in the daily contexts in which weakness of will is a practical problem.

Those influenced by economic theory may insist that the vengeful lover resolves according to her best judgment in the sense that she resolves to act in a way she believes will satisfy her strongest preference. This, however, is not the sense at issue when we say, "She knew it was not the best thing to do, but still she resolved to kill him." The point is that she resolved to kill, despite her awareness that this was foolish and immoral; that her resolution reflected her strongest preference is not denied.

These, admittedly, are difficult issues which cannot be adequately resolved without fuller discussion of evaluative judgments. For present purposes it suffices to raise doubts about the conventional wisdom that one cannot act contrary to one's current judgment about what is best to do, and to note how much of Amy's weakness can be described without presupposing a position on that controversial point.

IV

A weak-willed person does not lack willpower but wills weakly; that is, she fails to exercise appropriately the willpower which she has. This, at least, is the conception which I believe is presupposed by the common moral assessment with which we began. There is, however, a pervasive ambiguity in our talk about weakness of will, which easily confuses the issue. Sometimes, I think, we speak of a person as "having a weak will" when we mean that the person suffers from an abnormal incapacity; she cannot, by willing alone, overcome certain inner obstacles to doing what she sets herself to do even though most people in her position can do so. She lacks the ability, or has a diminished capacity, to do certain things which others can do, but not because she suffers from obvious physical limitations, low intelligence, misinformation, weak memory, extraordinarily difficult circumstances, apathy, or abnormal desires. On this conception the person with a "weak will" cannot do things which she wants and decides to do even though various familiar obstacles are absent. I prefer to call this disability "lack of willpower" to distinguish it from my conception of "being weak-willed," though of course merely labeling it does not explain it. One can suffer the disability to different degrees, but for simplicity I will focus upon extreme cases.

Some of the "will-less" persons considered earlier might also be said to lack "willpower," at least temporarily or with respect to certain matters; but typically we think of the person who lacks will*power* as having a will but being unable to carry it out. The person too depressed to act, for example, is more naturally described as lacking the will to act rather than as having little or no willpower.

On the other hand, the hopeless drug addict might be thought to lack both the will and the willpower to change his behavior if the reason he could not will (but only wish) to change his behavior was that he finally realized that, even if he were to will, the result would be the same. Without the hope of success, he cannot develop the will to change; but since he is not able to change even if he so willed, he lacks the willpower.

Though lack of willpower is an inability to do what one wills, not every inability to do what one wills is lack of willpower. Most obviously, when one is physically too weak to lift the weight one earnestly tries to lift, the problem is not with one's willpower. Similarly, magicians, even if mad enough to think otherwise, cannot levitate objects at a distance just by "willing" them to rise, but this is not seen as a defect of willpower. A paralyzed person, before discovering his condition, might be said to "will" to move his leg, but again it seems inappropriate to count his failure to move the leg as due to inadequate willpower. Sometimes we say that we "cannot" do what we (previously) resolved and committed ourselves to doing because the sacrifice is too great, our consciences would be offended, or we now see the activity as disgusting, embarrassing, or pointless. But what we are claiming here, typically, is not that we have deficient willpower but rather that we have reasons which justify or explain our giving up what we earlier resolved to do.

The classic cases of lack of willpower seem to involve physical addictions, compulsive behavior, and "irresistible impulses," though the idea, I think, leaves room for other patterns. These cases are complex and difficult to understand, partly because more empirical study is needed but also because we have both common-sense and theory-laden ways of describing and thinking about the same examples. The most I can hope to do here is to indicate briefly the main feature that seems to distinguish these (and other) ways of lacking willpower from the conception of weakness of will which is my main concern. It should be noted, too, that I am not arguing that everything we suppose to be weakness of will, as opposed to diminished willpower, is really so; in fact I am not even *arguing* that there actually are weak-willed persons as I conceive them. It would not be surprising if we are sometimes mistaken in our views about apparently weak-willed persons; and it is conceivable that we are thoroughly and systematically mistaken. But some attempt to distinguish ideas is necessary just to understand the common moral assessment.

An important feature of extreme addictions and compulsions seems to be that the agent is seen as unable to control the behavior in question even if, on reflection, he wants to and tries to. The problems are easiest to identify when the agent has actually decided, on reflection, that he does not want to behave as he does but finds, to his dismay, that all his efforts (without outside intervention) yield no results. But the problems are supposed to exist, in a less obvious way, even in persons who "gladly" behave as they do and never try to stop. Sometimes even the agent's insistence, to himself and others, that he is doing just what he wants may be taken in context as evidence that he has the problem. Some evidence may be taken from similarities in the pattern of his behavior with that of people who try but fail to change, from the incoherence of his "explanations," from correlations between his biological state with other addicts (human or animal), and from the way in which the behavior is manifestly destructive of what human beings need and the agent professes to value. But the inference drawn is something which of course cannot be directly observed, namely, that the agent cannot by his own efforts significantly change the behavior. The idea of irresistible impulses apparently requires the same inference, though without patterns of repeated behavior it is hard to see how the evidence could be as substantial.

In an admirable paper, Gary Watson attempts to distinguish compulsions from a more ordinary disability which he calls "weakness of will."[2] In both cases the agent is sometimes unable to act on his practical deliberations, but the explanations are different. Watson's weak-willed persons do not have a capacity of self-control to the degree that normal persons (in the comparison class) have this, and so they "give in to desires which the possession of the normal degree of self-control would enable them to resist."[3] Compulsive persons, by contrast, have desires that even the normal capacity of self-control would not enable them to resist. This, in my view, is a plausible contrast between compulsions and another type of diminished willpower; but since neither of Watson's types are able to act on the results of their deliberations, their problem is not weakness of will of the sort I propose to consider. Even Watson himself, we should note, points out that his idea of weakness of will is at odds with "the common account," though he argues (from assumptions I reject) that the common account is incoherent.

The idea of the weak-willed person that I think best fits the common moral assessment is different from the idea of a person suffering from a disability of any of the types mentioned above. Her problem is not that she is an addict, a compulsive, or even abnormal in her *ability* to carry out her resolutions, exert appropriate effort, etc. Her problem lies in the pattern of what she does when she could do otherwise. In saying this I do not mean that believing that people are weak-willed implies a belief in metaphysical indeterminism; what is meant is just that the weak-willed person, in displaying her weakness, was able to act differently in just the same (limited) sense that the ordinary (noncompulsive) liar could have told the truth, the common thief could have chosen not to steal, and the lazy student could have worked harder. The notions of "could have," "ability," and "self-control" are notoriously slippery, and it is controversial whether determinism poses a genuine challenge to any of our ordinary beliefs expressed in these terms. But my suggestion is that it is not a special problem about weakness

2   See footnote 1.
3   "Scepticism About Weakness of Will," p. 330.

or strength of will; if the ordinary liar, thief, and lazy student could act differently, then, in that sense, so could Amy.

V

To review, so far I have suggested that a weak-willed person has a will, has willpower, and does not necessarily act contrary to his best judgment. In characterizing someone as weak-willed, in this sense, we are describing him as the sort of person who repeatedly acts in certain ways but without implying that he is unable, or less able than people with other "vices," to act in alternative ways. The example of Amy suggests that weakness of will is a complex trait, which can be manifested in a variety of different patterns of action. The example also suggests we cannot identify weakness of will simply by looking to see whether at each moment the agent's acts correspond to his deliberative conclusions at that moment; we need to survey several aspects of the agent's history over time, including the degree of effort, the type of resolves, and the frequency and reasons for "changes of mind."

Our reflections so far point towards a complex conception of weakness of will which might be expressed as follows: Though not will-less or without willpower, weak-willed persons are the sort of persons who repeatedly and more than normal (a) make inadequate efforts, (b) resolve with too little determination, (c) break their resolutions, with or without a struggle, and/or (d) too readily abandon their undertakings.

Like the concept of "being hairy," this idea does not admit of precise determinations of "how much" and "how many parts" of the person (or the life) must satisfy the criteria, and what is considered "normal" may vary with the class to which the agent is compared. What is "inadequate" effort, "too little" determination, and "too readily" abandoning one's undertakings will also depend on what the agent's ends, projects, and undertakings are, and perhaps it is also to some extent relative to what is usual or commonly expected for the sort of activities in question. The idea of weakness of will, as I see it, is not so mysterious or obscure as many think, but it is many-sided and inexact.

A few comments on the different aspects of the account may be helpful. Consider first "inadequate effort." The point is that it counts towards a person's being weak-willed if the person, like Amy, characteristically exerts too little effort to achieve what she is aiming to do (assuming the end is attainable with more effort, she is not prevented in various familiar ways from exerting more effort, and the required level of effort is not extraordinary for that sort of activity).[4]

---

4 The sorts of things I have in mind that might be said to prevent a person from exerting more effort are, for example, ignorance of a remaining option, gross muscle fatigue (for some physical tasks), discovery that one lacks prerequisites (e.g., the mathematical knowledge to do a proof), not being able to conceive what more one could do that would count as "trying" (e.g., to recall

She wills weakly, we may say; but "exerting more effort" is not just one sort of thing for all activities, say, a special mental event like the flexing of an "inner" muscle. This seems obvious when we think, for example, of trying harder to win a chess game, to solve a logic problem, to run faster, to serve better in tennis, to recall a name, to identify brands of coffee by taste, or to be civil when very angry. Also, I should note that the standard of "inadequate effort" I have in mind is not a moral or prudential standard, nor is it what the agent believes at the time to be adequate. The standard has more to do with what is likely to bring off whatever it is she is up to.

Similar remarks apply to (b), e.g., Amy's "weak resolves." The standard of "too little determination" is not moral or prudential, nor is it what the agent thinks at the moment. The main question is what sort of resolve will best serve her purposes in resolving, no matter how foolish or immoral those purposes may be. And resolves may be weaker or firmer in two dimensions. Some resolves, first, are more "determined" in that the resolution has fewer significant loopholes and escape clauses enabling the agent to ignore it without "breaking" it. A weak resolution in this sense would be like a "weak law" which leaves plenty of room for citizens to defeat its purpose by taking advantage of its special provisions. The other dimension has to do with the attitude the agent takes towards her possible noncompliance in the future. One is more resolute, in this sense, when one puts one's self-image on the line, expecting and intending that if one fails one will chastise oneself and feel not merely disappointment but some self-contempt. The analogy here would be between a law without sanctions and a law "with teeth in it." One may, of course, question the utility or psychological wisdom of making strong resolutions of these sorts; but the point here is a conditional one. That is, if a person repeatedly makes only weak resolutions when stronger ones are needed for the purpose, then (given some further assumptions) this pattern is one of several which give evidence of weakness of will.

The third pattern, (c) above, presupposes a distinction between "breaking" a resolution and taking advantage of its (often implicit) option to "change one's mind" in the light of new information. Except when one anticipates a period of incompetence (as with Ulysses and the Sirens), one generally takes for granted that one's resolutions are meant to be revisable if various sorts of unanticipated circumstances arise. On the other hand, resolutions (in contrast to mere plans and policies) would be pointless if they did not direct one not to reconsider or deviate from the resolve for certain anticipated reasons (e.g., the arrival of an expected temptation or pres-

the smell of an exotic herb experienced once), extraordinary psychological domination by a Rasputin, and perhaps a hypothesized emotional "block" evidenced by repeated failures of efforts (of one sort, e.g., listening to martial music, lecturing oneself, asking others to offer rewards) to get oneself to "try harder" (in another way, e.g., to win at boxing). None of these are present in the ordinary case of weakness of will, and we cannot simply infer an "*inability* to exert more effort," in the sense intended here, from the general belief that all behavior is caused or from the particular fact that the agent *did not want* to exert more effort.

sure). One *breaks* the resolution only if one changes one's mind and deviates from it in circumstances and for reasons the resolution was designed to exclude. Sometimes, too, one may "revise" the resolution without breaking it when one deviates from the letter but not the spirit, just as one sometimes can satisfy the obligation from a promise by fulfilling its purpose in an alternative way. Given this distinction, the normative standard in (c) is built into the idea that the weak-willed person tends to *break* her resolutions rather than merely revise them or exercise an implicit option to respond to unforeseen circumstances. Breaking a resolution is not, of course, a paradoxical case of willingly acting against one's current will; rather, it is a willful refusal to be guided by a *prior* resolution in the very circumstances for which the resolution had been intended.

The last criterion, (d), most obviously requires us to look beyond the relation between the agent's acts and judgment at each moment. The person who "too readily abandons her projects" has her judgments and her acts in phase at each moment, but she vacillates in what she wills. She does not will weakly at each moment, we might say; but her will to fulfill particular projects is never strong and stable over time. One might object that what is weak here is not "her will" *per se* but her will to fulfill this or that end; however, despite this, I think that this tendency to abandon lightly particular projects that one has just energetically undertaken is among the patterns which characterize those we regard as weak-willed persons. In saying that they "too readily" give up their undertakings, I do not mean "to a morally undesirable degree" or even "to the detriment of their long-term interests"; the point is just that they are constantly pursuing ends which they give up before they can fulfill them and so, by their own voluntary choices, they systematically undermine what they work for.

To say that people are weak-willed, as I conceive this, is not to give a causal explanation of *why* they act as they do but to state *how* they characteristically act. The description may be compatible with a variety of explanations though not, on my view, with explanations that imply that weak-willed persons suffer from a special sort of inability to change their conduct that does not affect the garden-variety liar and thief. In saying that I was weak-willed in doing something, I do not even characterize my motives or reasons as specifically as if I reported that I acted from greed or malice or cowardice. I do indicate that what I did was not in accord with what I wholeheartedly and steadfastly endorse over time; for in calling my act "weak-willed," I place it with others in a class of acts which are at odds, in the various ways we have considered, with my own ends, projects, and previous commitments.

VI

Although I hope that my description of the weak-willed person avoids the worst paradoxes which action theorists have discussed, my aim has not been to solve the puzzles which they have raised but rather to prepare the way for the moral philosopher's traditional questions about a putative character defect. For this purpose it is important to have identified the trait in terms familiar enough to make it readily recognizable and clear enough to dispel genuine doubts about its possibility; but it is not necessary to resolve all theoretical questions that can be raised about the various concepts employed in the description, especially if these concepts are not unique to weakness of will but are pervasive in our ordinary understanding of human action. No doubt there are objections to my characterization of weakness of will even for our limited purposes, but let us set these aside for now so that we can, at least briefly, consider the main evaluative questions which prompted this inquiry.

These questions express the traditional concerns of moral philosophy about traits commonly supposed to be character defects: What reason does one have to avoid the trait, and why regard it as a *moral* defect? The questions seem particularly pressing about weakness of will as described here because that description does not itself imply that being weak-willed is always immoral or even disadvantageous to the agent. The weak-willed person, to be sure, exerts "inadequate effort," switches projects "too readily," etc.; but adequacy here is relative to the agent's own ends, which may themselves be foolish or immoral. The weak-willed person tends to break resolutions, but the resolutions may be more imprudent or morally objectionable than the decisions to break them.

Consider first the disadvantages of being weak-willed for the person who has this trait. Some of these are rather obvious. Even setting aside the disapproving and contemptuous reactions of others, weak-willed agents are more liable than most to fail in projects which they would find rewarding if they persisted in them and were moderately successful. Their feeble efforts, ineffective resolutions, and flip-flopping choices typically undermine their chances of gaining satisfactions they could have and would have if they were strong-willed. With such failures usually come feelings of disappointment and regret, often more disturbing than the external losses. But, though typical and important, these costs are not inevitable in every case and may even be compensated by lucky consequences of being weak. For example, those who have amply demonstrated their weakness may be less frequently called upon to make heroic sacrifices and to do more mundane chores which require effort and reliability. Weak memory and self-deception may reduce the liability to regrets. If a stupid resolution is made, weakness of will may block the bad consequences of carrying it out, even if one wishes that wiser planning or reconsideration could have done the job. There may be social rewards for the weak-willed in that others often find them easy to empathize with (in contrast, say, to the cruel), easy to pity (for their failures), and easy to bend to one's own will.

On balance, no doubt, even these considerations leave weakness of will a bad bet for most who weigh them wisely. But there is another important disadvantage of being weak-willed, namely, that weakness of will tends to undermine one's self-esteem and self-respect. This can happen in several ways. Most obviously, weakness of will tends to undermine self-esteem by making the agent less likely to reach levels of skill and accomplishment that he and others admire; for weak-willed persons, by definition, do "too little" of what they can do to fulfill their projects. Self-esteem, of at least one sort, depends upon belief that one has successfully completed undertakings that one counts important, or at least that one has done one's best towards this. Admiration and recognition by others tend to reinforce this self-esteem, but primarily because it leads one to suppose that one has earned it. One may still feel proud of one's natural good looks, one's distinguished heritage, etc., while knowing that one has failed at all one's projects; but one could not have the sort of self-esteem that amounts to recognition that one has oneself done what one regards significant. The problem is not that the weak-willed lack the ability to succeed but rather that they do not fully use their ability; and their low self-esteem stems not so much from doubting their *ability* to carry out their intentions as from their awareness that they typically choose to act in ways that prevent success.[5]

In another sense, I think, to respect oneself is to live up to one's minimal or base-line personal standards, where adopting "personal standards" is more than merely setting oneself an end which one wants very much to achieve.[6] To earn a higher salary, for example, may be an important end for me, but failure to achieve this will not make me "think less" of myself in the way, say, that failing to write intelligibly will. I do not put my self-respect on the line in pursuing the first as I do in working at the second. Being weak-willed, it seems, makes one liable to suffer diminished self-respect of this further kind. If one never sets personal standards, one cannot respect (or disrespect) oneself in this sense; and if one sets standards but constantly fails to meet them, one fails to respect oneself. The point here, unlike previously, is not that one lacks a welcome *feeling* (self-esteem) but rather that, by violating standards one has set for oneself, one *acts* with disrespect for oneself.

In addition, in their characteristic pattern of making and breaking resolutions, the weak-willed do not display full respect for themselves as rational deliberative agents. If one fully respected oneself as a rational agent, one would not make resolutions unless one had a good reason; for resolutions are our attempts at one time to constrain our deliberations at later times. Unlike mere intentions and tentative plans, they are like "orders" to oneself, prescribing how to act later and forbidding reconsideration (if later conditions are as anticipated). If we fully respected ourselves as rational agents, we would constrain our later deliberations

---

5 Compare John Rawls, *A Theory of Justice* (p. 440).
6 This idea of self-respect is developed in my "Self-Respect Reconsidered," in this volume. This is distinct from the sort of self-respect I discussed in "Servility and Self-Respect," also in this volume.

in this way only for good reasons; for example, if we foresaw obstacles to deliberating rationally at the later time (too little time, distracting pressures, or temporary incompetence). If the weak-willed make irrational resolutions, then, this is one way of not showing full respect for themselves as rational agents.

Suppose, on the other hand, they make only rational resolutions, constraining their later deliberations only for good reasons and leaving themselves room for reconsideration in case circumstances significantly change. In this case to break the resolution is irrational and shows a sort of disrespect for oneself as a person capable of rational self-control; for, by hypothesis, the resolution was made for good reasons and no change of circumstance or information warranted reconsideration. Respecting oneself as a rational agent does not require blindly following prior resolutions in all circumstances; but also it does not require, and may even rule out, trying to deliberate anew in each situation one faces.

Although some may not agree, or care, about the particular disadvantages I have mentioned, I suspect that few would deny that being weak-willed is generally disadvantageous to the agent. The more controversial issues concern the moral status of weakness of will. Although our account of weakness of will does not (and, I think, should not) settle these issues by definition, in various ways the account fits with the idea that weakness of will is a moral defect of character. By distinguishing, for example, between weakness of will and the disabilities we called "lack of willpower," the account helps to explain why weakness of will is not regarded as an adequate excuse for wrongdoing. Also the account, unlike some, fits the common idea that, even though weakness of will is a defect in character, many weak-willed acts are morally innocent, i.e., not wrong to do. The tendency of weakness of will to undermine self-esteem and self-respect helps to explain why weakness of will often provokes shame and contempt; and this may partially explain the moral disapproval of weakness of will, given the common belief that failure to maintain one's self-respect (in some relevant sense) is morally objectionable. Nevertheless, it remains a large and unsettled question whether weakness of will should be regarded a moral defect and, if so, in what sense. Disagreements about this, I suspect, result more from deep differences in how we see morality than from differences in what we think about the nature and effects of weakness of will. I conclude with a few tentative remarks on the problem.

First, the fulfillment of moral obligations and duties to others is often a difficult task, requiring at times strong effort, determination, and steadiness of purpose as well as sympathetic feelings and good intentions. As a result, an extremely weak-willed person is unlikely to meet all such obligations and duties. This is not because he suffers from a special debilitating condition; to the contrary, it is because if he did all he could to fulfill these obligations and duties he would not be the sort of person who displays the patterns we identified as weakness of will.

If this were the only moral argument against weakness of will, it would raise the possibility that a person might be *selectively weak-willed* without displaying any moral defect. That is, one might be vigorous, steadfast, and resolute in fulfilling one's obligations and duties to others but weak, vacillating, and self-defeating in the rest of one's life. If so, weakness of will (as I have described it) would not itself be a defect of moral character but only a pattern often associated with moral failings.

If, however, morality consists of more than fulfilling duties and obligations to others, then the room for being weak-willed selectively, without moral defect, shrinks. The virtues of justice, fidelity, and courage, for example, often call for just the sort of strength and stability of effort and resolution that the weak-willed person characteristically lacks. It is not that these virtues require a special *power* which the weak-willed lack. Both the weak-willed and the strong-willed have the power to be just, loyal, and courageous, but to have these virtues, given normal human liabilities and circumstances, one needs to use these powers in ways that tend to disqualify one from the category of the weak-willed. If we add that morality calls us, but does not command us, to tasks that are supererogatory, then there is further reason not to regard it as morally indifferent whether or not one is weak-willed so long as one fulfills one's obligations and duties to others. One can, of course, occasionally act in some of the ways typical of the weak-willed person without doing anything wrong, and not every act which actually manifests an agent's weakness of will need be morally significant. But it is not morally insignificant whether one rests content in a character, or characteristic pattern of action, which rules out leading the most worthy moral lives, which go beyond duty.

If we acknowledge obligations to oneself or self-regarding virtues and vices, we may find it even less likely that one can be weak-willed so selectively that one's weakness is morally indifferent. It can take strength of will, for example, to avoid servility, abuse of one's gifts, and various other forms of self-degradation. If it is a self-regarding virtue to respect oneself in any of the ways considered previously, this too would provide an argument.

All of these arguments (except perhaps the very last) treat the character trait, being weak-willed, not as inherently evil or vicious but as persistently liable, in normal human circumstances, to interfere with living by the demands and ideals of morality. Though this may be enough to qualify it for a place among the moral "vices," it does not by itself seem to warrant the kind of blame we give to cruelty, injustice, and dishonesty.

Some of the resistance to viewing weakness of will as a moral vice may come from the puzzle raised by our earlier example of the cruel Nazi who turns out to be strong-willed but is not thought to be a better person because of this. If weakness of will is a vice, one might think, then a Nazi with bad principles would be a better person if he had the strength of will to carry them out than if he failed to do so from weakness. But, one might continue, we are not inclined to think this; and so weakness of will must not be a vice. This reasoning is not compelling, however, for the moral worth of a person is not determined by simply adding points for virtues and subtracting for vices. The moral worth of having certain virtues, such as strength of will, may be conditional; that is, they may be to a person's credit only if that person also possesses certain other good traits. On this view, though no ideal person would be weak-willed, a weak-willed person does not automatically become better if, keeping all else the same, he or she becomes strong-willed. Strength of will would be an ideal to strive for along with charity, justice, etc., but it might be worthless by itself.

10

Promises to oneself

When one makes a promise to others, one puts oneself under obligation to them. Can one then incur an obligation to oneself by making a promise to oneself? If not, why not? Do the disanalogies between promises to others and "promises to oneself" show that "promises to oneself" are morally insignificant or, more generally, that obligations to oneself are impossible?

There are several reasons for raising these questions.

First, the idea of promises to oneself is familiar but puzzling. We often talk of such promises in jest, but sometimes quite seriously. Some find the idea quite natural, while others dismiss it as absurd. These phenomena suggest conceptual tensions of some philosophical interest in themselves, apart from any implications for larger issues.

Second, "promises to oneself" are frequently invoked in the controversy about whether one can have moral *obligations* to oneself. For example, some philosophers ridicule the idea of obligations to oneself by noting that I am not *morally* to blame if I "promise myself" a treat and then fail to take it. Obligations to oneself, it is assumed, would be self-serving requirements whereas morality is concerned with interpersonal relations. Other philosophers use the paradoxical idea of a "promise to oneself" to illustrate and support their general contention that "obligations *to* oneself," construed literally, are logically impossible.[1] The example is important to their case because promising is a paradigm of putting oneself under obligation *to* someone in the most *literal* sense.[2] To assess these arguments, then, we need to look closely at the analogy between promises to others and "promises to oneself."

Third, reflection on this analogy gives us a new angle from which to rethink the old question, why are promises *to others* morally binding? If, as I suppose, promises to others generally result in moral obligations and "promises to oneself" do not, what is the difference? Contrary to common assumptions, I suggest that the explanation is neither that obligations to oneself are logically incoherent nor that morality is concerned only with our relations to others. Moreover, there is

---

1 See, for example, M. G. Singer, "Duties to Oneself," *Ethics* 69 (1959): 202–5.
2 It is controversial, for example, whether we have obligations that are, in a literal sense, obligations *to* animals, deceased persons, or future generations. It may also be doubted whether obligations of charity are, literally, obligations *to* the needy persons who are the beneficiaries of their performance.

reason to doubt that rule–utilitarian and contractarian theories adequately explain the difference, for a "practice" of promising to oneself is possible and might prove useful.

Finally, though I agree with the common view that "promises to oneself" do not *generally* create moral obligations, the apparent exceptions to this negative conclusion lead to a more constructive suggestion. That is, if there are obligations to oneself, they are not simply obligations to promote one's own welfare or to follow the rules of a useful practice; they are more likely to be found among the moral requirements of self-respect.

My discussion will be divided as follows. In the *first section* I try to press as far as possible the idea that "promises to oneself" are, or rather could be, analogous to promises to others. There are, I suggest, far more similarities than one might suspect, and they help us to see what might be meant by speaking of an obligation as "*to* oneself." The *second section* takes up disanalogies, with particular attention to two that have been thought to make obligations to oneself logically impossible. While acknowledging differences, I argue that the disanalogies do not establish the logical impossibility of promises to oneself. In the *third section* I consider the moral significance of "promises to oneself." Although I agree with the dominant view that *these* do not *in general* create moral obligations, I suggest that this is for reasons other than the reasons that are supposed to exclude *all* obligations to oneself. Moreover, the apparent exceptions point to the sort of consideration that could more plausibly ground an obligation to oneself.

I

So that we can compare "promises to oneself," let us first consider some of the salient features of promises to others.

First, under what conditions do we say that a promise has been made? Clearly the person who makes the promise and the person to whom it is made must be at least minimally rational, capable of understanding a language, foreseeing to some degree likely consequences of their acts, *etc.* They must be conscious and aware of what they are doing at the time the promise is made: for example, not talking in their sleep, babbling in a drugged condition, and so on. One person, A, says something to another person, B, about a future act: typically, "I promise to X," but other expressions suffice when the context makes clear that this is what is intended. A and B must take what is said seriously, not in jest, as a line in a play or an example in philosophy class, *etc.* But, of course, A may not really intend to do X: lying promises are still promises. To distinguish promises from threats (e.g., "I promise I will kill you if you do that"), we should perhaps add that A believes that B has some interest in X and that B does have such an interest or at least lets A believe so. Both A and B must understand what promising means. This implies that they understand that, unless B releases A (e.g., says, "Forget it") or some other standard excusing condition obtains, then, by the conventional understanding of promising, A will be wrong not to do X and B will be entitled to complain. Though A may not actually intend to do X, A must intend that B believe that he intends to do X (or at least that B takes what he says as an attempt to have B believe this).[3]

Second, under what conditions is a promise, once made, fully binding? The concept of promising allows that if various circumstances arise, a promise is no longer binding. Most obviously, if the person to whom the promise was made, B, releases the promisor, the promise is cancelled. Again, unforeseen circumstances may arise so that it is obvious without B's saying anything that the original point of the promise will not be served by carrying it out. The promisor may, through no fault of his own, become incapable of fulfilling the promise. The promise may have been to do something morally wrong on other grounds, or conditions may have changed so that the only way to fulfill it is to violate some more stringent moral requirement. In these cases it is generally accepted that the original promise need not be kept, even though the promisor in some instances may still owe something to the promisee.

Third, what conditions must obtain in most cases if the practice of promising is to seem reasonable and to survive as a convention? Though particular promises could be made without the following conditions being satisfied, if these were not present as a rule, I think, we would not continue to make promises. (1) B actually has an interest in X. (2) There is some reason for A to make the promise, for example, A gains something in exchange or believes that B ought to be assured of A's Xing. (3) B believes that A is more likely to X if A promises. (4) A is really more likely to X if A promises. (5) In saying "I promise to X," A seriously resolves, makes it a matter of principle, to X; A regards this as more than a casual plan or intention and is willing to incur feelings of guilt and lower self-esteem in case of failure, except when there are conflicting obligations or excuses. (6) Others tend to think less of A if A fails to do as promised. (7) B remembers the promise and will be disappointed and prone to criticize A if A fails to keep it.

By analogy, then, what would be required for me to make a binding promise to myself? I must, of course, be sane and conscious. I would need to say something, at least silently, to myself. The words could be "I promise myself that I will X." I must not be joking, merely amusing myself, illustrating a philosophical point, *etc.* I must have some reason for wanting to do X, for example, a belief

---

3 This last qualification seems required to account for the following case. A tells a friend that he does not intend to do X and asks him to convince B of this without saying how he knows. Then A says "I promise to do X" to B, not intending to cause him to believe that he intends to do X but meaning for B to think him to be trying to fool him with a false promise. B, for reasons of his own, pretends to believe that A will do X. A promise, I think, has been made. The example is from Holly Thomas.

that it promotes my interests or furthers some morally worthy end. I must intend to do X, for, unlike the case of promises to others, there is no possibility of getting the promisee (myself) to believe that I intend to do X unless I really do, at least if we set aside the half-believing and half-disbelieving condition of self-deception. Crucially, if what I say is to be more than an expression of intention, I must understand that my words "I promise myself" imply that I will be wrong and liable to legitimate self-criticism if I fail to do X, barring standard excuses and justifications.

Consider next conditions which must be met for a promise, once made, to be fully binding. One can easily imagine promises to oneself analogous to promises to others insofar as they would not be regarded binding under certain conditions, for example, if circumstances so change that keeping the promise becomes obviously pointless, if it conflicts with more stringent obligations, or if it turns out to be impossible through no fault of the person who makes the promise. We can even imagine that those who make promises to themselves have a well-understood procedure for releasing themselves from the promise when necessary. Suppose, for example, it is understood that one can cancel the promise if, but only if, one has *reconsidered* it carefully in the light of *new*, unanticipated *information, without* the *immediate pressure* of expected temptations, and one has reached a definite decision that it is best, all considered, that the promise no longer remain in force. Taking the point of view of the recipient of a promise to myself, I could cancel it when unforeseen events make it clearly detrimental to my original aims and values; but taking the point of view of the promisor, I could not escape my obligation at will but only when special circumstances arise. These circumstances might be understood to include an explicit statement to myself that the promise is cancelled, though, as we shall see, they must include more than this. In the absence of these special circumstances, failure to do what one promised oneself to do would be viewed as breaking the promise, not releasing oneself from it.

So far, setting aside for now possible disanalogies, it seems as if promises to oneself are conceivable. But would anyone have adequate reasons to make them? Could such promises, understood as I have described, serve the purposes of enough people so that they would continue to understand the words "I promise myself" in the required way? Let us review the conditions that must obtain in general if we are to continue to make promises to others. Are the analogous conditions met for promises to oneself?

(1) Typically, I suggested, B must have an interest in the fulfillment of the promise. This would be so for promises to oneself if persons typically promised themselves to do only what in their best deliberative moments they wanted themselves to do at a later time. An example would be the reformed drug addict who promised herself to refuse all offers of the drug she used to crave. She has an interest in doing what she promised herself.

(2) Promising would continue only if there are reasons for A to promise, e.g., sometimes A believes that promising will promote A's own interests. This condition is easily satisfied in the case of promises to oneself provided the previous condition is met and that making the promise substantially increases the likelihood that the desired future act will be performed (see [4] below). Since, by (1), B stands to benefit from the proposed act and, by hypothesis, A and B are identical, it follows that A has an interest in making the promise if doing so makes it more likely that the act will be done.

(3) B typically must believe that A is more likely to perform if A makes the promise. This condition will be met if the next condition, (4), is satisfied, provided only that the persons who make promises to themselves are reasonably well informed. That is, informed persons will believe themselves more likely to do something if they promise themselves to do it, provided that in fact this is true.

(4) Promising would not survive as a practice unless promising typically makes the promisor more likely to do the thing promised. Now we have supposed that promises to oneself are usually made when the agent, on due deliberation, wants to perform some future act and is capable of performing it. Let us suppose further that such promises are normally made only when the agent, in deliberative moments, anticipates impulses and temporary pressures that will be temptations to deviate from the plan judged best. In this situation one would have good reason to want to ensure, or at least make more probable, that one will overcome the anticipated obstacles and act on the plan that, under deliberation, seemed best. If, by making a promise oneself, one makes oneself liable to feelings of guilt for yielding to contrary impulses, one increases the likelihood that one will do the desired act. Making the promise to oneself also strengthens one's motivation by making one liable to the disapproval of others who may know of the promise or liable, if others do not know, to the unpleasant feeling of hiding to avoid disapproval. By hypothesis, if I make a serious promise to myself I must believe that noncompliance, barring special circumstances, is wrong, and so I should expect to feel guilty. Others who accept promises to oneself in the same way and who learn of my noncompliance must also believe that I have done wrong and so can be expected, in general, to think less of me for it.

It should be noted that even if the viability of promises to oneself depends in this way on the sanctions of others, this does not imply that the resulting obligation is *to* others. Liability to criticism by persons other than the promisee is also a supporting feature of the practice of promising to others, and this does not mean that all such promises are *to* society or *to* the would-be critics.

(5) Promising would continue, I suggested, only if typically the promisor genuinely intends to do as promised. In the case of promises to oneself this condition is readily met, for one cannot promise oneself to do something that one has no intention of doing. For A must intend for B to believe that A intends

to comply, and this is impossible if A knows that B (here = A) knows that A has no intention to comply. In order to make a promise to oneself one *has* to intend to do as one promises.

(6) The maintenance of promising, I have assumed, is conditional on the sanction of public opinion. This sanction could work to motivate us to keep promises to ourselves as well as promises to others provided that there are others who believe that breaking a promise to oneself is wrong and that they know when these promises are made and broken. We could keep our promises to ourselves secret; but insofar as their purpose is to increase the likelihood that we will resist anticipated temptations and carry out best deliberative plans, we would always have a reason not to be secretive about such promises. Others may have less motivation to express disapproval when one breaks a promise to oneself than when one breaks a promise to another, but most people are already so willing to condemn the weakness and imprudence of others that we can hardly expect that they would refuse to add pressure to those known to have made promises to themselves.

(7) Because one will normally have a self-interested reason for wanting to see one's promises to oneself fulfilled, one should be even less inclined to forget them than to forget promises to others. But, one may wonder, would people have adequate motive to impose sanctions on themselves for breaking promises to themselves? In the case of a promise to oneself the person especially entitled to complain about nonfulfillment, the promisee, must be the very person who made the promise. To be an object of complaint and criticism, especially self-criticism, is not pleasant, and so we might expect unfulfilled promises to oneself to provoke less spontaneous and vehement criticism than is typically aroused by broken promises to others. When one offends against oneself, one is tempted to forgive if not forget. Nevertheless, though painful, self-criticism is a familiar fact of life, and in fact people are often harder on themselves than on others. Thus it is reasonable to suppose that people would often be self-critical upon breaking promises to themselves and knowing this would increase the likelihood of their fulfilling such promises.

II

The discussion so far suggests that genuine promises to oneself are possible; but have we overlooked crucial differences between promises to others and "promises to oneself"? Surely there are differences, and these may make all the difference.

The most obvious dissimilarity is that promises normally relate two or more persons whereas a promise to oneself is a reflexive relation involving only one person. This fact alone, however, is no obstacle; for, while some relations are the sort one can have only with others (e.g., marrying, dragging by the heels), other relations are of a kind that one can have either with others or oneself (e.g., being attorney for, hitting). Such relations do not necessarily require a schizo-phrenic view of the person, dividing him, for example, into phenomenal and noumenal selves, actual and ideal selves, or present and futures selves. The question is whether the particular relation, promising, is a relation that one can have to oneself without troublesome metaphysical dualism. To determine this we need to look more specifically at the differences between promises to others and "promises to oneself."

One difference was noted in passing earlier: there can be no full-fledged lying promises to oneself. When one person makes a promise to another, the promisor can, with full intention and awareness, completely deceive the promisee about what he really intends to do, but no one can thoroughly deceive oneself in this way. Does this make a difference as to whether one could make a promise to oneself? Clearly not, for the practice of promising to others would in no way suffer if, miraculously, lying promises became impossible. Suppose, for example, that everyone's eyes would flash purple whenever they tried to make a deceptive promise and that, as a result, no one would take seriously such a would-be "promise." Then, because there would be no deceptive promises, the practice of promising would be even more useful than it is now. So the impossibility of making *lying* promises to oneself is hardly a reason for denying the possibility of *any* promises to oneself.

Controversies about private languages might call attention to the following apparent disanalogy: making promises to oneself is a language game that is parasitical on promising to others. The latter presupposes a public setting, a shared "form of life." If there were no such observable promises to others, we could not have learned to understand "promises to oneself."

This may well be true, but it does not show that promises to oneself are impossible. Presumably one could not talk to oneself if one had not first learned to talk to others, but this does not mean that one cannot talk to oneself. To say that promises to oneself are possible is not to say that one could make such promises if one grew up, like Wolf-boy, without human contact or in a society without public promises.

Another difference worth considering is this: when a person violates his prom-ises to another to gain something for himself, typically the other person loses completely in the transaction; but when a person violates his promise to himself in order to get something for himself, no one loses completely.[4] That is, assuming the original promise to himself continues to be in his best interest, when he breaks the promise he sacrifices long-term interest for some lesser (usually more immediate) gain; but the broken promise is not altogether opposed to his wants and interests. By contrast, a broken promise to another person may completely oppose that person's wants and interests.

4   This point was suggested to me by Morton Beckner.

In the absence of further information, we should no doubt prefer (a) a situation in which no one loses completely and someone gets something (though less than what is best for him) to (b) a transaction in which one person loses completely and another gains something (perhaps even what is best for himself). Typically broken promises to oneself exemplify (a) and broken promises to others exemplify (b). But the most we could infer from this is that, typically, breaking promises to others is more objectionable than breaking promises to oneself. Our question, however, is whether promises to oneself are impossible, and the disanalogy under consideration fails to show this. It is not essential to promising that the parties have radically diverse interests. Suppose, for example, that two persons, John and Mary, have interests so similar or complementary that (for a range of choices in question) whatever benefits John to some degree benefits or pleases Mary, and vice versa. Now if John, to pursue an immediate desire, breaks a promise to Mary, Mary is not completely the loser, though she may not get what she most prefers. But this does not mean that they cannot make promises or that they would have no reason to do so. Promises may help them to count on each other to carry out coordinated plans for their mutual benefit, and they will also enable Mary to be more assured that John will do what she most wants in certain cases even when he might prefer to do something else (and *vice versa.*) If we were fortunate enough to live in a world so empathetic that everyone shared in the joys and sufferings of everyone else, promises would still be possible and would have a point.

The last disanalogy suggests another. Promises between two (or more) persons are often useful because each needs to be assured how the other person will act when they are not together to consult and coordinate their activities. Suppose, for example, that A and B know that they will not be able to communicate for a while and that during this period it is mutually advantageous if both do X or both do Y but harmful to each if one person does X and the other Y. They might select a plan, e.g., that both do X, and then assure each other by promising that they will stick to the plan despite anticipated temptations to deviate from it. The promise should increase their motivation to carry out the plan because it makes them liable to complain and to feel guilty if they should fail. Promises to oneself, however, do not serve a strictly analogous function. Despite normal memory lapses, *etc.*, no sane person is as completely "out of touch" with himself as two persons can be with each other. The left hand always knows, to some extent, what the right hand is doing. So, after all, the person who makes a promise to himself is not like John and Mary in the previous example: they needed promises because they were not in constant communication but there is no similar communication gap to give a point to a promise to oneself.

This objection notes a genuine dissimilarity, but not one that shows promises to oneself to be impossible or pointless. The objection calls attention to one rationale for promises to others that seems inapplicable to promises to oneself, but this rationale does not seem necessary to promises of any kind. Suppose John and Mary are handcuffed together and capable of reading each other's minds. Suppose further that their relevant wants and interests are not only similar in content but identical in intensity and importance: that is, the events that satisfy John satisfy Mary to the same degree, and *vice versa*.[5] Now, as in the case of one person, there is no communication gap and no diversity of interests. Would they have any use for promises? Apparently so; for, assuming that making a promise increases the likelihood of performance, John has an interest in Mary's promising to do what is mutually advantageous, and vice versa. In fact in the special circumstances we have imagined, John also has a self-interested reason for making the promise, and so does Mary. The rationale is similar to that behind a promise to oneself, namely, by promising one makes it more likely that one will overcome temptations and do what, all considered, one sees as best.

I turn now to two influential objections succinctly stated by M. G. Singer.[6] The first disanalogy Singer notes is that in the case of obligations to others the second party can release the first from obligation whereas, according to Singer, no one can release *himself* from an obligation. That is, if A has an obligation to B, B can release A from obligation; no one can release himself from an obligation; therefore no one can have an obligation to himself.

Some of Singer's critics understood him to mean by the first premise that if A has an obligation to B then B can *at any time* release A; but, so construed, the premise is open to numerous counterexamples, as they readily noted. Infants and deceased friends cannot release us from our obligations, and yet it seems that we still have obligations to them. We would not lose our obligations to a friend if he fell into a coma and so became temporarily unable to release us. Again, suppose you promise a friend to take her money or drugs in trust for an anticipated period of stress, with the understanding that you will refuse to listen to any of her requests for the money or drugs in that period. Then under stress, as anticipated, she asks for the money or drugs, professing to release you from your promise. It seems that, despite what she says, she cannot release you then.

In response to this sort of example Singer explained that what is in question is the logical possibility of release, not whether in fact the promisee is so situated that he can actually do it. Being in infancy, comatose, or even deceased, Singer suggests, can be regarded as contingencies that do not establish that it is *logically* impossible for the promisee to release the promisor. If the friend under stress were to prove herself thoroughly competent, she could release you from your promise.

---

5   This is no doubt possible only within a limited range of events, but we can imagine that the promises concern only such events. An example might be two persons playing a gambling machine which has equal payoffs and costs.

6   *Op. cit.* Singer's position is discussed by Warner Wick, Daniel Kading, Mary Mothersill, and Frank Knight in *Ethics*, 70, 71 (1962–63). Singer's reply is "Duties and Duties to Oneself," *Ethics* 73 (1962–63): 133–42.

The first premise, then, is that if A has an obligation to B, it is *logically possible,* under some conceivable circumstances, for B to release A from the obligation. For the conclusion to follow, the second premise must be similarly qualified. That is, this second premise must state that it is logically impossible for a person, under any circumstances, to release himself from an obligation. But given the understanding of "promises to oneself" I have hypothesized, this second qualified premise is not true. There is a way in which one could release oneself from an obligation to oneself: by reconsidering the promise to oneself in the light of unanticipated new information, in the absence of immediate pressures of anticipated temptations, judging that it is best, all considered, to cancel the promise, and then explicitly declaring the promise cancelled. Admittedly, there remains a difference between the two-person case and the one-person case; for when one person promises another to do something, the second can release the first *simply* by saying (seriously, with awareness), "Forget it." There need be no new, unanticipated information, careful reflection, absence of temptation, etc. But all that is required to nullify Singer's argument is that release from promises to oneself is possible, not that it is possible in all the same circumstances as release from promises to others.

Singer's insight, I think, is valuable but less troublesome than he supposes. To extend the metaphor, I cannot be literally *bound* by ropes if they are so loosely draped around me that I can "free" myself *at will,* but this does not mean that if I am bound there is no way I can release myself. I might with some effort cut or undo the knots if appropriate objects happen to be around. Similarly, I could hardly have an obligation to myself if I could release myself at will, e.g., by simply saying "I release myself." But I could be bound by a promise to myself if release was not easy or automatic but still possible in special circumstances.

We might also question whether Singer's first premise is logically necessary. Suppose A promises B to give B no hard drugs no matter what B says. A and B, let us say, agree that the promise is for all time, not just for a momentary period of stress. It seems that B cannot release A, under any circumstances, for if A takes what B says as a release A will violate the original promise. Singer counters, cleverly, with the suggestion that the original promise really consists of two promises:[7] (a) to refuse to give B hard drugs and (b) to refuse to accept anything B says as release. B can release A from the first promise (a) by first releasing A from the second promise (b). If B tries to make release from (b) impossible by adding a further promise [e.g., (c) to refuse to accept a release from (b)], then this will obviously lead to an infinite regress.

Singer's way of construing the promise, however, is not obviously the only or best way. Unless one is already committed to releasability as a precondition of an obligation to someone, why not view the original promise as one promise

---

7 "Duties and Duties to Oneself," *Ethics* 73 (1962–63): 133–42.

with a special content, i.e., to refuse-to-give-B-drugs-no-matter-what-B-says? Perhaps we believe as a matter of moral judgment that circumstances could arise in which A is no longer under obligation, e.g., the drug B has foresworn proves to be less harmful than previously thought and is in fact necessary to B's survival. But then it is questionable whether B has released A or whether the obligation is simply cancelled by changed circumstances. In any case, the possibility of release seems more a matter of moral judgment than of conceptual necessity. If A believed that nothing B said would release him from his promise, would his mistake, if it is one, be a failure to understand the concept of an obligation to someone or would it rather be that he has unduly rigorous moral principles?

Singer's second argument calls attention to the apparent fact that making promises to others confers rights in a way that "promises to oneself" cannot. Briefly, he argues: if A has an obligation to B, then B has a right against A; it is absurd to suppose that a person could have a right against himself; and so no one can have an obligation to himself.

At least part of the force of this argument is borrowed from the previous one, for one function of saying that B has a right against A is to imply that B can release A (if anyone can). As this point has already been discussed, what we need now to consider is whether there is anything more to the argument.

To refute, or support, Singer's premises in the most thorough way, we would need a detailed analysis of "having a right against someone." But because necessary and sufficient conditions for having a right are so controversial, I suggest that instead we review features which are at least characteristic of the situation in which one person has a right against another. Whether the features are necessary becomes important only when it is clear that they are absent in the case of promises to oneself.

Characteristically, when B has a right against A (that A do X), the following is true: (1) If, without B's informed free consent, A fails to do X, then, barring special excuse or justification, A is wrong. (2) In case of such failure, B is regarded as an especially injured party (even if in fact others suffer as much). (3) Similarly, B is the person normally regarded in a special position to complain (though others may sometimes rightly chastise A for failing in an obligation to B). (4) B is normally the person in a special position to release A from the obligation, if anyone can. (5) B is justified, barring special circumstances, in demanding that A do X, whether A wants to or not. (6) B is justified, barring special circumstances, in demanding that A do X, whether or not X is in A's best interest. (7) B is justified to demand compensation or at least apology if A should fail to do X without B's free informed consent and in the absence of special excuse or justification.

Though admittedly it sounds odd for us to speak of "rights against oneself," at least the first five characteristic features of rights could conceivably be generated by "promises to oneself" as well as by promises to others. Imagine, as before, a community that acknowledges and reinforces a practice of "promises to oneself" that is as closely analogous as possible to the common practice of promises to others. Suppose, then, that with these conventional understandings I make a serious "promise to myself," thereby assuming the roles of both A and B for purposes of the conditions (1)–(7). Now, by our previous discussion, the following should be at least logically possible. I make a promise to myself but I can, in the special circumstances described earlier, release myself from the promise (4); but if I fail to keep the promise to myself, without such a release or special excuse, I do something wrong (1); nevertheless, I am the injured party, the recipient and usually the intended beneficiary of the broken promise (2); so I am in the most appropriate position to complain and criticize (3); and if release is impossible, I am justified in demanding of myself that I fulfill the promise, whether at that time I want to or not (5).

It may seem more doubtful that I would be justified in demanding of myself that I keep the promise whether or not it serves my best interests (6). For, after all, the point of promises to oneself, as imagined here, has been to reinforce one's motivation to carry out one's best deliberative plans. But, on closer consideration, there is less disanalogy here than it seems.

First, some promises to oneself may be to do what one believes one ought to do, on independent grounds, even though it is not in one's self-interest. In this case, the fact that keeping such a promise turns out to be against my best interest is not a "new circumstance" permitting release, and so, believing in promises to oneself, I would be justified in demanding of myself that I carry out such a promise even against my interests. The point of this unselfish promise, after all, was just to strengthen my motivation in anticipated circumstances of this sort.

Second, consider promises to oneself designed to further one's own interest without harming others. If new information (even that one's desires changed in unanticipated ways) shows the previous deliberation mistaken, then, provided immediate anticipated temptations are absent, I can simply release myself from the promise. Because special circumstances permit release, I need not (even according to [6]) demand of myself that I keep the promise contrary to my best interests.

Third, consider a case in which the promise to oneself was self-interested but release is impossible because one is under the pressure of immediate, anticipated temptations. Then would I be justified in demanding of myself that I keep the promise contrary to self-interest? Two replies might be given. One might argue that, even from a self-interested point of view, the *policy* of sticking to one's promises to oneself until one is again in a pressure-free position to reassess the promise is best in the long run, even if on some particular occasions it leads one to sacrifice maximum self-interest. Alternatively, one could argue that the release conditions I described for promises to oneself are too stringent and should be loosened to allow release under temptation when new information makes the promise *obviously* obsolete. In any case, there is no need to deny (6) for promises to oneself.

The final characteristic feature of rights, (7), seems at least partly inapplicable to promises to oneself. If the heart of an "apology" is a frank admission of wrongdoing together with implied recommitment to avoidance of similar behavior in the future, then one might at least do this much in the case of a broken promise to oneself even though one cannot, literally, "apologize" to oneself. To demand compensation would be pointless, for the same person who demands would be receiving the compensation. Payment would, so to speak, go from one pocket to the other. Perhaps because no meaningful compensation is possible, people who break their promises to themselves tend to feel a need to *punish* themselves. When we break promises to others we can sometimes "pay them back"; but we cannot do this with broken promises to ourselves.

To conclude this survey, it seems far from clear that most characteristic features of "having a right against someone" must be absent in the case of promises to oneself. Where the analogy is weakest (regarding [7]), it is not entirely obvious that the feature is a *necessary* condition of rights rather than merely a typical or characteristic one. The notions of self-criticism, making demands on oneself, releasing oneself, and the like, are admittedly in need of further analysis; but there seems little reason to suspect that they can be understood only if we presuppose an untenable metaphysical dualism of "selves." Again, I concede that talk of *violating* one's own rights, *pressing* one's rights against oneself, and the like, seems either metaphorical or out of place. Still, our imagined practice of promising to oneself mirrors enough of the characteristic features of rights that it seems quite misleading, if not false, to insist that promises to oneself are conceptually impossible.

III

The thesis that it is conceptually impossible for obligations to arise from "promises to oneself" is often accepted uncritically, I suspect, because most people have an intuitive sense that in fact we do not in general put ourselves under *moral* obligation when we say, "I promise myself." When, for example, we say, "I promise myself a treat tonight," we rarely, if ever, understand this in the serious way required to make such a "promise" analogous to promises to others. In particular, we do not really believe that we will be morally wrong not to give ourselves a treat even if no unanticipated special circumstances arise. Such "failures" do not typically arouse guilt feelings. Even if we *could* make binding promises to ourselves, then, we rarely do so because we do not meet the conditions that would give our words ("I promise myself") the appropriate seriousness.

But suppose a person did meet the required conditions. That is, imagine both that there exists the conventional understanding of "promises to oneself" that I have described and that a particular person satisfies all the criteria for making a promise to herself. Would we then say that she had put herself under a genuine moral obligation? Not in general, I think. We might be prepared to grant that she has a personal obligation to herself, reminding ourselves that legitimate uses of "obligation" are not restricted to the moral sphere but also have a place in games, in the law, and elsewhere; but, except in special cases, most would rightly resist the suggestion that a moral obligation was generated.

Suppose, for example, a young woman solemnly promised herself that she would become rich by the age of forty. Satisfying our conditions for serious promises to oneself, she actually believes that if she does not do so, barring unanticipated special circumstances, she will be morally wrong. Again, imagine that she promised herself, in all seriousness, that she would taste all thirty-one flavors of Baskin-Robbins ice cream. She had always been inclined to order the same flavor but became convinced that she might be missing something better, and so, to resist the old habit and gain more pleasure in the long run, she makes the promise, not merely resolving to taste all the flavors but intending to make it wrong for her to fail to carry through. Suppose, further, that when she later lets ample opportunities pass and does not taste all the flavors or make much money, she feels guilty. Our intuitive response, I suspect, would be that her guilt feelings are misplaced, that she was not really under a moral obligation to become rich and taste the thirty-one flavors even though she thought she was.

The situation would be quite different, however, if she had made the promises to some other interested person. Suppose, for example, she had promised her aged grandfather that she would become rich in order to assure the old man that his descendents would be well off and she promised the Baskin-Robbins flavor master that she would taste all thirty-one flavors so she could give the company a comparative evaluation. Then, though the ensuing obligations may not be viewed as especially stringent, there seems little doubt that they qualify as moral ones.

The contrast with promises to oneself is evident when we consider how the promisor might rebut a claim that she ought to be doing something that conflicts with what she promised to do. Suppose, for example, someone tells the woman, "You should spend less time making money and more time with your grandfather" and "You should save your ice cream money for famine relief." She would offer at least partially counterbalancing moral considerations if she replied, "But I promised my grandfather that I would be rich by forty and the Baskin-Robbins flavor master that I would taste all thirty-one flavors." By contrast, to say "I promised *myself* that I would be rich and taste all thirty-one flavors" would not be accepted as a claim to competing moral obligations. It might be acknowledged as a legitimate insistence on a *right* to pursue self-interest in these matters, but hardly as a claim that she is not morally free to do otherwise.[8]

One might object that in failing to keep her serious promises to herself the young woman is at least morally at fault for not living up to her own moral convictions for, by hypothesis, *she* believes that it is wrong not to fulfill the promises to herself. But this objection misses the mark. By not fulfilling what she mistakenly believes to be a moral obligation, she displays a defect of character; but this does not mean that she has really failed to meet her moral obligations. As some would say, what she does is objectively right and only subjectively wrong. The proper advice when the woman feels guilty for not keeping her promise *to herself* to become rich and taste all thirty-one flavors seems to be this: "Of course a good person will try to live by her honest moral convictions, but in this case you are mistaken about what your moral obligations are. Saying 'I promise myself,' however seriously, does not in general make a moral requirement out of what you were previously free to do or not to do." By contrast, if she had made her promises to her grandfather and the flavor master, that sort of response would be inappropriate.

To summarize, the conclusion suggested by our investigation so far is this. A practice of "promising to oneself" is logically possible, and might serve a useful purpose. By considering this in some detail we found that we can make sense of the expression that an obligation is "*to* oneself," even when treating the term as more or less parallel with "obligation *to* another." But, nevertheless, we do not in fact regard promises to oneself as morally binding in most cases.

If correct, this conclusion should reopen for further consideration the old question, why are promises *to others* morally binding? This is, of course, a large and controversial topic, too much to undertake here. But our reflections on the analogy between promises to oneself and promises to others at least have some implications for the larger question.

First, we cannot explain the fact that promises to others are in general morally binding whereas promises to oneself are not by dismissing the latter as incoherent.

Second, it would oversimplify the difference to say that moral obligations are requirements to benefit others whereas promises to oneself are merely devices to benefit oneself. For one could make a promise to oneself to underscore one's resolve and strengthen one's motivation to pursue altruistic ideals as well as self-interested goals. Moreover, one can make a binding promise to another (e.g., one's mother) that one will take care of oneself (e.g., quit smoking).

Third, there is reason to doubt that rule-utilitarian and contractualist theories adequately explain the difference, for a "practice" of promises to oneself is at least conceivable and could both promote general utility and appeal to rational

---

8 Singer, in "Duties to Oneself," suggests that the characteristic function of claims to "obligations to oneself" is to affirm a right to do what, misleadingly, one says one has an obligation to do.

self-interested "contractors."[9] Whether the practice would in fact have these advantages would depend, of course, not only on its benefits but also on the costs of "making a moral issue" out of what most now regard as morally indifferent. But this is an empirical question, and we may well wonder whether the moral status of promises to oneself really depends on this empirical question. Suppose that, on balance, a practice of promises to oneself (taught, sanctioned by peer pressure, etc.) promotes general utility and appeals to rational self-interested (e.g., Rawlsian) contractors simply *because* it serves the interests of those who use it or, more generally, because it is a device (like "behavior modification" therapy) that enables them more effectively to pursue their goals, whatever these may be. Then rule-utilitarians, it seems, would have to conclude that promises to oneself would be morally binding. But would they be? Would they, special cases aside, give us anything more than hypothetical imperatives?

These doubts naturally raise further doubts about an underlying assumption of the rule-utilitarian and (Rawlsian) contractualist treatment of promises, an idea also taken for granted in my discussion here: namely, that promising should be construed as a "practice," defined by conventional rules that we have some independent moral ground to accept. If we viewed the personal commitment expressed in promising in a different way, the comparison of promises to others and promises to oneself might yield quite different results.

Turning now to special cases, recall that so far I have only argued that we do not regard persons as *in general* morally bound by their promises to themselves. But there are certain cases in which it is hard to deny the moral significance of such promises. Moreover, I suspect that the temptation to view promises to oneself as morally binding stems from concentration on these special cases, just as the facile dismissal of promises to oneself results from focus on a different range of examples (e.g., promising myself a treat). To illustrate, consider the following. The once honored sheriff, humiliated by one act of cowardice, has become the town drunk, despising himself and ridiculed by all. When he hears that the outlaws from whom he ran are now coming back to town, he "promises himself" most solemnly to dry out and face them with courage. He will not do it for others, he thinks, but for himself, as one last chance to be true to himself. He deliberately places his last shred of self-respect on the line, fully accepting that if he makes and then breaks this "promise" he will be rightly condemned by himself and others more than if he simply skips town at once.

This story is a fiction from a romantic Western film, but similar scenarios closer to home are not hard to imagine. In these cases there is some morally

---

9   For rule–utilitarianism see John Rawls' "Two Concepts of Rules," *Philosophical Review* 64 (1955): 3–32 and Richard Brandt, "Towards a Credible Form of Rule–Utilitarianism," in George Nakhnikian and H. Castañeda, eds., *Morality and the Language of Conduct* (Detroit, Mich.: Wayne State University Press, 1963) pp. 102–43. A contractualist position on promising is represented by John Rawls, *A Theory of Justice* (Cambridge, Mass.: Harvard University Press, 1971) pp. 342ff.

significant reason, independent of the "promise to oneself," to do what one promises, and thus the agent does not see the promise as transforming what was previously morally *neutral* into a moral obligation (as is typical with promises to others). However, the agent does regard the promise as making a moral difference, and not merely as a device to make performance more likely (like a shot of adrenalin, a coach's "pep talk," or burning one's bridges for escape). The promise puts one's self-respect on the line, making failure more than ordinary weakness of will (as shown, say, in backsliding on diets and breaking trivial New Year's resolutions). The moral interest in the outcome does not stem from the promise alone, as it may with promises to others, but, once made, these special commitments to oneself seem to transform the situation, making nonperformance worse, and limiting the range of reasons for which one can honorably decide to abandon the project. Failure naturally brings disapproval of oneself, not merely disappointment or acknowledgement that one missed an opportunity to do what is morally good but supererogatory.

These special cases of serious promises to oneself seem to have a moral significance that is not adequately explained by our working model of a "practice" useful as a device to strengthen motivation. The examples remain puzzling, and no doubt controversial, but they at least point the direction that may prove more fruitful for further discussion of obligations to oneself. That is, they suggest that the ultimate ground of what is most plausibly called an obligation *to* oneself is self-respect, not a quasi-contractual relation with oneself, a need to bolster one's motivations in general, or a moral requirement to promote one's own welfare.

Self-respect, in fact, seems to be what underlies serious claims to obligations to oneself quite apart from any promise to oneself. When, for example, in Ibsen's *A Doll's House* Nora leaves her patronizing husband, saying "I have obligations to myself too," she is telling him that she cannot find or maintain her self-respect while living with him as before. Had she added, "I promised myself a trip to Paris," she would hardly have strengthened her case, though perhaps a subsequent promise to herself not to live again as anyone's doll would not be morally insignificant.

Social snobbery and human dignity

The Revolution that raised banners to "Liberty, Equality, and Fraternity" was more than a political revolution.[1] It was also a social revolution that spread radical ideas about how one should view one's fellow human beings. Revolutionaries demanded increased recognition of the rights and needs of the common man, but they also insisted on respect. They charged that an elite had misappropriated to itself not only wealth and privilege but also symbols of "honor" and "dignity" unwarranted by inheritance, achievement, or individual merit. Even more radically, some argued that all humanity has a dignity independent of social class and individual distinctions. Among these, Rousseau was the most eloquent, and Rousseau was instrumental in convincing Kant to place human dignity at the core of his ethical theory.

The political implications of this idea of human dignity have been much discussed, but the implications for our social attitudes and personal relations have been comparatively neglected. This may be because various forces have conspired to reduce the more obvious manifestations of *class* snobbery, which was the immediate target of the social revolution. In our more individualistic world, however, class snobbery readily gives way to new forms of *merit* snobbery that are also incompatible with human dignity. In fact the most familiar ground for opposing *class* snobbery, i.e., respect for *individual merit,* is often stretched to serve as the basis for more modern forms of elitism. Thus, even though old style class snobbery is not our primary problem, it should be worthwhile to look for common threads between this and newer forms of snobbery and to consider how the once radical idea of human dignity stands opposed to both.

In pursuing these aims, I plan to proceed as follows. *First,* I sketch an example that illustrates several types of snobbery and helps to distinguish these from other vices that are often associated with snobbery. The example suggests a general characterization of snobbery that, I hope, will be adequate for subsequent discussion. My aim here is not to give an analysis that exactly fits all linguistic uses of that term, nor is it to provide a psychological account of the development of snobbish attitudes. The intent is merely to isolate certain central characteristics

---

1   This paper was first written for a conference at Virginia Polytechnic Institute and State University in May, 1989. The conference theme was the motto of the French Revolution, "Liberty, Equality, and Fraternity." Thanks are due to William Williams, the other participants at that conference, and several colleagues for helpful comments.

of those commonly regarded as snobs, traits that are morally objectionable but distinct from other familiar vices (such as conceit, cruelty, and injustice).

Second, I distinguish several types of snobbery and discuss the common idea that what is wrong with snobbery is that the snob does not base his esteem and contempt for people on their true merits and faults as individuals. This idea provides a familiar objection to *class* snobbery, and, on reflection, it poses a challenge to *talent* snobbery and *achievement* snobbery as well. However, standards of individual merit are notoriously variable and controversial, reflecting different ideas about what constitutes an individual herself (as opposed, say, to her good fortune). Moreover, no matter how merit is measured, one remains a snob if one lets assessments of merit become an exclusive and all-pervasive criterion for grouping people as honorable (insiders) and contemptible (outsiders). Even if one judges individual merit only by character and moral desert, one may be a *moral* snob if these moral judgments dominate one's attitudes towards others.

Third, I contrast individual merit with a Kantian ideal of human dignity. This ideal attributes a basic worth to all human beings independently of class, talent, achievement, and even moral effort. To acknowledge this worth fully we must do more than respect rights and be charitable; we must value and respect all persons as persons, regardless of status and merit, in attitude as well as in deed. Thus dignity stands opposed to all forms of snobbery and places a severe limit on the kind and degree of contempt that we may legitimately have towards even the most defective and vicious human beings. From this Kantian perspective, the main fault in snobbery is not error in judging the merits of individuals but rather failure to acknowledge the basic worth of human beings as persons.

My interest in this project stems from several sources. These include a long-standing interest in Kant's ethics and a strong personal aversion to snobbery, extreme enough to raise worries about "reverse snobbery." More significantly for others, I find that, like servility and some other vices, snobbery has three features that tend to be neglected in contemporary ethics. *First,* though there are obvious utilitarian objections to snobbery, these seem far from the whole story about what is wrong with snobbery. On my Kantian account, by contrast, snobbery is not merely derivatively wrong because it tends to have bad social consequences; it is an attitude that is itself inconsistent with a basic moral point of view regarding the worth of persons. *Second,* contemporary ethics is mostly focused upon right and wrong *action,* duty and supererogation, or rights and welfare, but our questions about snobbery belong to the ethics of *attitudes.* Too often it is assumed that objectionable attitudes are simply those that lead to wrong *actions,* but in some cases, such as snobbery, this seems to have matters backwards. On the present Kantian account, snobbish acts are wrong, in part, because of the objectionable attitudes they manifest, not the reverse. *Third,* snobbery seems to be an attitude towards oneself in relation to others that is inappropriate not only in the way it views others but also in the way it conceives oneself. The Kantian case against snobbery is not entirely other-regarding; for, on this view, by measuring the worth of persons entirely by the variables of social class and/or individual merit, snobs fail to appreciate their own unconditional worth as persons.

I

Consider the Honorable I. M. LeGrand, who is a paradigm of many sorts of snobbery without a confusing array of other faults.[2] He is honest, truthful, generously charitable, and scrupulous in conforming his conduct to duty and the rights of others. But he sees himself as superior to ordinary folk in virtually every respect he acknowledges as important. For example, he is enormously proud that he belongs to the noble LeGrand lineage, an illustrious and wealthy family in an historically prominent and culturally superior nation. Though charitable and sometimes affectionate towards those born less fortunate, he can only laugh at the thought of such people bearing themselves with the sort of dignity he accords himself and his few peers. LeGrand does not place his superiority entirely in class connections, however; he also feels quite puffed up over the fact that he as an individual is extraordinarily intelligent, good-looking, and artistically gifted. Nor does his pride rest exclusively on his gifts, for he also looks down on his self-indulgent peers who neglect their talents. By contrast, he has exerted himself with self-discipline to cultivate his gifts, and he has effectively used them to win both popular fame and esteem from exacting critics. External troubles bother him less than most people, for he remains buoyed up by his constant awareness that he has few, if any, equals and that no one is *more* deserving of esteem, honor, and pride. Only good manners, in which he also takes pride, prevent him from bragging to others and informing them of his superiority, though we can hardly imagine that his attitude has altogether escaped the notice of others.

The flip side of LeGrand's pride, we may suppose, is his contempt for anyone he deems deficient in the very ways in which he himself is so superior. Although he acknowledges equality before the law as well as duties of self-restraint and charity, he sees no merit in talk of "honor" and "dignity" among people who are "low born," ignorant, unrefined, lazy, or morally lax. The idea that the low born and even hardened criminals have "dignity," and are owed "respect," seems to him pure nonsense. A person must be entitled to respect by birth, talent, prodigious effort, or at least good character. Charity and pity may be freely given, he thinks, but one can honor and respect only excellence. The proper attitude to those who are deficient, then, is some degree of contempt; and for the most extreme cases the only reasonable attitude is utter contempt.

LeGrand exemplifies several types of snobbery and his attitude illustrates that

2 Snobbery is not a frequent topic in contemporary moral philosophy, but Judith Sklar gives a stimulating discussion, rich with examples, in *Ordinary Vices* (Cambridge, Mass.: Harvard University Press, 1984), pp. 87–137.

snobbery can be distinct from other familiar vices. Normally we find extreme snobbery, such as LeGrand's, entangled in a cluster of unsavory traits, including callous disregard for the rights and well-being of "inferiors," inflated self-evaluation unresponsive to counterevidence, and perhaps a pathetic need to define oneself by association with some "in-group." Pretense, self-deception, insecurity, and closed-mindedness are often part of the package. But, though frequent companions, these traits are not essential to snobbery, at least not to the attitude I want to consider here. My sketch of LeGrand omits these commonly associated faults, and so makes LeGrand a somewhat unusual snob; but this helps to focus on the residual vice that, for subsequent discussion, I take to be snobbery.

To sharpen this focus, consider again two important vices that LeGrand lacks, namely, disregard for others' rights and insensitivity to their welfare. One can be a snob, I suggest, with or without these faults. For example, a snob with no sense of justice or decency might treat servants as if they had no right to demand a living wage or to expect an apology for a breech of privacy; but, as we see with LeGrand, one can be quite scrupulous about such matters and still remain a snob. One can grant others' their rights while still "looking down one's nose" in an objectionable way.

Further, though snobs are often insensitive to the feelings and general welfare of those they consider their inferiors, this is not essential. One may pay loving attention to the feelings and general welfare of another person, as one might to one's prize poodle, while still snobbishly looking down on that person as having a status in every way inferior to one's own. Alternatively, if one lacks affection, a sense of duty might lead one to attend carefully to another's welfare and feelings even though one had nothing but contempt for the person himself, just as a conscientious dog sitter might fulfill a contract to care for an ugly and ill-trained mongrel that she detested. One cannot escape snobbery, then, simply by avoiding the insensitive and uncaring treatment of "inferiors" that so frequently accompanies it.

Generally, though the snob lacks an important pro-attitude towards persons he deems inferior, he may have a variety of other pro-attitudes towards them. For example, the snob may appreciate the utility of those he looks down on. He may like them and enjoy their company. He may feel that deferential behavior and tokens of respect are required by the role or office the person has been assigned by a higher authority (e.g., the president, the pope, or the executive board). Having these pro-attitudes may help to conceal snobbery, but it does not prevent one from being a snob, for one may still secretly harbor a pervasive and ill-founded contempt for those outside one's esteemed circle. And because snobbery is compatible with having the pro-attitudes of liking, enjoying, and appreciating one's "inferiors," lacking such attitudes cannot be what constitutes snobbery.

That snobbery is not simply absence of such favorable attitudes towards "inferiors" becomes more evident when we reflect on remarks like the following:

"She is a *good* maid, and I confess that I enjoy having her around, but one mustn't forget, after all, that she's still *just* a maid (black woman, high school drop out, etc.)." Or: "Those people are worthless scum, as we all know, but one must at least accord this one the honor due to his *position* as the ambassador (a priest, my sister's boss, etc.)." Or, again: "I must admit that she is very smart *for a woman* (hardworking *for a Mexican,* articulate *for a Southerner,* etc.)."

When we hear people defend themselves against a charge of bigotry with the reply, "Some of my best friends are . . . (blacks, Jews, etc.)," we do not automatically absolve them of the suspicion of bigotry. The same is true when we hear that defense from someone we suspect of snobbery. The reason is not merely that we doubt the bigot and the snob have the friends they claim. The reason is that bigotry and snobbery can coexist with many pro-attitudes towards those regarded as inferiors, even with a truncated form of friendship. "Making friends" with outsiders is no guarantee against snobbery.

Very commonly snobs have inflated opinions of themselves, thinking themselves to be more intelligent, accomplished, famous, powerful, or impressive to others than they are. But a person is not a snob *simply* because of such false empirical beliefs or "errors of fact." To be sure, snobs typically begin and end with mistaken empirical beliefs. For example, they may begin by thinking that they, or their ancestors or associates, have more talents, achievements, and influence than they actually have, and they often end by falsely inferring that others admire them for these things more than they do. But, though we may not know any, we can easily imagine snobs who are not mistaken or self-deceived in these ways. Like LeGrand, they may *be* just as talented, influential, etc., as they suppose, but their snobbery is still revealed in the importance they attribute to such matters as they look down upon others.

Similarly, at various periods in history certain widely held false beliefs no doubt encouraged snobbery but did not necessitate it. For example, people once believed that racial and sexual stereotypes were biological necessities, that privileged families were favored by God, and that existing class structures were underwritten by natural law. Generally, people too often supposed the things in which they took pride were due to something grander than luck and circumstance. However, merely sharing these dubious assumptions did not by itself make anyone a snob. One could, in principle, believe that one was given superior ability and position by God or Nature without measuring one's personal worth by these assets and using them to justify a pervasive contempt for inferiors.

Even without such dubious empirical and metaphysical beliefs, snobs are often puffed up about themselves and contemptuous of others on the basis of aesthetic and other *evaluative* judgments that are unwarranted. For example, they may be haughty about their supposed fine taste in music, art, literature, and manners although in reality they slavishly conform to the passing fashions of a tasteless self-appointed elite. We expect to find a host of snobs among the ranks of the pseudointellectuals, phony connoisseurs, and those who treat provincial standards of etiquette as if they were categorical imperatives. But bad taste and provincialism are no more essential to snobbery than factual error. They make the snob more ridiculous, and so perhaps more tolerable; but they cannot be the core of the problem, for good taste and cosmopolitan outlook are no guarantee against snobbery. Even if truly "refined," well-read, and possessed of the most sophisticated tastes, one may manifest snobbery in one's unqualified contempt for those who are boorish, illiterate, and uncultured. It is the same with taste as with empirical beliefs: what matters is not so much the correctness of one's judgments as what one supposes this justifies in one's attitudes towards others.

So far we have focused on what is *not* essential to snobbery. To review, snobbery is an attitude, or evaluative stance, towards others in relation to oneself; but it is *not* essentially a matter of respect vs. disregard for rights, concern vs. indifference to welfare, liking vs. disliking, showing outward tokens of respect vs. openly displaying contempt, having true vs. mistaken beliefs, or good vs. bad taste. But then if a person, like LeGrand, is genuinely refined, realistic about his talents, justly proud of his record, scrupulous about others' rights, sensitive to their welfare, and respectful in demeanor, what more is required for him to avoid being a snob?

To begin somewhat vaguely, the core attitude in snobbery, as I see it, has to do with what one views as contemptible and base vs. what one sees as honorable and noble. These are terms not often used in contemporary moral philosophy, perhaps because the terms call to mind aristocratic class structures that we are glad to be rid of. As postrevolutionary philosophers we would rather focus on attitudes usually taken towards persons by virtue of their individual characteristics independently of class associations: loving, liking, approving, and hating, disliking, disapproving, etc. Nonetheless, the notions of the contemptible and the honorable are at least implicit in our everyday judgments and attitudes, especially, I suggest, in the attitudes we consider snobbish.

Though we may think of the honorable and the contemptible as categories rooted in class structures, they are not essentially so. In fact it is one of the merits of Rousseau, Kant, and the French Revolution that they attempted to shake loose the traditional associations of these ideas by urging the ideas of the honorable citizen, the nobility of labor, and the dignity of humanity. We can view people as worthy of honor on various grounds and to various degrees, independently of social class, office, and natural assets. Although praise, admiration, and approval seem to imply comparative judgments of individual merit, one can deem a whole class of persons, even all of humanity, as worthy of honor to some degree independently of individual effort and achievement. Similarly, though blame and disapproval seem to imply judgments of individual fault, contempt is an attitude one can take towards whole groups regardless of individuating features. People differ, of course, on what constitutes a proper ground for viewing someone as honorable or contemptible, and to a large extent, I suggest, disagreement about this is what separates the snob from the believer in human dignity.

We are perhaps inclined to associate the idea of "honoring" someone with twenty-one gun salutes, red carpets, and brass bands, or at least trophies, medals, gold watches, and congratulatory speeches. We use such tokens when we honor people differentially, singling out a few for special notice. "Honors" intended for this purpose tend to become meaningless as they are more and more widely distributed. A cartoon from the Second World War makes the point: Willie, a bedraggled infantryman, asks the well-dressed award-giver for a pair of dry socks instead of another "Purple Heart," as the dry socks are rarer and more useful than the supposed "honor." If viewing someone as "worthy of honor" necessarily implied wanting to single that person out for special celebration, then of course there would be something ridiculous about the idea that all human beings, no matter what their status, are worthy of honor.

But it is possible to understand a more limited, but still important, notion of honoring where selectivity and comparison are not the point. When we "honor" someone *as* a member of a cherished group (former classmates, fellow citizens, or human beings), we express in various symbolic ways our *respect* for the person *as a member* as well as (what we take to be) well-based pride, pleasure, or glad acceptance of comembership with that person. "Honor" is perhaps the extreme manifestation of at least one sort of "respect," an attitude opposed to "contempt" and implying a basis in something important about the object of respect.[3] This respectful attitude is not essentially acknowledgment of rights or an esteem earned by a comparatively high degree of achievement.[4] Nevertheless it implies a sincere acknowledgment that there is something about the person (as member of the group in question) that is valuable, in some sense. The relevant sense of "valuable" here is not "useful," "likeable," or "meritorious," but something more like "fine," "worthy of favorable notice," "not to be put down." Understanding the attitude in this way, we can "honor" and "respect" all human beings as such, though, of course, the snob doubts that we should.

My suggestion, then, is that the core of snobbery is an attitude towards oneself (and one's associates) in relation to others that has to do with "honoring" (in a broad sense) and holding in contempt. More specifically, *it is a disposition to count*

---

3 Unfortunately the word "respect" has many uses, some of which (misleadingly for my purpose) suggest acknowledgment of rights or special individual merit. For this reason I continue to use the sometimes awkward expression "honor" for ideas that, but for the ambiguity, might more naturally be expressed in terms of "respect."

4 Thus the sense of "respect," or at least its immediate ground, is not quite the same as those discussed in "Servility and Self-Respect" and "Self-Respect Reconsidered," in this volume. One might argue, however, that dignity is the ultimate ground for each of these types of respect: respect for human rights, (selective) respect for individuals who set and live by standards for themselves, and respect for persons as "honorable" fellow human beings.

people as worthy of "honor" and "contempt" on inadequate grounds, in inappropriate contexts, or to an unwarranted degree.[5]

Any example must presuppose answers to controversial questions yet to be considered: what are "inadequate grounds," "inappropriate contexts," etc.? But, admittedly making assumptions on these matters, we can illustrate the general idea of snobbery by returning to our paradigm. LeGrand not only takes pride in his ancestry; he mistakenly supposes that it justifies contempt for others. He does not merely recognize and honor individual merit in its context, praising the superior artist in his reviews and selecting the brightest tutors to teach his children; he transforms these judgments of special merit into measures of personal worth across all contexts. And because LeGrand's contempt knows no bounds, the degree of his ("utter") contempt marks him as a snob even when it is a response to truly deplorable traits. In addition, LeGrand regards himself as more worthy of honor than other *deserving* people on the "inadequate grounds" of his good fortune in heritage and natural gifts. Though justly proud of his accomplishments, he also "puffs up" about them in social contexts where his attention should be focused elsewhere (e.g., weddings, funerals, political discussions). Though (by hypothesis) accurate in ranking his gifts and achievements relative to others, he goes beyond this in supposing that one's ranking on such matters, by itself and without limit, determines the degree of one's worthiness of honor and respect compared to others.

Because of the terms "inadequate," "inappropriate," and "unwarranted," my general description of the core of snobbery implies that snobbery is necessarily objectionable, even if it should prove to have advantages. Characterizing snobbery in normative terms, however, is only natural and not a special problem, for "snob" and "snobbery" are, after all, pejorative terms that express condemnation of certain attitudes. Moreover, though the account implies that snobbery is objectionable, it does not pretend to settle the main substantive issues by definition. It leads us to expect, what seems true, that people disagree about who counts as a "snob" according to their different views about what constitute reasonable grounds for holding people worthy of honor and contempt in various contexts and to various degrees. Because the general characterization of snobbery does not settle this, it is in a sense "incomplete," leaving room for different views about what makes persons worthy of honor and contempt. Disagreements about this are what distinguish the several types of snobbery, to which I now turn.

---

5   It is important to note that what I propose here is a general characterization of "the core of snobbery," not a definition of snobbery. Racism and sexism may in fact share a common core with the kinds of social snobbery with which I am mainly concerned in this essay. Although it should become clear as we proceed that the forms of snobbery considered here do not logically presuppose (and at times even oppose) racism and sexism, I do not attempt to give a general account of the differences between snobbery, racism, and sexism.

II

My aim in this section is not merely to review familiar types of snobbery but to suggest that the most common diagnosis of the fault of snobbery is not adequate for all types. In sum, my argument runs as follows. The classic snob is a *class snob,* and the usual objection to class snobbery is that it refuses to respond appropriately to individual merit. Standards of individual merit shift, however, as one takes a narrower and narrower view of what excellences belong to the individual herself as opposed to her good fortune. Accordingly, the criticism that class snobbery neglects individual merit can lead to a series of new forms of snobbery as the conception of merit progressively narrows. Even if pressed to an extreme (and controversial) limit, this meritarian line of objection would still leave untouched a kind of *moral* snobbery that is objectionable for other reasons. And this suggests a critique of snobbery from a quite different perspective.

Consider first snobbery based on *social class:* that is, the attitude that one deserves special honor or contempt, apart from special context, simply by virtue of being a member of a group identified not by the individual talents or merits of its members but rather by features such as inherited wealth, land ownership, kinship with royalty, historically prominent families, traditional privileges, and the like. Insofar as social conventions group together people with similar skin color, location of birth, ethnic background, religion, etc., for purposes of allocating honor and contempt, these too are social classes for our purposes. Often, of course, those who regard their own class as especially worthy of honor do so, or pretend to do so, in the belief that members of that class generally have admirable features other than those that define the class, e.g., higher intelligence, leadership capacities, artistic sensibility, and superior character. But to the extent that these persons differentiate the honorable from the base by the criterion of class rather than *individual* possession of the other features, we may suspect them of being class snobs, i.e., persons whose judgments of honor and contempt are based on the inadequate ground of membership in social class.[6]

The sort of special contexts that might warrant occasional and limited honoring members of one's "social class" could be, for example, family reunions, national centennials, religious conventions, and the like. But, admitting possible exceptions, even a limited practice of "honoring" social class members as such naturally raises suspicions of class snobbery. Imagine, for example, having a festival to honor rich white Protestants with English surnames. Dividing individuals into groups by certain criteria is for most purposes, as the Supreme Court puts it, "inherently suspect."

---

6 So far they are merely "suspect" rather than "guilty" because the charge of snobbery presupposes what has yet to be argued, namely, that mere membership in a social class is an *inadequate* ground for honor and contempt, apart from very special contexts.

The usual argument that social class is an inadequate basis for honor and contempt is that merely belonging to a social class is not an excellence or merit of the individual. Though people often "identify" themselves by social class, from a meritarian perspective, membership in a favored social class is simply good fortune, or occasionally an advantage acquired by marriage or self-interested effort, and therefore not a basis for counting people as honorable or contemptible. Your class membership, one is inclined to say, is not really *you* in the relevant sense; and, even if it were, its distinguishing marks (wealth, family, nationality, ethnic origin, etc.) are not themselves excellences or merits.

Reflections of this sort may move some class snobs to become *talent snobs:* that is, without deeper change, they may merely shift the basis of their self-honoring and contempt for others from class membership to possession of natural assets, such as high intelligence, artistic talent, inherited physical advantages, etc. (This transition may be made easier by the self-serving belief that members of one's social class generally share these natural assets.) Talent snobs seem to be on firmer ground than class snobs, for, at least in some cases, there may be no doubt that, unlike social class, the talent snob's grounds for honor really are ways in which some individuals are "better" *in some sense* than others. Moreover, few would doubt that there are *some* contexts in which preferential treatment is warranted for individuals with finer natural assets: for example, talent can be a legitimate criterion for selecting trainees for various jobs and professions.

But, again, if worthiness of honor and contempt are determined by individual merit, there are natural objections to talent snobbery. High intelligence, native good looks, athletic ability, perfect pitch, etc., are admittedly assets to those who possess them and potential resources for service to others, and they may often be reasonable grounds for allocating opportunities that enable the recipient eventually to earn applause for extraordinary achievements. But our *merits,* it seems, depend not on what we are "given" but on what we do with our gifts. If individual merit is what counts, why should anyone *honor* the mere possession of talent, apart from any effort to develop it or put it to good use? And why should anyone hold others in contempt for lacking it through no fault of their own? The attitudes appropriate to natural talent are recognition of the possessor's good fortune, wishing it not to be wasted or abused, and so forth; and even these responses make sense only in the limited contexts where the particular asset may matter, not throughout all interpersonal relations. We may concede that, for political purposes, people "own" their talents, and we can reasonably credit those who develop their talents for good ends; but talents themselves are worthless when neglected, not something one "earns," and (arguably) not essential features of a person. Thus it seems foolish to make mere possession or lack of natural assets a basis of honor and contempt, especially the primary basis.

Thoughts of this sort might lead some talent snobs to rely on achievement, rather than natural gifts, as the dividing mark between the honorable and the contemptible. Suppose, for example, they now applaud themselves and others only for fine artistic performance, not mere talent, for recognized intellectual contributions, not high I.Q., and for evident public service, not mere leadership ability. Similarly, we can imagine, they come to have as much disdain for talented nonachievers as for ungifted plodders.

This attitude would not be snobbery, but rather good sense, if duly measured and restricted to the appropriate contexts: for example, to music reviews, book recommendations, and selections for service awards. There is nothing wrong, surely, in congratulating people (even oneself) for excellent achievements and honestly deploring bad performances in fields one is competent to judge.

But talent snobbery has merely given way to *achievement snobbery* if these limited and measured responses are extended to other contexts, infecting all one's dealings with others outside the area where the excellence and achievements are relevant, and if the worth of the person (for honor or contempt) is *equated* with what he or she has managed to achieve. Achievements depend on both effort and luck. Initial talent and opportunities are good fortune, not personal merit, and the efforts behind both artistic achievement and public service may have been motivated by attitudes that have no claim to honor. To express our delight we reasonably applaud *the result,* and to encourage like efforts by others we praise the *diligence and devotion* it required. But if the necessary conditions were talents and opportunities unavailable to others, it seems unreasonable to make achievements the *sole* basis for honoring some persons above others outside the special contexts of prizes and awards. And if, further, the achiever's underlying *motive* was self-serving (e.g., love of power or glory), then the achievements will be reasonable grounds for the achiever to be pleased with himself but not for him to expect others to view him as worthy of honor as a person.

Carrying these reflections to their limit, the meritarian critic of snobbery may conclude that only well-motivated *effort* can make one worthy of honor. Because class, talent, and the success of one's efforts are so dependent on circumstances and luck, true merit, it seems, must be what is most "up to the individual," namely, the degree to which one *tries* to live the best one can. If two persons have an equally well-motivated and strong *will* to achieve a good end, on this view, they are equally meritorious even though one succeeds and the other fails.

Though perhaps few take this final step, it seems a natural progression in the sort of reflections we have been considering. As the basis of snobbery shifts from social class to natural talent, then to achievements, we have an ever-narrowing idea of what it is about the person that primarily and pervasively merits our honor or contempt. Correspondingly, the idea of what constitutes the "identity" of a person, or its significant features, shrinks as gradually we strip away, first, historical roots and *social connections,* then *native capacities,* next one's *record* of accomplishments, leaving at last only the strength and goodness of the individual's *will.*

To philosophers this is a familiar progression, but it is also highly controversial. Some would argue that it has been carried too far, and others would insist on pressing it still farther. The latter, for example, may argue that both determinism and indeterminism imply that an individual's motives, effort, and will are just as much "due to luck" as talents and achievements.[7] Therefore, they may argue, since luck excludes merit, nothing is really an individual merit, not even a "good will." Others, seeing this conclusion as absurd, may try to block the argument by denying the sharp contrast between luck and merit, thereby reopening the possibility that achievements and talents may, after all, be "merits." Disputes of this sort may be unresolvable, as they seem to hinge on deep metaphysical issues about what traits are essential to the "identity" of individuals. Moreover, arguments on these issues, I suspect, are often confused expressions of evaluative disagreements about what is important in individuals.

The fact that the meritarian critique of snobbery tends to bog down in such disputes, however, is not the only reason for wanting to consider another approach. After all, most philosophical arguments will become mired in controversy if pressed hard enough. My main objection to relying on the meritarian critique is a moral one rather than a worry about its metaphysical commitments. That is, even if successful against the forms of snobbery previously considered, the objection that snobbery miscontrues individual merit fails to give the whole case against snobbery and, unless supplemented, invites a *moral snobbery* that may be as insidious as the previous kind.[8]

Consider again the reformed achievement snob who has been convinced to count only well-motivated efforts as meritorious. Now he is determined to give no credit for achievements unless they are reflections of the achievers' efforts, from morally worthy motives, to make the most of whatever talents and opportunities are allotted to them. Also he is prepared to honor conscientious effort in even those who are untalented and have few opportunities regardless of whether their efforts accomplish anything worthwhile. He reserves his contempt exclusively for those who make no good efforts, which includes selfishly motivated achievers as well as the morally apathetic and the flagrantly immoral.

So far, perhaps, the reform is all to the good. But in switching to a moral standard for individual merit, our reformed achievement snob may simply become a *moral snob*. For example, suppose that, confident at last that he has an adequate ground for assessing who is worthy of honor and contempt, he sees no reason to restrict the use of these judgments to special contexts or to hold them in moderation. He does not merely mistrust the proven liar and refuse to tolerate cruelty and injustice; he dismisses the person who has these vices as "moral garbage."

7 This line of reflection is explored in an interesting way by Thomas Nagel's "Moral Luck" in *Mortal Questions* (Cambridge University Press, 1979), pp. 24–38.
8 Here I am admittedly stretching the word "snobbery" beyond its customary use as well as taking a moral stand with which I expect many will disagree.

He does not simply try to emulate his moral saints and honor them on ceremonial occasions, in obituaries, and the like. Instead he constantly idolizes them and looks down on the morally inferior with great disdain. If possible and when duties permit, he will associate only with the former and have nothing to do with the latter. He chooses not only his friends but also his books, films, clubs, bumper stickers, and grocery products to express honor for the virtuous and scorn for the vicious. He likes to join boycotts less for their effects than to condemn worthless manufacturers and government leaders. Though he is committed to working hard for good causes, failure to get results does not dampen his spirits because he is constantly glowing with self-satisfaction from the thought that his efforts make him so much more worthy than most others. Though he is scrupulous of the rights and welfare of his moral inferiors, it pains him to give even these tokens of respect to people who do not deserve it.

The problem with this moral snob is obviously not that he has too little regard for individual merit. Moreover, if we acknowledge individual merit at all, it does not seem plausible to say that his problem is a faulty criterion of merit, one that treats as meritorious what is largely due to good fortune. So the usual meritarian arguments against snobbery are ineffective here. If the attitude I call "moral snobbery" is really objectionable, this must be for other reasons.

Two arguments against moral snobbery will no doubt occur to everyone; and, though not the whole story, these undeniably have some force. The first argument, made famous by Kant, is simply that we are too ignorant to categorize people as the moral snob does. We know too little of our own deepest motives ever to be morally self-satisfied, and, all the more, we cannot tell from others' external conduct who among them, if any, really have good wills. Moreover, Kant would add, even the most condemning empirical evidence that a person is morally evil cannot justify the inference that there is no spark of goodness in his will. Thus, though there should be no limit to our efforts to do what is right, comparative judgments of the moral merits of persons should have little place in our lives.[9]

No doubt extreme moral snobs are often guilty of ignoring the limitations of knowledge stressed in this argument, but there are at least two reasons not to rest our case here. *First,* though a sound warning against overconfidence in our moral assessments, surely the argument exaggerates the degree of our ignorance of human motivation. We are far from infallible, and sometimes without a clue, about people's motives and intentions; but these are in general empirically accessible, not features of a world utterly hidden from us. Calling attention to our limited knowledge should moderate the moral snob's attitude, but it does not strike at its core. "Judge not, for you may be mistaken" is a useful warning against excess, but, as the snob may retort, "Why not make the most of the evidence we have?"

9   This theme in Kant's ethics is stressed in my paper "Kant's Antimoralistic Strain" in *Theoria* 44 (1978): 131–51.

Second, the argument from ignorance is not the whole case against moral snobbery because that attitude would be objectionable even if the snob knew everyone's motives. Imagine, if you can, a moral snob who makes no mistakes in categorizing people as virtuous and vicious and who can determine exactly each person's comparative degree of moral merit. Suppose, further, that he knows that his own ranking is quite high (setting aside, of course, the controversial matter of his snobbery). Even then there seems to be something about his attitude that is objectionable, for his bottom line is that people are fundamentally worthless except when, like himself, they manage to earn moral credit by their good efforts. The moral snob's problem is not merely that he makes comparative moral judgments or that he makes such judgments without adequate evidence; the problem is more that these judgments dominate his relationships, generating a moral contempt that knows no proper bounds.

The other obvious argument against moral snobbery is, of course, that this is an attitude that has bad consequences. Moral contempt is hard to hide, and yet overt expressions of contempt tend to poison social relations. Few will accept that they are worthy of contempt, even if they admit wrongdoing. So contemptuous judgments tend to cause pain and resentment rather than moral improvement. They inhibit compromise among people of different moral views. Energies spent in judging and condemning people could be better spent elsewhere. Moral self-congratulation may lead to moral complacency, and so on. No doubt, as utilitarians will insist, these and other negative consequences outweigh both the pleasures of being a moral snob and whatever other good it may cause. But, as with many undesirable traits, the case against moral snobbery is overdetermined. One need not deny the obvious utilitarian considerations against it in order raise a different sort of objection. Moreover, to see snobbery as an inherently objectionable attitude, rather than merely one with undesirable consequences, we need to look for a diagnosis elsewhere.

III

Kant once wrote that he had been inclined to think that dignity and respect should vary with intellectual achievement and that therefore professors should be accorded the highest dignity, presumably vastly superior to that of common laborers.[10] But, he says, Rousseau saved him from this error and taught him that the important ground of dignity is in every human being. Thus Kant seems to admit a temptation to what I call talent and/or achievement snobbery, but he found this to be incompatible with his idea of human dignity. But what is this idea, how does it oppose snobbery, and why should anyone accept it?

10 See Schilpp, *Kant's Pre-Critical Ethics,* (Evanston, Ill.: Northwestern University Press, 1960), pp. 47–8.

For Kant *human dignity,* in contrast with "social dignity" that varies with one's position, is a kind of "unconditional and incomparable worth" and "admits of no equivalent."[11] It is compared to mere "price," which is a conditional value that allows comparison and "admits of equivalents." To say that dignity is "unconditional" means that it is a kind of worth not dependent upon contingent factors, such as serving as a means to desired ends, being liked, enjoyed, etc. It is a worth that any rational agent, when being fully rational, must necessarily recognize; and whoever has it continues to have it, in all contexts, so long as he exists. To say the worth is "incomparable" means at least that it is "above all price," that is, it should take precedence, in case of conflict, over any degree of merely conditional value (such as market value and sentimental value).

More controversially, Kant seemed to conceive of dignity as "without equivalent" in a stronger sense: that is, dignity is not a quantitative dimension of value along which items are compared and rated for purposes of determining what "exchanges" are reasonable. Thus, even in difficult moral dilemmas, one cannot justify sacrificing or violating the dignity of one person on the ground that this will thereby preserve *more* net dignity in others. "Price," by contrast, is a value relative to contingent desires and circumstances, and so in principle one can reasonably exchange or sacrifice anything of very high "price" for the sake of things of higher price.

Kant regarded neither dignity nor price as a metaphysical feature of the world independent of the will and wants of rational agents, something "out there" to be discovered. Rather, to attribute value to something is to say that rational agents do or should will to pursue or cherish it. Thus material things have "price" because some rational agents want them; and rational agency itself has "dignity" because, Kant argues, rational agents necessarily regard it as an "end in itself," something to be cherished, maintained, and honored.

Kant attributes human dignity to virtually all sane adult human beings because of their "autonomy" of will. This implies at least a minimum capacity and disposition to acknowledge rational and moral principles. Significantly, however, moral virtue is not a prerequisite of dignity; even the grossly immoral have it. To these the message of Kantian morality is not "You worthless creature, try to make yourself into something valuable!" but rather "Realize that as a rational/ moral agent you have an unconditional and incomparable worth, and now live in a way befitting such a splendid creature!"

Kant appeals to the idea of human dignity repeatedly when arguing for more specific moral conclusions.[12] It is, for example, a premise in his doctrine of rights/

---

11 My interpretation of Kant on these points is developed in my paper "Humanity as an End in Itself," *Ethics* 91 (October, 1980): 84–99.

12 The views mentioned here are presented in Kant's *Metaphysics of Morals,* which is published in translation in two volumes. See John Ladd, tr., *The Metaphysical Elements of Justice* (Indianapolis, IN: Bobbs-Merrill, 1965) and James Ellington, tr., *The Metaphysical Principles of Virtue* (Indianapolis, IN: Bobbs-Merrill, 1964).

justice, and it seems to underlie a minimal principle of beneficence and mutual aid. More important for our purposes, Kant often appeals to the idea when condemning practices and attitudes that "dishonor" our humanity. We acknowledge human dignity not only by promoting welfare and not violating rights but also by "honoring" and "respecting" persons as rational/moral agents. Thus we must not engage in "mockery," which treats others as worthless, or "servility," which denies one's own worth. Again, though justice may demand severe punishment, human dignity forbids degrading punishments that fail to respect the criminal as a human being.

Aspects of this Kantian idea of dignity may be too extreme for some, and few today can accept the whole system of ideas in which Kant embedded his discussion. But the core of his idea, I suspect, is widely acknowledged, at least in principle. What seems less fully appreciated is the way in which the basic idea of dignity opposes snobbery of all types, even moral snobbery. On reflection, however, this seems undeniable. For the root idea of dignity is simply that virtually everyone, regardless of social station, talents, accomplishments, or moral record, should be regarded with respect as a human being. Although of course we may protect ourselves from the vicious and choose our special friends, our basic attitude towards human beings should be as honorable fellow members of a common association. To extend the metaphor, membership need not be earned and cannot be forfeited or resigned; we are qualified as lifetime members simply by being rational/moral agents. For fellow members, presumed able to understand and appreciate the common cause, we reserve a kind and degree of moral criticism that we would never bother to lay on aliens and beasts; but nonetheless utter contempt for fellow human beings, whatever they have done, is incompatible with our respecting them as "one of us."

Human dignity not only requires some minimum respect for the worst moral agents, it also places limits on the *contexts* in which one can appropriately honor some people more than others for their talents and accomplishments. One who regards all persons as having an unconditional and incomparable worth cannot rely on any selective standard to sort people for honor, as the snob does, across all contexts. To do that would be to go beyond honoring them *as* musicians, scholars, athletes, etc., and to use the selective criteria as a measure of their worth as persons. Granting dignity to all need not, of course, prevent us from giving special tokens of deference to officeholders or special recognition to extraordinary talent and achievement, provided the occasion leaves no doubt that this is all we are doing. Similarly, we need not deny that some people are morally better than others and that their conscientious efforts have a "moral worth" in a sense distinct from "dignity." However, to *use* such judgments, as the moral snob does, as a ground for pervasive contempt for "moral inferiors" expresses the attitude, contrary to dignity, that one's worth is exclusively or primarily something one earns. We respect erring fellow human beings by refusing to equate them with their moral records and by instead acknowledging their capacity to improve.

A consequence of this view of snobbery is that snobs, in a sense, undervalue themselves as well as others. Though LeGrand does not suffer from an excessively low opinion of himself, he has rested his self-respect on an unstable ground. He expects others to honor him for advantages that most cannot find in themselves and will be pleased if he loses. He himself is committed to abandoning his sense of self-worth to the extent that his talents fade and his record becomes tarnished. Even now, if deeply reflective, he must see that his snobbish attitude does not allow him to count himself as valuable just as a human being, standing naked, as it were, without his medals on. Like a child who cannot see why his mother should love him unconditionally, he cannot believe that anyone, including himself, should cherish and respect him apart from his gifts and record. Like most of us, no doubt he actually does value just existing as the author of a human life, but his snobbish attitude requires him to see this as a mere personal preference, not a claim to a value worthy of anyone's respect. It implies that, were it not for special contingent facts about him, even his death and disgrace would not in themselves be worthy of others' notice. To live with such an attitude seems a misfortune, not only for others but for the person who has it.

Why should one accept the idea of human dignity? To someone utterly hostile to the idea, there may be no effective answer. But for the rest of us a line of reflection suggested by Kant may carry some weight.[13] In simplest terms, the argument is this. First, those of us rational enough to be concerned to govern ourselves by reasons will find, on reflection, that we conceive of ourselves, for all practical purposes, in a certain way: able to choose policies and goals for ourselves, surveying our particular desires without assuming that they are all good reasons for acting, and capable of resisting them if we have reason to do so (negative freedom). Moreover, we find ourselves committed to standards of rationality that we did not arbitrarily invent but with which we "identify" (as if we had "legislated" them to ourselves – positive freedom). These rational standards, which we may not always follow in practice, include a recognition that when we value something in itself, not merely as a personal preference, but as something with an objective claim to respect by other rational agents, we must honor that value wherever it is, not just when we ourselves possess it.

Next, although we do not generally attribute such objective value to our particular projects and enjoyments, we cannot help but view ourselves, as existing rational agents and the authors of our lives, as having a special kind of value that anyone should acknowledge whether they like us or not. That is, if we reflect deeply, we find that we inevitably value ourselves as "ends in ourselves," as

13 Here I draw freely from Kant's *Groundwork of the Metaphysic of Morals*, tr. H. J. Paton (New York: Harper & Row, 1964). See also my "Kant's Theory of Practical Reason," *The Monist*, 72, no. 3, (1989): 363–83.

agents with a "dignity" not dependent on the details of our social position, our utility to others, our popularity, our record, or even the degree to which we like and approve of the particular way our lives are going. We attribute this value to our rational agency not because it is *ours*, but because of what it is.[14] Thus, in consistency, we cannot fail to acknowledge its claims in anyone else who has it. One cannot attribute dignity to oneself, or any favored person, on a ground that others share and then consistently fail to grant dignity to the others. Thus we cannot reasonably deny dignity to any human being who is the sort of (minimally) rational agent we take ourselves to be.

Stupidity, foolishness, laziness, failure, bad attitudes, and even serious crimes do not prove that a person lacks that basic humanity on which, Kant believed, we rest our own claims to dignity. Even when heinous crimes raise the gravest doubts, it may be better to err on the side of faith that there is humanity in even the worst person than to dismiss anyone as utterly worthless.

To conclude, this Kantian case against snobbery admittedly leaves many reasonable questions unanswered. For example, some people may persist in denying dignity even to themselves; and if so, the argument sketched above will not move them. Others will worry that attributing dignity to ourselves as rational agents leads to undervaluing animals (and even our own "animal nature"). But, even if overstated, the Kantian argument at least poses some pertinent questions for us to consider when tempted to snobbery: Are the differences that make us feel so puffed up about ourselves and so contemptuous of others really the sole or primary basis for our self-respect? Would we count ourselves as worthless human beings if we lost these assets? Are we not, even without these superior traits, persons with a claim to at least some minimum respect and honor in the human community? Can we honestly deny that others have the same basis for that minimum claim? Is it not inconsistent, then, to deny respect and honor to others as persons? And, finally, is not this denial of human dignity, when wrapped in elitist excuses, the very core of snobbery?

---

14   It is important to note that the argument requires more than the egoist's admission, "*I* cherish *my* living as a rational agent," namely, "living as a rational agent is a thing to be valued," i.e., something of "agent-neutral" value.

Pains and projects: justifying to oneself

My reflections start from three directions.[1] First, in his very stimulating new book, *The View From Nowhere,* Thomas Nagel argues that pains and projects give us quite different sorts of reasons for acting.[2] Pains, he says, are bad in themselves whereas the nonfulfillment of individuals' personal projects is not; pains, unlike projects, are inherently reasons for acting. In deciding how to treat others, then, it is irrational, barring counterreasons, to fail to alleviate another's pain but not to fail to contribute to another's projects. While this is intuitively plausible in the examples he considers, I am doubtful about the general thesis.

Second, as I review classic theories of practical reason, and recent modifications, I often find their implications for particular cases counterintuitive. Present-time preference theories, for example, require too little concern for one's future, and prudential theories go too far when they try to make up this deficiency by insisting that rational choice requires maximization over time of some special factor, such as desire, cognitively refined desire, or balance of pleasure and pain. But intuitions differ, and many theorists seem little concerned about counterintuitive results. This leads me to suspect that much of the disagreement is rooted in the fact that theories of practical reason are designed for quite different purposes. A theory that works well enough for one purpose, say, explanation and prediction, may fail to serve other purposes, such as those of moral theory or analysis of ordinary meaning.

A third concern is my long-standing, and sometimes painful, project of trying to understand and reconstruct Kant's theory of practical reason. Although I have no intention of doing Kant exegesis here, I would like to explore some main themes which I think are at least Kantian in spirit. My concern is not to defend the label ("Kantian") or to borrow whatever aura of authority it may invoke; it is rather to articulate the view in question, compare it with some others, hopefully in a way that shows it to be an understandable, perhaps even plausible, alternative for the purposes for which it was intended.

My focus here will be almost entirely limited to reasons for action that do not

---

1 Earlier versions of this paper were given at the Pacific Division Meetings of the American Philosophical Association, March, 1987, and the Oberlin Colloquium, April, 1987. Thanks are due to commentators Michael Bratman and Christine Korsgaard, to participants, and to several colleagues, especially Geoffrey Sayre McCord, Gerald Postema, and Bernard Boxill.
2 New York and Oxford: Oxford University Press, 1986, chapter 8.

have to do with the welfare, rights, or interests of others.[3] Probably no decisions are completely without effect on others, but my concern will be with decisions insofar as the welfare, rights, and interests of others are set aside. The question is: what must rational agents count as reasons in those aspects of their deliberations in which effects on others are not the issue?

The several interests with which I began are meant to converge in the following plan. *First,* because the value of a theory of reasons depends on its purpose, I begin by describing a special sort of deliberation which raises the questions that, for now, I take theories of reason to be addressing. That is, I want to specify the background aims (and consequent assumptions) against which various accounts of practical reason are to be measured here. *Second,* I consider the merits, from this point of view, of a (Kantian) negative thesis: that, for the range of choices at issue here, there are no substantive considerations that always provide reasons from which we can and must determine the rational thing to do. *Third,* because this principle, if unsupplemented, leads to the same counterintuitive results as some contemporary preference theories, I consider a (Kantian) supplementary principle that requires rational concern for one's future and one's self-respect. *Finally,* I conclude with a brief note on the problem posed by Nagel concerning other people's pains and projects.

I

Suppose I am considering whether or not to undertake a challenging long-term project, say, to learn to play all of Beethoven's piano sonatas (Nagel's example) or to finish writing a book on which I have labored, off and on, for years. To do so, let us imagine, will require some sacrifice of other projects and even some pain (given, say, my incipient arthritis or limitations as a writer). Others may be affected, of course, but for now I am setting that aside and considering first whether, apart from others, I ought to undertake the project. I am asking myself what *reasons* I have for deciding one way rather than the other, and this concern to do what reason indicates is not just one preference among others but the background presupposition of my question.

It is important that I am deliberating about what to do, not trying to predict what I will do or to anticipate how I, or others, might causally explain my choice once made. In my deliberation I take for granted my commitment (or "will") to do what is rational, and I deliberate only over options that I assume I have the willpower to carry out. Whether or not I believe in metaphysical determinism is irrelevant to my task, for in deliberating I must presume, for practical purposes, that I face genuine options. For similar reasons, principles of ideal rationality

---

3 To avoid misunderstanding it is very important to keep this restriction of scope in mind. Except in my last paragraph, I shall be discussing *only* deliberation about reasons *other* than the usual moral considerations we must take into account in dealing with others.

will be irrelevant to my problem if they refer to information that is inaccessible to me. For some other purposes, my final decision may be assessed or explained as "rational" or "irrational" by reference to facts of which I cannot be aware in deliberation; but my best deliberation can only make use of what is available to me prior to the decision. Thus remote consequences I have no way of predicting are irrelevant to my task; and also, even if it is a fact that at the moment of decision I will be in a certain psychological state that will causally determine the outcome, this is not a fact that I can use. If I were to know it, I would no longer be deliberating.

Now deliberation often takes place against a background of unquestioned ends and commitments that the agent takes for granted. The questions then are what are the most efficient *means,* what are the risks, costs, sacrifices in terms of resources, etc.? So long as the relevant ends are fixed, or at least presumed to have a certain *prima facie* weight, deliberation can proceed along the familiar lines of instrumental, or means-end, reasoning. In theory, though rarely in practice, this can have the form of a search for the solution to an intellectual problem, ideally a calculation over fixed quantities.

But the sort of deliberative reflection I have in mind is one in which the agent regards all his previous ends and commitments as subject to rational review. Like Cartesian meditation in the practical realm, nothing is beyond doubt – unless seriously doubting it proves to be incompatible with the very undertaking the deliberator has set about. From this perspective instrumental principles are insufficient; for we are questioning the ultimate ends, or initial value assignments, without which instrumental principles cannot be applied. The "preferences" that decision theory needs to take as given are just what is under scrutiny.

Even when we deliberate about ends, and accept each only provisionally, ordinarily our concern is with how a particular end would fit with other possible ends that we find appealing: for example, is it compatible with these other ends, will it enhance them, or detract from them? In our deeper review, however, I imagine that the inquiry goes beyond these factual questions. For each end we ask: do we consider this, in itself, to be worth pursuing, setting aside its effects on other ends?

This sort of deep reflection on the ends and commitments one normally takes for granted is a philosophical enterprise that is impractical for everyday decision making but may nonetheless have its place. We cannot, of course, question everything at once, and we cannot live long with suspended commitment about the major ends of life. But as Kant, Aristotle, and others remind us, we can review in turn the main ends we take for granted in ordinary deliberation and ask whether it would be rational to make them our ends apart from how pursuing them affects our resources and other ends.

To say that we can reflect in this way does not mean that we will find the action-guiding answers we might hope for. Such questions may be in principle unanswerable. For example, some argue that rational assessment of ends can only be made relative to other ends which are taken for granted but are not rationally required. Possibly, our ultimate ends are fixed by our natural desires, not by reason, and reason merely tells us how to achieve our ends rather than constraining our choice of ends. This skeptical position is a natural conclusion to draw when one surveys a number of unpersuasive philosophical attempts to establish that there are intrinsically rational ends. But let us not assume the skeptical position at the outset; for the project at hand is to examine some alternatives.

The deep deliberation I have in mind has two further features that are an important part of its aim. The first is that the deliberators are looking for what we might call *justifying* reasons, not merely considerations which can *motivate* them or *explain* why they act as they do. But they are not looking to justify their choices *to others*. Their aim, rather, is to justify their choices *to themselves*.

Most often, no doubt, the context in which we give justifying reasons for our choices is one in which we try to justify ourselves to others under a presupposed system of shared norms. For example, we give reasons to justify our conduct in a legal trial, at a conference of business associates, or before "the court of public opinion." But *our* deliberators, I imagine, are looking for something different, namely, reasons by which they can, in a sense, justify decisions to themselves. This is not to say that their own satisfaction and happiness are their sole and final concerns; for these ends too must come under scrutiny, and so far it remains a possibility that other ends can, and even must, be given weight.

Justifying one's choices is called for when there is a suggestion that one's choice is criticizable or objectionable in some way. Justifying reasons then deflect the potential criticism and disapproval. To justify a choice to oneself, then, one needs reasons that show one's choice not liable to self-condemnation or self-disapproval when thoroughly scrutinized in the most thoughtful reflection.

Such reasons are typically based on one's ends, but we cannot suppose that all ends can be justified by further reasons. What we are looking for are the ultimate ends that, for us, justify particular choices but themselves require no further justification.[4]

A further feature of deep deliberation of the sort I have in mind is that our deliberators will not affirm a prospective choice, whatever its other outcomes, unless they are reflectively satisfied *with what the choice reveals (or makes) of themselves* as agents.[5] To put the point in a European manner, they aim for choices that will stand up not only under criticism *by* the self but also under criticism *of* the

4 I oversimplify here in order to avoid complications that must eventually be considered. That is, I suppose too readily that ultimate ends can be isolated from other considerations and assessed independently, but in fact we may need to assess "packages" of ends (together with their necessary means) in a more holistic fashion, according to G. E. Moore's principle of "organic unities" (i.e., the value of a whole is not necessarily the sum of the values of the parts).

5 I draw here from Charles Taylor, "Responsibility for Self," in Amelie Oksenberg Rorty, ed., *The Identities of Persons* (Berkeley: University of California Press, 1976), 281–99.

self. The perspective of a deep deliberator, then, is not merely that of a "consumer," focused on how the choice will affect her experiences, or a "producer," focused only on the external states of affairs it will produce. These concerns are encompassed in the primary perspective of one who is both the would-be "author" of a piece of her biography and at the same time its reflective critic. From this point of view, one reviews potential choices not only as choices that will produce certain experiences and external results but also as choices that will be *hers* and will partly constitute the sort of agent she will be. Thus to withstand reflective self-scrutiny one must consider not only what outcomes one prefers, apart from how they came about, but also *who* brought it about, and why, and what one thinks of oneself for having done so.

The point is not that the deep deliberator has an obsessive concern to avoid all self-disparaging *feelings;* for such feelings may be both unwarranted and unavoidable. What one wants to avoid is the sustained, all-considered, reflective conclusion that one's choice was unjustifiable. Also the aim is not simply to maintain a pleasing self-*image* to which one would sacrifice future welfare and other aims. On the contrary, how one's choices affect one's future and other interests will normally be crucial to whether one is content that the choice is to be one's own. The point, rather, is that, what is chosen must be an option that, all considered, the agent can accept without self-disapproval and in full awareness that the choice itself, and not just its benefits and costs, are the agent's own.

Something like this, I imagine, characterizes some minimal features of the deliberative point of view that Kant and others have presupposed when they rejected some alleged rational principles in favor of others. Historical questions aside, some may object that certain "preferences" (or "ends") have been built into the deliberative situation, and these, it might be argued, are not necessary for *rational* deliberation. In a sense, of course, our deliberators do *prefer* what they can "justify to themselves" on thorough scrutiny, and agents could be called "rational" in *some* senses even though they lacked such a concern. For example, we can imagine that *cognitively* rational and well-informed agents might aim exclusively to maximize certain outcomes (e.g., pleasure/pain balance), taking liability to self-criticism into account only so far as it is a liability to pains that cannot be avoided by selective attention, self-deception, and tranquilizers. They might have no interest in what I call "deep deliberation." In fact, considering how painful self-examination can be and the pleasures it may lead one to forego, they might desire to avoid it whenever possible.

My concern here is not to deny these possibilities but rather to see how, if we begin with the aims of deep deliberation, certain (Kantian) ideas about reasons and rational choice may be more understandable and plausible than some familiar alternatives. It should be noted, however, that the "preferences" or "ends" that I have attributed to deep deliberators are not highly variable first order values, like a love of chocolate or philosophy; nor are they the substantive controversial values that philosophers have debated since ancient times, like fame, power, wealth, pleasure, and peace of mind. The alleged "end" or "value" I presume deep deliberators to have, as implicit in the questions they raise, is just the procedural, second-order concern that one's choices, whatever their content, be capable of surviving a kind of deeply reflective scrutiny of and by oneself. Kant, I take it, would not call a person a fully "rational" agent if that person utterly lacked this concern; and, though the term "rational" has its various uses, I suspect that there is some sense in which most of us would endorse Kant's assessment.

II

Even though one may begin with a specific question about undertaking to learn all the Beethoven sonatas or to finish a book, deep deliberation searches for basic grounds for choosing and so is quickly led to more general philosophical questions about the sorts of things one must count as reasons. The philosopher's dream, of course, is to find just one category of reasons in terms of which all others can and must be measured. Among the most common candidates, I suppose, have been desire, pleasure/pain, peace of mind, and "intrinsic value."

Kant, Hume, and many contemporary philosophers, however, reject the idea that rational choice must or can be simplified in this way. Kant, for example, denies that there are substantive (or "material") principles of practical reason. Material principles say that we ought to act to realize certain specific ends or values, such as pleasure, avoidance of pain, power, peace of mind, satisfaction of desire, and the like. To say that they are principles of practical reason would be to say that, for everyone, rational choice is necessarily determined by reference to the selected values. If, for example, pleasure and avoidance of pain are the selected values, then the fact that an act will bring me a pleasure is in itself always a reason for doing it, and if I fail to do it, for the sake of something that is neither pleasant nor a way of avoiding pain, that would necessarily be irrational.

In denying that such substantive, or material, principles are principles of practical reason, one is not, of course, saying that it is irrational to pursue the alleged values, that rational deliberation can sometimes ignore them, or that they cannot often be cited appropriately as one's "reasons" for acting. What is denied is only that everyone *must count* them as (justifying) reasons on pain of being irrational. Perhaps everyone should *consider* them, for the most thorough rational reflection aims to review all the ends commonly assumed to provide reasons. Perhaps also there are ends that, *as it happens,* everyone after deep reflection is prepared to weigh, or even to pursue. What our negative thesis denies is not *this* but that the material principles are rationally *compelling:* or, in other words, that the selected values give us reasons that determine rational choice, or at least must be counted, *simply because of what they are and what it is to be rational in deep deliberation.*

The issue here is not simply one of conceptual analysis, for example, whether the concept of rational agents entails that they always aim for the selected end. Some philosophers seem to try to support their material principles on such conceptual grounds. But since others assert that their material principles are necessarily rational without claiming that this is an analytical or conceptual truth, the issue cannot be settled simply by asking whether it is self-contradictory to say that an agent is "rational" but "lacks the (selected) end."

At this point formal argument becomes difficult. One strategy, which may be the best one can do, is simply to take up the point of view of deep deliberation about ends and to consider for oneself the ends that are supposed to be rationally compelling. So rather than argue directly for the negative thesis, I want to sketch briefly the sort of reflection that might lead to it.

Suppose it occurs to me that finishing the book will likely affect my reputation, for good or ill, and I acknowledge that, whether I am proud of the fact or not, I do care about reputation. But now I wonder whether reputation is something I must consider as a final end. I can only guess whether finishing the book would realize my highest hopes or my worst fears; but the question I raise now is whether a justified belief that my reputation would be enhanced is in itself a reason for finishing the book, and whether a justified fear that the book would damage my reputation is in itself a reason to abandon the book. Reflection on my past behavior may convince me that I have in fact counted good reputation as an end in itself; but would I be irrational if I decided now to discount this, treating it as insignificant in choices and self-assessments except so far as it may have consequences for other things I value, like increased opportunities, financial rewards, and *self*-esteem? The choice, it seems, is up to me, assuming that I will be content with it in the future. Though I may not be able to help *caring* about reputation, I may decide on reflection that I am not satisfied to be the sort of person who acts for reputation and so may refuse to count reputation itself as a justifying reason. Surely there is nothing irrational in this, and I might reflect in a similar way about most of the particular ends (like power) that some favor but others do not.

But now I think further: I *want* to finish the book, and, though I may discount reputation, I wonder whether I can so easily discount my *desires*. After all, the most common way to *explain* our choice of basic ends is to say that we desire them, and some say that rational selection of ends is simply a matter of discovering what we most desire. To simplify the issue, let us set aside future and past desires because their reason-giving status is more controversial than that of current desires and, in any case, no one argues that a future or past desire has *more* weight *per se* than a present one. Can I, then, rationally discount a present desire?

Well, supposing the "present" means the duration of my deliberation, if I now desire something but lose my desire for it as I reflect more thoroughly about its object, then, surely, I *can* reasonably discount the initial desire. The question then is whether I must count as reasons all the desires that I *continue* to have as I reflect thoroughly (with my best information). This is the sort of thing I *usually* count as a reason, of course, and I would regard myself quite silly if I did otherwise. But then again the desires that usually come to my attention in deliberation have already been filtered through evaluative screens that were fixed in place by a long history of past decisions and now merely appear as the background of my conscious reflections. Also when I count a desire as a reason, usually I am assuming that its fulfillment will be pleasant or have some other payoff. It remains a question, then, whether my desiring itself, apart from these, must count as a reason.

This seems doubtful. Suppose that I find myself desiring something quite extraordinary even though I expect no further "pay off" in its fulfillment: for example, I want to be buried in an expensive bronze casket; I want to learn to play all the piano pieces that my sister played as a child, no matter how distasteful I find them; or I have a desire to trample the flowers in the virgin forest when hiking alone. Suppose, further, that these strange desires do not extinguish, as one might expect, upon persistent reflection on available facts. Even when I reflect on the probable roots of these desires in childhood envy, fantasy, etc., the desires remain. By hypothesis, I do not expect pleasure, or relief from frustration, if the desires are fulfilled, but the desires persist. Now it is undeniable that the desires are dispositions to act and so may figure in *explanations* of what I do, but must I count them as *justifying reasons?* It seems obvious, from the deliberative point of view, that I *can* refuse to regard the fact that I have such desires as any reason to act; and, if on reflection I have some contempt for the sort of person who has and honors such desires, then denying them status as justifying reasons seems not irrational but rather quite appropriate to my aims in deliberating towards self-justifiable choices.

A spirit of toleration might prompt me at first to suppose that I must at least *weigh* each persistent desire even if I choose in the end to squelch it in favor of a desire to satisfy some evaluative standard. But though all potentially relevant factors should no doubt be *considered,* why must I give them weight in my deliberations? Weighing reasons in deliberation is not just estimating the relative intensity of the desires one has (even after reflection). What weight a desire has, and even whether one counts it as worth weighing, is partly a matter for reflective decision.

At this point I may wonder whether my present deliberations are too limited and unsophisticated to isolate the desires that necessarily give reasons for acting. The strange desires I mentioned above (bronze coffin, etc.) might survive my layman's scrutiny but how would they fare under cognitive psychotherapy? Perhaps the desires that I must weigh in rational deliberation are just the desires that I would have after subjecting myself to this deeper, more thorough and systematic exposure to potentially relevant facts.[6] If so, then these especially filtered desires might be the common denominator in terms of which all reasons could be cashed out and so, at last, rational deliberation would be (in principle) a sort of calculation over given quantities.

But suppose I have reason to believe, from the experience of others in such treatment, that desires I detest would survive the treatment. I know that I have them and would continue to have them; but, disapproving of them as I do, must I nevertheless count them as reasons now? I might also learn that cognitive psychotherapy would extinguish my interest in the evaluative standards I now affirm on my best reflection. I should take this information seriously, of course, as it suggests that my current reflective preferences may be rooted in ignorance and prejudice. But this is not the only possibility: the treatment may radically change the sort of person I am, not merely by destroying wants and values based on misunderstanding but in a variety of other ways as well. Admittedly, whether learned in therapy or without it, "the truth" may set me free from desires and aversions that have currently unrecognized features of a kind that even now I deplore. I may, for example, lose self-frustrating aversions and desires formed by childhood conditions irrelevant to my current life. But what changes cognitive psychotherapy would cause is an empirical question. Conceivably, I could lose harmless desires, like wanting the home team to win, and I could lose more serious concerns, like my attachments to individuals and career, which are central to the sort of person I now am and want to be. Unlikely as it may be, the outcome might even be that the overriding desire that survives treatment is a desire to commit suicide. The point, however, is *not* that one should hide from facts, fear psychotherapy, or even disregard what indirect evidence one can get about which of one's desires would survive a more thorough and systematic exposure to information. The point is simply that the mere fact, by itself, that one's desire would or would not survive cognitive psychotherapy does not determine whether one *must*, to be rational, count it as a reason in deliberation. Given what I am looking for in deep deliberation, there is still a choice to be made even after I learn what I can about what my desires would be after cognitive psychotherapy.

Having rejected desire, I might wonder whether pleasure and pain provide the necessary common denominator of rational choice. This seems quite implausible, however. Consider first the extreme hedonism that *identifies* rational choice with choice that maximizes the agent's balance of pleasure over pain, and so

6 This suggestion, of course, is drawn from Richard Brandt's *A Theory of the Good and the Right* (New York: Oxford University Press, 1978). The type of objection that I raise to Brandt's view is developed in Alan Gibbard's "A Noncognitive Analysis of Rationality in Action," *Social Theory and Practice* 9 (1983): 199–221, and also in my review essay, "Darwall on Practical Reason," *Ethics* 96 (1986): 604–19.

counts nothing but pleasure and pain as ultimate reasons. Quite arbitrarily, this would dictate that it is always irrational to forego innocent pleasures for the sake of highly desired and valued states of affairs after one's death (unless, perchance, there are counterbalancing secondary pleasures and pains of contemplating the future, etc.).

Let us consider, then, the more modest claim that, though pleasure and pain are not the *only* ultimate reasons, they are, necessarily, *always* ultimate reasons. Even this restricted claim seems uncompelling. If, for example, in my more perverse moments I would take pleasure in the wanton destruction of beauty, in undermining the very projects I have labored hard to achieve, or in viewing photographs of mutilated animals, I need not count this as a (justifying) reason in favor of the corresponding activities. It seems quite unconvincing to insist that, in deciding that I cannot justify the activities to myself, I *must*, on pain of irrationality, list these pleasures in the "pro" column and then find stronger counterbalancing reasons for the "con" column. The nature of the pleasures themselves is such that I do not count them as justifying reasons.

The main argument philosophers seem to have given for the contrary view is that it is impossible not to *care* about the pleasure, to be to some extent drawn by it. But even if true, this "being drawn" has no more necessary rational status than the *desires* we have just considered. Perhaps I cannot help caring, but in deliberation the fact that I care need not be counted as a reason even *tending* to justify the corresponding choice.

A last ditch stand of hedonism, suggested by Nagel, claims that at least *severe physical pains* necessarily provide everyone with ultimate reasons for acting. Surely, one might argue, we cannot imagine that any human being whom we would regard rational could refuse to count his own present severe pains as justifying reasons for taking the steps to alleviate them. Here at last we seem to find bedrock: a substantive reason that no one in his right mind could discount.

Although I am inclined to agree with the *practical* implications of this suggestion, I have doubts about the theory it presupposes. *Why* do severe physical pains have this special status? Is it to be explained by saying (with Nagel) that by their nature such pains *just are* "bad in themselves," or that they are inherently reasons for choice rather than reasons by choice? Though tempting and innocuous for practical purposes, I suspect that this way of putting the matter obscures more than it explains. Human nature being what it is, probably no one who is cognitively rational and understands what he is doing would seriously think of discounting severe physical pain. Anyone who *said* that he did not count such pain as any reason for acting at all would be naturally suspected of being insincere, self-deceiving, or quite "out of his mind." Some professed values and preferences are so contrary to what we know of human nature that we have good evidence to suppose that the person who professes them does not understand the question, does not mean what he says, or is quite mad.

But, setting aside insincerity and misunderstanding, is the madness explained by calling it a failure to recognize intrinsic badness or objective reason-giving force? These, I suspect, are either untenable metaphysical claims or else merely other ways of saying that people who understand and reflect deeply and coherently always *do* count severe physical pain (etc.) as justifying reasons apart from other considerations. The latter, though no doubt true, does not identify the reason-giving force of severe pain as something prior to and independent of the procedural conditions on rational deliberation; it merely asserts that severe pain *is* always counted by us as a justifying reason when we satisfy those constraints. In other words, claiming to discount severe pain is a good *sign* of a disorder in one's thinking about practical matters, but it does not constitute it or explain it independently of procedural principles of rational deliberation.

These informal remarks about the rational status of pains, desires, etc., take for granted some presuppositions inherent in the stand-point of deep deliberation. That is, one's inclinations are not viewed as forces which fix one's ends without one's cooperation. Rather, one actively reviews and examines one's inclinations as background facts about which one has a decision *to make*, presupposing that one can discount and act contrary to any given inclination even if one continues to *feel* it after full reflection. Naturally, one assumes that one *will* not choose to discount inclinations without a reason, and acknowledging something as a reason implies caring about it. But searching for reasons is not simply trying to discover one's inclinations, just as weighing reasons is not simply trying to introspect the relative strengths of one's inclinations. One may find that one "cannot" discount certain factors, but in deliberation this "cannot" typically expresses a refusal, not a disability. Like Martin Luther's remark, "Here I stand, I can do no other," it does not complain of powerlessness but rather expresses sustained commitment.

III

The negative remarks so far suggest the following ideal of rational (deep) deliberation: first, in choosing ends, one must critically scrutinize one's actual and potential ends, in the light of one's best available information, asking whether one can rest content not only with the outcome of the selection but also with oneself as the person who made it; then, without assuming any substantive principles about what is necessarily a reason for choosing, one must *simply decide* what ends *at this moment* one can best justify to oneself; after this, one must rely on familiar instrumental principles for the choice of the best means to one's ends.

So construed, our account would be similar in an important respect to the familiar view that rational choice is relative to the agent's *current* considered preferences. This similarity, however, invites similar objections. In particular, theories that make rational choice depend entirely on current preferences may not square with common intuitions about the weight we should give to our future concerns. To be sure, we all care about our futures, the more so, perhaps, the more we reflect deeply and clearly. This fact ensures that even if current preferences give us our basic reasons for acting, we all have *some* reasons to make provisions for our futures. Still, this leaves open the possibility that those with unusually now-centered preferences might "rationally" choose to sacrifice (what are generally regarded as) important future interests for relatively minor present ones. For example, suppose that a young woman's reflections on her increased prospects for an early death by lung cancer did not arouse a strong present concern to prevent this; and suppose, further, that the ends she reflectively endorses now will not be undermined by such a painful early death. Then, it seems, present-oriented theories may have to allow that she has little reason now to avoid cancer-causing activities.

One advantage of the substantive theories we have just rejected is that they have a ready answer to this sort of objection. Hedonism, for example, holds that all one's potential pleasures and pains over time necessarily give one reasons for acting. The fact that smoking will likely cause me pain in the future, then, is a reason that I cannot rationally discount. Similarly, desire theories may hold that future desires count as much as present ones, provided these are equally intense, likely to be satisfied, etc. But our (Kantian) negative thesis denies the basic premise of these theories, namely, that certain states of affairs (like pain, desire-satisfaction) in themselves necessarily give us reasons to act. One wonders, then, how our (Kantian) account might be supplemented to handle the objection.

Another objection invited by both present-preference theories and many substantive theories is that these theories do not give proper regard to the *quality* of life. What I have in mind is the sort of complaints that Mill and Moore made about unrefined hedonism: that is, the pleasures and activities preferred by the pig and the fool are not worth as much, and so are less rational to choose, than the pleasures and activities of a human being and especially a Socrates. A similar objection may be raised to any theory that allows each reflective agent to select basic ends without insisting on extra weight for "higher quality" ends: if agents place their priority on ends that are (generally regarded) "base," "animalistic," or "frivolous," the theory must concede that for such people these are rational ends. Present-oriented theories seem especially vulnerable to the objection, for they do not even require that one refine one's ends by giving weight to what one would prefer *over time*. Again, though the objection itself is controversial, I want to consider how our (Kantian) proposal, suitably modified, would respond to it.

A positive modification of the (Kantian) view described so far is suggested by looking at the way prudentialists sometimes support their claim that one must (rationally) give regard to one's future. The thought seems to be this: immediate pleasures, desires, etc., necessarily give me reason to act; I am the same person, or subject of experiences, now and later; and so if an experience is of a kind to give me reason to favor it for myself now, the same features must give me reason, other things being equal, to favor it for myself later. In other words, insofar as the thing I will receive is the same and I, the recipient, am the same, there is the same reason to have it later as now. This argument is not uncontroversial, but even if unobjectionable on its own grounds, it will not serve my purposes because it starts by denying our negative thesis. That is, it presupposes that certain ends (e.g., immediate pleasures or satisfactions) in themselves necessarily give us reasons to act. But the argument suggests an analogous line of thought.

A central feature of common sense and Kantian conceptions of a person is that one is the same rational *agent* over time. Though my habits, tastes, and values may change, along with my physical attributes, I, the person who chooses now, am the same agent as I, the person who chooses ten years hence, will be. For our purposes, this need not be construed as a metaphysical claim so much as a claim about a set of attitudes typically presupposed in the deliberative enterprise: for example, I am now responsible for and to myself later, and I later will be responsible for my choices now as well as then, and responsible to myself still later.

The notion of "responsibility" here is not merely a causal one, as in "Lightning was responsible for the fire"; nor is it social role-requirements, as in "The secretary is responsible for the minutes"; nor is it public "answerability," as when one is liable to be hauled into court to answer charges. What is meant, however, is a partly causal and partly normative notion that we may understand by analogy with these. For example, when we take a deliberative standpoint we assume that we have not only an ability to influence our future choices indirectly but also a capacity to make plans and resolutions *for* our future, which should have a prima facie authoritative influence in later deliberations. Again, we take the attitude that in the future I will be "responsible" *for* my present choices in the sense that I will have to acknowledge that I myself am the author of the character and consequences resulting from my current choices. Accordingly, I may later take a dim view of myself for making certain choices now, and, as the same person, I am the one who must then bear the criticism. I am not, of course, two persons, a "future self" and a "past self," one of whom can call up the other before its court for trial. But still, because I am the same person, I must accept that I am the accused as well as the prosecutor when I critically reflect on my earlier choices.

These reflections, however vague, suggest a line of thought leading to the positive (Kantian) thesis that requires concern for one's future. Instead of starting with the premise that certain *experiences* are necessarily reason-giving, we might start with the (Kantian) idea that, in deep deliberation, rational agents necessarily want to *respect themselves* as agents at least at the time of deliberation. This is just a consequence, or perhaps restatement, of the presuppositions of deep deliberation: the one value or end inherent in the deliberative project is that the deliberators are concerned to choose so that their choices stand up, at least at that time, to the most thorough critical scrutiny of and by themselves. This may be viewed as a procedural standard that is rationally required for consistency with their own aims. By itself it does not require any particular substantive values, nor even (so far) concern for the future, but it is a starting point.

Next let us suppose that, like most of us, our deep deliberator sees herself as one rational agent over a lifetime, e.g., the same agent now as the person who will have her body and memories in the future, barring brain transplants, etc. When one reflects on what is involved in this complex normative conception of oneself, one may see that it includes recognition that one is responsible not only *for* what one will be later but also *to* oneself later. That is, in acknowledging that the later critic is *myself,* not another, I am already acknowledging that I am not (even now) indifferent to that critic's best reflective judgments.

My concern to withstand my own critical scrutiny now seems not to be based on special features of myself (as rational chooser or critic) that I have now but will generally lack in the future. What may vary with time are the particular values and inclinations I have, but these are what I subject to scrutiny and not a fixed presupposition of it. Given this view of myself, the commitment to make my choices justifiable to myself later seems implicit in my project of deep deliberation.

Though this line of thought may not convince anyone who does not share the self-conception that it presupposes, it suggests a (Kantian) principle independently worth considering, namely, that each person should choose in such a way that he can maintain his self-respect over time. This does not mean, of course, doing whatever one can to preserve *feelings* of self-respect, for often the best way to do *that* is to be self-deceiving and forgetful. The point is just that one must extend the attitude of the deep deliberator to include, as part of one's task, an effort to make present choices so that they can withstand one's own critical self-scrutiny not merely now but at later times as well.

There are at least three important implications of this idea, which I shall mention but cannot develop here. *First,* though future pains and desires have no more necessary reason-giving force in themselves than present pains and desires do, one must consider them, even if one currently feels apathetic about them, for one must give weight to what one will later think, on due reflection, of one's current choice. Moreover, future severe pains will be particularly difficult to discount because, human nature being what it is, one will rarely be satisfied later with current decisions made without serious regard to averting these pains. If any later concern is one that I would then reflectively endorse, then I cannot with full self-respect discount it now.

These remarks are not meant to suggest that somehow one can divide one's expected future into equal time-slices that should each be given equal, or "impartial," treatment. This picture belongs more naturally to the theory that says that each pleasure or desire has, *per se,* equal reason-giving force. The ideal of maintaining respect for oneself as a rational agent does not lend itself to maximizing strategies or calculations over given quantities. Sometimes one may find that one now deplores certain desires that one expects oneself later to endorse, or that one will later lose ideals that one now holds dear. These problems are complicated by the fact that what one now chooses can directly or indirectly influence what one will feel and think later. In such cases the ideal of maintaining self-respect may be at best a heuristic ideal, something to try to approximate, rather than a rigid requirement of reason.

The *second* consequence of the self-respect requirement is that one will normally have strong reasons to preserve for oneself the necessary conditions for future rational choosing and for realizing one's future ends, whatever they may be. Thus, for example, one has reason to avoid not only mental incapacity and ignorance but also to avoid bodily damage and squandering of one's resources. Why? One must choose now so that one can withstand scrutiny of one's choice by oneself later, and, though one may not know in particular what one will later want and endorse, one can reliably predict that these enabling goods will be (justifiably) wanted, whatever else one may choose.

The *third* consequence of the self-respect principle is that, given human nature, it is unlikely that many people will rationally chose ends that are *persistently and widely* regarded "base," "frivolous," and "animalistic" over viable alternatives which they understand. Why? Not because these "lower" ends are always or inherently contrary to reason. Rather, given that these epithets are persistently applied to them across many cultures, they probably have features that most human beings are unwilling to endorse, on reflection, over time. And, unless one is quite extraordinary in one's make up or unless one's reflection turns up something that others have missed, one is unlikely to find that opting for those ends is something one can justify to oneself, as a part of oneself, over time. One might, just conceivably, maintain self-respect for a time while choosing to pick blades of grass instead of more challenging human pursuits, but it is less likely that one could do so, in deep reflection, for long.

I conclude with a brief remark about the suggestion by Nagel with which I began. So far nothing has been said about why or how we should take into account the interests of others, but let us assume for a moment that my present remarks could be expanded to include a rational or moral requirement to respect other people as rational agents. (This is obviously the next move in a Kantian program.) Well, when my choices affect others, how should I weigh their pains relative to their projects? Is it more important, other things being equal, to see to a person's comfort than to promote that person's projects? The problem is complicated because human beings are not just "rational agents" but also (like nonrational animals) creatures with feelings, and, despite Kant, there seems to be more to morality than what is required by respect for rational agency.

Nevertheless, insofar as the respect for others as rational agents gives us reasons, it seems to favor our weighing others' comfort relative to their projects in more or less the same way that those persons would do for themselves. For neither pains nor desired projects have necessary reason-giving force, even in one's own case, and so their rational value to a person as ends depends on that person's deliberative choices. Thus, it seems, the standard of what to value about the lives of others, when we are trying to respect their rational agency, should *prima facie* be *their own choices,* unless those choices cannot withstand their own critical scrutiny (which we are rarely in a position to know) and unless, on reflection, their choices are ones that we cannot aid without losing our own self-respect.

13

The message of affirmative action

Affirmative action programs remain controversial, I suspect, partly because the familiar arguments for and against them start from significantly different moral perspectives. Thus I want to step back for a while from the details of debate about particular programs and give attention to the moral viewpoints presupposed in different *types* of argument. My aim, more specifically, is to compare the "messages" expressed when affirmative action is defended from different moral perspectives. Exclusively forward-looking (e.g., utilitarian) arguments, I suggest, tend to express the wrong message, but this is also true of entirely backward-looking (e.g., reparation-based) arguments. However, a moral outlook that focuses on crosstemporal narrative values, such as mutually respectful social relations, suggests a more appropriate account of what affirmative action should try to express. Assessment of the message, admittedly, is only one aspect of a complex issue, but a relatively neglected one. My discussion takes for granted some common sense ideas about the communicative function of action, and so I begin with these.

Actions, as the saying goes, often *speak* louder than words. There are times, too, when only actions can effectively communicate the message we want to convey and times when giving a message is a central part of the purpose of action. What our actions say to others depends largely, though not entirely, upon our avowed reasons for acting; and this is a matter for reflective decision, not something we discover later by looking back at what we did and its effects. The decision is important because "the same act" can have very different consequences, depending upon how we choose to justify it. In a sense, acts done for different reasons are not "the same act" even if otherwise similar, and so not merely the consequences but also the moral nature of our acts depends in part on our decisions about the reasons for doing them.

Unfortunately, the message actually conveyed by our actions does not depend only on our intentions and reasons, for our acts may have a meaning for others quite at odds with what we hoped to express. Others may misunderstand our intentions, doubt our sincerity, or discern a subtext that undermines the primary message. Even if sincere, well-intended, and successfully conveyed, the message of an act or policy does not by itself justify the means by which it is conveyed; it is almost always a relevant factor, however, in the moral assessment of the act or policy.

189

These remarks may strike you as too obvious to be worth mentioning; for, even if we do not usually express the ideas so abstractly, we are all familiar with them in our daily interactions with our friends, families, and colleagues. Who, for example, does not know the importance of the message expressed in offering money to another person, as well as the dangers of misunderstanding? What is superficially "the same act" can be an offer to buy, an admission of guilt, an expression of gratitude, a contribution to a common cause, a condescending display of superiority, or an outrageous insult. Because all this is so familiar, the extent to which these elementary points are ignored in discussions of the *pros* and *cons* of social policies such as affirmative action is surprising. The usual presumption is that social policies can be settled entirely by debating the rights involved or by estimating the consequences, narrowly conceived apart from the messages that we want to give and the messages that are likely to be received.

I shall focus attention for a while on this relatively neglected issue of the message of affirmative action. In particular, I want to consider what message we *should try* to give with affirmative action programs and what messages we should try to avoid. What is the best way to convey the intended message, and indeed whether it is likely to be heard, are empirical questions that I cannot settle; but the question I propose to consider is nonetheless important, and it is a *prior* question. What do we want to say with our affirmative action programs, and why? Since the message that is received, and its consequences, are likely to depend to some extent on what we decide, in all sincerity, to be the rationale for such programs, it would be premature and foolish to try to infer or predict these outcomes without adequate reflection on what the message and rationale should be. Also, for those who accept the historical/narrative perspective described in Section IV, there is additional reason to focus first on the desired message; for that perspective treats the message of affirmative action not merely as a minor side effect to be weighed in, for or against, but rather as an important part of the legitimate purpose of affirmative action.

Much useful discussion has been devoted to the constitutionality of affirmative action programs, to the relative moral rights involved, and to the advantages and disadvantages of specific types of programs.[1] By deemphasizing these matters

---

1 See, for example, the following. John Arthur, ed., *Morality and Moral Controversies,* 2nd ed. (Englewood Cliffs, N.J.: Prentice-Hall, Inc., 1986), pp. 305–47. William T. Blackstone and Robert D. Heslep, eds., *Social Justice and Preferential Treatment* (Athens, Ga.: The University of Georgia Press, 1977). Bernard Boxill, *Blacks and Social Justice* (Totowa, N.J.: Roman and Allanheld, 1984). Marshall Cohen, Thomas Nagel, and Thomas Scanlon, eds., *Equality and Preferential Treatment* (Princeton, N.J.: Princeton University Press, 1977). Robert K. Fullinwider, *The Reverse Discrimination Controversy* (Totowa, N.J.: Roman and Littlefield, 1980). Alan H. Goldman, *Justice and Reverse Discrimination* (Princeton, N.J.: Princeton University Press, 1979). Kent Greenawalt, *Discrimination and Reverse Discrimination* (New York: Alfred A. Knopf, 1983). Barry R. Gross, ed., *Reverse Discrimination* (Buffalo, N.Y.: Prometheus Press, 1977). Thomas A. Mappes and Jane S. Zembaty, eds., *Social Ethics,* 2nd ed. (New York: McGraw-Hill Book Company, 1982), pp. 159–98.

here, I do not mean to suggest that they are unimportant. Even more, my remarks are not meant to convey the message, "It doesn't matter what we do or achieve, all that matters is what we *say*." To the contrary, I believe that mere gestures are insufficient and that universities cannot even communicate what they should by affirmative action policies unless these are sincerely designed to result in increased opportunities for those disadvantaged and insulted by racism and sexism.

I divide my discussion as follows: *First,* I describe briefly two affirmative action programs with which I am acquainted, so that we can have in mind some concrete examples before we turn to controversial principles. *Second,* I summarize why I think that affirmative action programs need not be illegitimate forms of "reverse discrimination" that violate the rights of nonminority males. This is a large issue, well discussed by others, but it must be considered at least briefly in order to open the way for more positive considerations. *Third,* I discuss two familiar strategies for justifying affirmative action and give some reasons for thinking that these should not be considered the whole story. The "forward-looking" strategy appeals exclusively to the good results expected from such programs, and the "backward-looking" focuses on past injustice and demands reparation. One of my main points is that this very division leads us to overlook some other important considerations. *Fourth,* in a brief philosophical interlude, I sketch a mode of evaluation that seems to provide a helpful alternative or supplement to the traditional sorts of evaluation that have dominated discussions of affirmative action. This suggestion draws from recent work in ethical theory that stresses the importance of historical context, narrative unity, and interpersonal relations. *Fifth,* combining these ideas with my proposal to consider the message of affirmative action, I present some analogies that point to an alternative perspective on the aims of affirmative action programs. Seen from this perspective, programs that stress outreach, encouragement, and development opportunities appear in a more favorable light than those that simply alter standards to meet quotas.

I

Affirmative action programs take various forms and are used in many different contexts. To focus the discussion, however, I shall concentrate on hiring and admission policies in universities and colleges. Even in this area there are many complexities that must be taken into account in the assessment of particular programs. It may matter, for example, whether the program is voluntary or government-mandated, quota-based or flexible, fixed-term or indefinite, in a formerly segregated institution or not, and so on. Obviously it is impossible to examine all these variations here. It is also unnecessary, for my project is not to defend or criticize specific programs but to raise general questions about how we should approach the issue. Nonetheless, though a full range of cases is not needed for this purpose, it may prove useful to sketch some sample programs that at least illustrate what the more abstract debate is about.

A common feature of affirmative action programs is that they make use of the categories of race and gender (more specifically, blacks and women) in their admission and hiring policies, and they do so in a way that gives positive weight to being in one or the other of these latter categories. Policies use these classifications in different ways, as is evident in the cases described below.

When I taught at Pomona College in 1966–68, for example, the faculty/student Admissions Committee was blessed, or cursed, with applications numbering several times the number of places for new students. After a careful study of the correlation between grade-point averages of graduating seniors and data available in their initial application dossiers, a professor had devised a formula for predicting "success" at the college, where success was measured by the student's academic average at graduation and the predictive factors included high school grades, national test scores, and a ranking of the high school according to the grades its previous graduates received at the college. All applicants were then ranked according to this formula, which was supposed to reflect purely academic promise. The top 10 percent were automatically admitted; and a "cutoff" point was established, below which candidates were deemed incapable of handling the college curriculum. Then committee members made a "subjective" evaluation of the remaining candidates in which the members were supposed to give weight to special talents, high-minded ambition, community service, intriguing personality, and, more generally, the likelihood of contributing to the sort of college community that the evaluators thought desirable. Another cut was made, reflecting both the "pure academic" criteria and the subjective evaluations. Next (as I recall) the football coach, the drama instructor, the orchestra leader, and others were invited to pick a specified number from those above the minimum cutoff, according to whether they needed a quarterback, a lead actor, a tuba player, or whatever. Then those identified as minorities but above the minimum cutoff line were admitted, if they had not been already, by a procedure that started with the most qualified academically, moving down the list until the minority applicants to be admitted made up at least a certain percentage of the final number of students to be admitted (10 percent, as I recall). The rest were admitted by their place on the academic list.

Pomona College is a private institution, but some state colleges and universities have adopted policies that are similar in important respects. At the University of California at Los Angeles in the 1970s, I became familiar with a significantly different kind of affirmative action regarding graduate student admissions and faculty hiring and promotion. The emphasis here was on positive efforts to seek out and encourage qualified minority applicants, for example, through recruitment letters, calls, and campus visits. Special funds were allocated to create new faculty positions for qualified minority candidates, and special fellowships were made available to release minority faculty from some teaching duties prior to tenure. Teaching and research interests in race and gender problems were officially recognized as relevant to hiring and promotion decisions in certain departments, provided the usual academic standards were maintained. Guidelines and watchdog committees were established to require departments to prove that each time they hired a nonminority male they did so only after a thorough search for and examination of minority and female candidates. Since decisions to hire and promote were still determined by the judgments of diverse individuals, I suspect that some deans, department heads, and voting faculty members carried affirmative action beyond the guidelines, some countered this effect by negative bias, and some simply refused to deviate from what they perceived as "color-blind" and "sex-blind" criteria.

II

Is affirmative action *necessarily* a morally illegitimate form of "reverse discrimination" that *violates* the rights of white male applicants?

The question here is not whether some particular affirmative action program is illegitimate, for example, because it uses quotas or causes the deliberate hiring of less qualified teachers; rather, the question is whether making gender and race a relevant category in university policy is *in itself* unjust. If so, we need not go further with our discussion of the message of affirmative action and its advantages and disadvantages: for however important the need is to communicate and promote social benefits, we should not do so by unjust means.

Some think that the injustice of all affirmative action programs is obvious or easily demonstrated. Two facile but confused arguments seem to have an especially popular appeal. The first goes this way: "Affirmative action, by definition, gives preferential treatment to minorities and women. This is discrimination in their favor and against nonminority males. All discrimination by public institutions is unjust, no matter whether it is the old kind or the newer 'reverse discrimination.' So all affirmative action programs in public institutions are unjust."

This deceptively simple argument, of course, trades on an ambiguity. In one sense, to "discriminate" means to "make a distinction," to pay attention to a difference. In this evaluatively neutral sense, of course, affirmative action programs do discriminate. But public institutions must, and justifiably do, "discriminate" in this sense, for example, between citizens and noncitizens, freshmen and seniors, the talented and the retarded, and those who pay their bills and those who do not. Whether it is unjust to note and make use of a certain distinction in a given context depends upon many factors: the nature of the institution, the relevant rights of the parties involved, the purposes and effects of making that distinction, and so on.

193

All this would be obvious except for the fact that the word "discrimination" is also used in a pejorative sense, meaning (roughly) "making use of a distinction in an unjust or illegitimate way." To discriminate in this sense is obviously wrong, but now it remains an open question whether the use of gender and race distinctions in affirmative action programs is really "discrimination" in this sense. The simplistic argument uses the evaluatively neutral sense of "discrimination" to show that affirmative action discriminates; it then shifts to the pejorative sense when it asserts that discrimination is always wrong. Although one may, in the end, *conclude* that all public use of racial and gender distinctions is unjust, to do so requires more of an *argument* than the simple one (just given) that merely exploits an ambiguity of the word "discrimination."

A slightly more sophisticated argument runs as follows: "Affirmative action programs give special benefits to certain individuals 'simply because they are women or blacks.' But one's color and gender are morally irrelevant features of a person. It is unjust for public institutions to give special benefits to individuals solely because they happen to have certain morally irrelevant characteristics. Hence affirmative action programs are always unjust."

A special twist is often added to this argument, as follows: "What was wrong with Jim Crow laws, denial of the vote to women and blacks, and segregation in schools and public facilities was just the fact that such practices treated people differently simply because they happened to have certain morally irrelevant characteristics. Affirmative action programs, however well-intentioned, are doing exactly the same thing. So they are wrong for the same reason."

Now people who argue in this way may well be trying to express something important, which should not be dismissed; but, as it stands, the argument is confused, unfair, and historically inaccurate. The confusion and unfairness lie in the misleading use of the expression "*simply* because they are women or blacks." It is true that typical affirmative action programs, such as those I described earlier, use the categories of "black" (or "minority") and "female" as an instrumental part of a complex policy. This does not mean, however, that the fundamental reason, purpose, or justification of the policy is nothing more than "this individual is black (or female)." To say that someone favors a person "*simply because* that person is black (or female)" implies that there is no further reason, purpose, or justification, as if one merely had an utterly arbitrary preference for dark skin as opposed to light, or female anatomy over male anatomy. But no serious advocate of affirmative action thinks the program is justified by such personal preferences. On the contrary, advocates argue that, given our historical situation, quite general principles of justice or utility justify the temporary classificatory use of race and gender. That being black or white, male or female, does not in itself make anyone morally better or more deserving is acknowledged on all sides.

Thus even if one should conclude that the attempts to justify affirmative action fail, the fair and clear way to express this conclusion would be to say that the grounds that have been offered for using gender and race categories as affirmative action programs do are unconvincing. Unlike the rhetorical claim that they favor individuals "merely because they are black (or female)," this does not insinuate unfairly that the programs were instituted for no reason other than personal taste. And, of course, those of us who believe that there are good reasons for affirmative action policies, with their sorting by gender and race, have even more reason to reject the misleading and insulting description that we advocate special treatment for individuals *merely because* they are blacks or women.

The argument we have been considering is objectionable in another way as well. As Richard Wasserstrom points out, the moral wrongs against blacks and women in the past were not wrong just because people were classified and treated differently according to the morally irrelevant features of gender and color.[2] There was this sort of arbitrary treatment, of course, but the main problem was not that women and blacks were treated differently *somehow* but that they were *treated as no human being should be treated.* Segregation, for example, was in practice not merely a pointless sorting of individuals, like separating people according to the number of letters in their names. It was a way of expressing and perpetuating white contempt for blacks and preserving social structures that kept blacks from taking full advantage of their basic human rights. The mistreatment of women was not merely that they were arbitrarily selected for the more burdensome but still legitimate social roles. It was, in large part, that the practices expressed an attitude towards women that subtly undermined their chances of making use of even the limited opportunities they had. The proper conclusion, then, is not that any current program that makes use of race and gender categories is simply committing the same old wrongs in reverse. The worst wrongs of the past went far beyond merely the arbitrary use of these categories; moreover, it has yet to be established that the new use of these categories in affirmative action is in fact arbitrary (like the old use). An arbitrary category is one used without good justification, and the charge that affirmative action programs use race and gender categories unjustifiably is just what is at issue, not something we can assume at the start.

Another argument to show that affirmative action is unjust is that it violates the rights of white males who apply for admission or jobs in the university. This is a complex issue, discussed at length in journals and before the Supreme Court; rather than review that debate, I will just mention a few of the considerations that lead me to think that, though certain *types* of affirmative action may violate the rights of white males, appropriately designed affirmative action programs do not.

2 See Richard Wasserstrom, "Racism and Sexism" and "Preferential Treatment" in his *Philosophy and Social Issues* (Notre Dame, Ind.: University of Notre Dame Press, 1980), pp. 11–21, 51–82.

First, no individual, white male or otherwise, has an absolute right to a place in a public university, that is, a right independent of complex considerations of the functions of the university, the reasonable expectations of actual and potential taxpayers and other supporters, the number of places available, the relative merits of other candidates, and so on. What rights does an applicant have? Few would dispute that each individual has a right to "formal justice."[3] That is, one should not be arbitrarily denied a place to which one is entitled under the existing and publicly declared rules and regulations. Any university must have rules concerning residency, prior education, submission of application forms, taking of entrance tests, and the like, as well as more substantive standards and policies for selecting among those who satisfy these minimal requirements. Formal justice requires that individual administrators do not deviate from the preestablished rules and standards currently in effect, whether from personal preference or high-minded social ideals. But this is not to say that old policies cannot reasonably be changed. One does not, for example, necessarily have a right to be treated by the rules and standards in force when one was born or when one first thought about going to college.

Formal justice is quite limited, however, for it is compatible with substantively unjust rules and standards. In addition to formal justice, each individual citizen has a right that the rules and standards of the university to which he/she applies be made (and when necessary changed) only for good reasons, consistent with the purposes of the university and the ideals of justice and basic human equality. This is a more stringent standard; and it does establish a *presumption* against using race and gender categories in policies which affect the distribution of opportunities, such as jobs and student status. This is because race and gender, like being tall and muscular, are not *in themselves* morally relevant characteristics. Considered in isolation from their connections with other matters, they do not make anyone more, or less, deserving of anything. As the Supreme Court says, they are classifications that are "suspect."[4] But this does not mean that it is always unjust to use them, but only that their use stands in need of justification. What counts as a justification depends crucially upon our assessment of the legitimate purposes of the institution that uses the categories.

No one denies that the education of citizens and the pursuit of knowledge are central among the purposes of public universities. But, when resources are limited, decisions must be made as to what knowledge is to be pursued and who is to be offered education in each institution. Here we must consider the role of a

---

3   William K. Frankena, "The Concept of Social Justice", in *Social Justice* edited by Richard B. Brandt (Englewood Cliffs, N.J.: Prentice-Hall Inc., 1962), pp. 8–9. Henry Sidgwick, *Methods of Ethics*, 7th ed. (London: The Macmillan Company Ltd., 1907), pp. 379, 386f. John Rawls, *A Theory of Justice* (Cambridge: Harvard University Press, 1971), pp. 56–60, 180, 235–39, 504f.
4   Regents of the University of California v. Allan Bakke, 98 S.Ct. 2733, 46 L.W. 4896 (1978). Reprinted in Wasserstrom, ed., *Today's Moral Issues,* second edition. (New York: Macmillan Publishing Co., 1975), pp. 149–207. (See especially pp. 156–57.)

university as one of a complex network of public institutions in a country committed to democratic ideals and faced with deep social problems. It has never been the practice of universities to disregard their social roles in the name of "purely academic" concerns; given current social problems, few would morally defend such disregard now. The more serious issue is not whether this role should be considered but rather whether the role is better served by affirmative action or by admission and hiring policies that admit only classification by test scores, grades, and past achievements. To decide this, we must look more closely at the purposes that affirmative action is supposed to serve.

III

Some arguments for affirmative action look exclusively to its future benefits. The idea is that what has happened in the past is not in itself relevant to what we should do; at most it provides clues as to what acts and policies are likely to bring about the best future. The philosophical tradition associated with this approach is utilitarianism, which declares that the morally right act is whatever produces the best consequences. Traditionally, utilitarianism evaluated consequences in terms of happiness and unhappiness, but the anticipated consequences of affirmative action are often described more specifically. For example, some argue that affirmative action will ease racial tensions, prevent riots, improve services in minority neighborhoods, reduce unemployment, remove inequities in income distribution, eliminate racial and sexual prejudice, and enhance the self-esteem of blacks and women. Some have called attention to the fact that women and minorities provide alternative perspectives on history, literature, philosophy, and politics, and that this has beneficial effects for both education and research.

These are important considerations, not irrelevant to the larger responsibilities of universities. For several reasons, however, I think it is a mistake for advocates of affirmative action to rest their case exclusively on such forward-looking arguments. First, critics raise reasonable doubts about whether affirmative action is necessary to achieve these admirable results. Thomas Sowell, a noted conservative economist, argues that a free-market economy can achieve the same results more efficiently; even if affirmative action has beneficial results (which he denies), it is not necessary for the purpose.[5] Though Sowell's position can be contested, the controversy itself tends to weaken confidence in the entirely forward-looking defense of affirmative action.

An even more obvious reason why affirmative action advocates should explore other types of defense is that the exclusively forward-looking approach must give

---

5 Thomas Sowell, *Race and Economics* (New York: David McKay Co., 1975), chapter 6. *Markets and Minorities* (New York: Basic Books, Inc., 1981), pp. 114–15.

equal consideration to possible negative consequences of affirmative action. It may be, for example, that affirmative action will temporarily increase racial tensions, especially if its message is misunderstood. Even legitimate use of race and sex categories may encourage others to abuse the categories for unjust purposes. If applied without sensitive regard to the educational and research purposes of the university, affirmative action might severely undermine its efforts to fulfill these primary responsibilities. *If* affirmative action programs were to lower academic standards for blacks and women, they would run the risk of damaging the respect that highly qualified blacks and women have earned, by leading others to suspect that these highly qualified people lack the merits of white males in the same positions. This could also be damaging to the self-respect of those who accept affirmative action positions. Even programs that disavow "lower standards" unfortunately arouse the suspicion that they don't really do so, and this by itself can cause problems. Although I believe that well-designed affirmative action programs can minimize these negative effects, the fact that they are a risk is a reason for not resting the case for affirmative action on a delicate balance of costs and benefits.

Reflection on the *message* of affirmative action also leads me to move beyond entirely forward-looking arguments. For if the sole purpose is to bring about a brighter future, then we give the wrong message to both the white males who are rejected and to the women and blacks who are benefited. To the latter what we say, in effect, is this: "Never mind how you have been treated. Forget about the fact that your race or sex has in the past been actively excluded and discouraged, and that you yourself may have had handicaps due to prejudice. Our sole concern is to bring about certain good results in the future, and giving you a break happens to be a useful means for doing this. Don't think this is a recognition of your rights as an individual or your disadvantages as a member of a group. Nor does it mean that we have confidence in your abilities. We would do the same for those who are privileged and academically inferior if it would have the same socially beneficial results."

To the white male who would have had a university position but for affirmative action, the exclusively forward-looking approach says: "We deny you the place you otherwise would have had simply as a means to produce certain socially desirable outcomes. We have not judged that others are more deserving, or have a right, to the place we are giving them instead of you. Past racism and sexism are irrelevant. The point is just that the sacrifice of your concerns is a useful means to the larger end of the future welfare of others."

This, I think, is the wrong message to give, and it is unnecessary. The proper alternative, however, is not to ignore the possible future benefits of affirmative action but rather to take them into account as a part of a larger picture.

A radically different strategy for justifying affirmative action is to rely on backward-looking arguments. Such arguments call our attention to certain events in the past and assert that *because* these past events occurred, we have certain duties now. The modern philosopher who most influentially endorsed such arguments was W. D. Ross.[6] He argued that there are duties of fidelity, justice, gratitude, and reparation that have a moral force independent of any tendency these may have to promote good consequences. The fact that you have made a promise, for example, gives you a strong moral reason to do what you promised, whether or not, on balance, doing so will have more beneficial consequences. The Rossian principle that is often invoked in affirmative action debates is a principle of reparation. This says that those who wrongfully injure others have a (prima facie) duty to apologize and make restitution. Those who have wronged others owe reparation.

James Foreman dramatically expressed this idea in New York in 1969 when he presented "The Black Manifesto," which demanded five hundred million dollars in reparation to American blacks from white churches and synagogues.[7] Such organizations, the Manifesto contends, contributed to our history of slavery and racial injustice, and as a result they incurred a debt to the black community that still suffers from its effects. Objections were immediately raised: for example, both slaves and slave-owners are no longer alive, not every American white is guilty of racial oppression; and not every black in America was a victim of slavery and its aftermath.

Bernard Boxill, author of *Blacks and Social Justice*, developed a more sophisticated version of the backward-looking argument with a view to meeting these objections.[8] Let us admit, he says, that both the perpetrators and the primary victims of slavery are gone, and let us not insist that contemporary whites are guilty of perpetrating further injustices. Some do, and some do not, and public administrators cannot be expected to sort out the guilty from the nonguilty. However, reparation, or at least some "compensation,"[9] is still owed because contemporary whites have reaped the profits of past injustice to blacks. He asks

6   W. D. Ross, *The Right and the Good* (Oxford: The Clarendon Press, 1930).

7   James Foreman was at the time director of international affairs for S.N.C.C. (Student Nonviolent Coordinating Committee). The "Black Manifesto" stems from an economic development conference sponsored by the Interreligious Foundation for Community Organizations, April 26, 1969, and presented by Foreman at the New York Interdominational Riverside Church on May 4, 1969. Later the demand was raised to three billion dollars. See Robert S. Lecky and H. Elliot Wright, *Black Manifesto*. (New York: Sheed and Ward Publishers, 1969), pp. vii and 114–26.

8   Bernard Boxill, "The Morality of Reparation," *Social Theory and Practice*, Vol. 2, no. 1., (1972), pp. 113–22, and *Blacks and Social Justice*, chapter 7.

9   In the article cited in footnote 8 Boxill calls what is owed "reparation," but in the book he calls it "compensation." The latter term, preferred by many, is used more broadly to cover not only restitution for wrongdoing but also "making up" for deficiencies and losses that are not anyone's fault (e.g., naturally caused physical handicaps, damages unavoidably resulting from legitimate and necessary activities). We could describe the backward-looking arguments presented here as demands for "compensation" rather than "reparation," so long as we keep in mind that the compensation is supposed to be due as the morally appropriate response to past wrongdoing.

us to consider the analogy with a stolen bicycle. Suppose my parent stole your parent's bicycle some time ago, both have since died, and I "inherited" the bike from my parent, the thief. Though I may be innocent of any wrongdoing (so far), I am in possession of stolen goods rightfully belonging to you, the person who would have inherited the bike if it had not been stolen. For me to keep the bike and declare that I owe you nothing would be wrong, even if I was not the cause of your being deprived. By analogy, present-day whites owe reparations to contemporary blacks, not because they are themselves guilty of causing the disadvantages of blacks, but because they are in possession of advantages that fell to them as a result of the gross injustices of their ancestors. Special advantages continue to fall even to innocent whites because of the ongoing prejudice of their white neighbors.

Although it raises many questions, this line of argument acknowledges some important points missing in most exclusively forward-looking arguments: for example, it stresses the (intrinsic) relevance of past injustice and it calls attention to the rights and current disadvantages of blacks (in contrast with future benefits for others). When developed as an argument for affirmative action, it does not accuse all white males of prejudice and wrongdoing but, at the same time, it sees the fundamental value as justice. As a result, it avoids giving the message to both rejected white males and reluctant affirmative action applicants that they are "mere means" to a social goal that is largely independent of their rights and interests as individuals.

There are, however, serious problems in trying to justify affirmative action by this backward-looking argument, especially if it is treated as the exclusive or central argument. Degrees of being advantaged and disadvantaged are notoriously hard to measure. New immigrants have not shared our history of past injustices, and so the argument may not apply to them in any straightforward way. The argument appeals to controversial ideas about property rights, inheritance, and group responsibilities. Some argue that affirmative action tends to benefit the least disadvantaged blacks and women; though this does not mean that they are owed nothing, their claims would seem to have lower priority than the needs of the most disadvantaged. Some highly qualified blacks and women object that affirmative action is damaging to their reputations and self-esteem, whereas the reparation argument seems to assume that it is a welcome benefit to all blacks and women.

If we focus on the message that the backward-looking argument sends, there are also some potential problems. Though rightly acknowledging past injustice, the argument (by itself) seems to convey the message that racial and sexual oppression consisted primarily in the loss of tangible goods, or the deprivation of specific rights and opportunities, that can be "paid back" in kind. The background idea, which goes back at least to Aristotle, is that persons wrongfully deprived of their "due" can justly demand an "equivalent" to what they have lost.[10] But, while specific deprivations were an important part of our racist and sexist past, they are far from the whole story. Among the worst wrongs then, as now, were humiliations and contemptuous treatment of a type that cannot, strictly, be "paid back." The problem was, and is, not just that specific rights and advantages were denied, but that prejudicial attitudes damaged self-esteem, undermined motivations, limited realistic options, and made even "officially open" opportunities seem undesirable. Racism and sexism were (and are), *insults,* not merely tangible *injuries.*[11] These are not the sort of thing that can be adequately measured and repaid with equivalents. The trouble with treating insulting racist and sexist practices on a pure reparation model is not merely the practical difficulty of identifying the offenders, determining the degree of guilt, assessing the amount of payment due, *etc.* It is also that penalty payments and compensation for lost benefits are not the only, or primary, moral responses that are called for. When affirmative action is defended exclusively by analogy with reparation, it tends to express the misleading message that the evils of racism and sexism are all tangible losses that can be "paid off"; by being silent on the insulting nature of racism and sexism, it tends to add insult to insult.

The message suggested by the reparation argument, by itself, also seems objectionable because it conveys the idea that higher education, teaching, and doing research are mainly benefits awarded in response to self-centered demands. The underlying picture too easily suggested is that applicants are a group of self-interested, bickering people, each grasping for limited "goodies" and insisting on a right to them. When a university grants an opportunity through affirmative action, its message would seem to be this: "We concede that you have a valid claim to this benefit, and we yield to your demand, though this is not to suggest that we have confidence in your abilities or any desire to have you here." This invitation seems too concessionary, the atmosphere too adversarial, and the emphasis too much on the benefits rather than the responsibilities of being a part of the university.

IV

Here I want to digress from the explicit consideration of affirmative action in order to consider more abstract philosophical questions about the ways we evaluate acts and policies. At the risk of oversimplifying, I want to contrast some assumptions that have, until recently, been dominant in ethical theory with alternatives suggested by contemporary philosophers who emphasize historical

10 Aristotle, *Nicomachean Ethics,* translated by J. A. K. Thomson (Baltimore, Md.: Penguin Books, Inc., 1955), Book V, especially pp. 143–55.
11 See Boxill, *Blacks and Social Justice,* pp. 132ff, and Ronald Dworkin, "Reverse Discrimination" in *Taking Rights Seriously* (Cambridge, Mass.: Harvard University Press, 1978), pp. 231ff.

context, narrative unity, and community values.[12] Although these alternatives, in my opinion, have not yet been adequately developed, there seem to be at least four distinguishable themes worth considering.

First, when we reflect on what we deeply value, we find that we care not merely about the present moment and each future moment in isolation but also about how our past, present, and future cohere or fit together into a life and a piece of history. Some of our values, we might say, are cross-time wholes, with past, present, and future parts united in certain ways. Thus, for example, the commitments I have made, the projects I have begun, what I have shared with those I love, the injuries I have caused, and the hopes I have encouraged importantly affect both whether I am satisfied with my present and how I want the future to go.

Second, in reflecting on stretches of our lives and histories, we frequently use evaluative concepts drawn more from narrative literature than from accounting. Thus, for example, we think of our lives as having significant beginnings, crises, turning points, dramatic tension, character development, climaxes, resolutions, comic interludes, tragic disruptions, and eventually fitting (or unfitting) endings. The value of any moment often depends on what came before and what we anticipate to follow. And because our lives are intertwined with others in a common history, we also care about how our moments cohere with others' life stories. The past is seen as more than a time of accumulated debts and assets, and the future is valued as more than an opportunity for reinvesting and cashing in assets.

Third, evaluation must take into account one's particular historical context, including one's cultural, national, and ethnic traditions, and the actual individuals in one's life. Sometimes this point is exaggerated, I think, to suggest a dubious cultural relativism or "particularism" in ethics: for example, the thesis that what is valuable for a person is defined by the person's culture or that evaluations imply no general reasons beyond particular judgments, such as "That's our way" and "John is my son."[13] But, construed modestly as a practical or epistemological point, it seems obvious enough, on reflection, that we should take into account the historical context of our acts and that we are often in a better position to judge what is appropriate in particular cases than we are to

---

12   See, for example, Alasdair MacIntyre, *After Virtue* (Notre Dame, Ind.: Notre Dame University Press, 1981). Similar themes are found in Carol Gilligan's *In A Different Voice* (Cambridge: Harvard University Press, 1982) and in Lawrence Blum, *Friendship, Altruism and Morality* (Boston: Routledge and Kegan Paul, 1980).

13   Regarding cultural and moral relativism see, for example, David B. Wong, *Moral Relativity* (Berkeley and Los Angeles: University of California Press, 1984), with an excellent bibliography, and Richard B. Brandt, *Ethical Theory* (Englewood Cliffs, N.J.: Prentice-Hall, Inc., 1959), pp. 271–94. Versions of particularism are presented in Andrew Oldenquist, "Loyalties," *The Journal of Philosophy* 79 (1982), pp. 173–93, Lawrence Blum, *Friendship, Altruism and Morality* (Boston: Routledge and Kegan Paul, 1980) and Bernard Williams, "Persons, Character and Morality" in *Moral Luck* (New York: Cambridge University Press, 1981), pp. 1–9.

articulate universally valid premises supporting the judgment. We can sometimes be reasonably confident about what is right in a particular context without being sure about whether or not there are relevant differences blocking the same judgment in seemingly similar but less familiar contexts. We know, as a truism, that the same judgment applies if there are no relevant differences, but in practice the particular judgment may be more evident than the exact scope of the moral generalizations that hold across many cases. Thus, although giving reasons for our judgments in particular contexts commits us to acknowledging their potential relevance in other contexts, moral judgment cannot be aptly represented simply as deducing specific conclusions from clear and evident general principles.

Fourth, when we evaluate particular acts and policies as parts of lives and histories, what is often most important is the value of the whole, which cannot always be determined by "summing up" the values of the parts. Lives, histories, and interpersonal relations over time are what G. E. Moore called "organic unities," i.e., wholes the value of which is not necessarily the sum of the values of the parts.[14] The point is here not merely the obvious practical limitation that we cannot measure and quantify values in this area. More fundamentally, the idea is that it would be a mistake even to try to evaluate certain unities by assessing different parts in isolation from one another, then adding up all their values. Suppose, for example, a woman with terminal cancer considered two quite different ways of spending her last days. One way, perhaps taking a world cruise, might seem best when evaluated in terms of the quality of each future moment, in isolation from her past and her present ties; but another way, perhaps seeking closure in projects and with estranged family members, might seem more valuable when seen as a part of her whole life.

Taken together, these ideas cast doubt on both the exclusively forward-looking method of assessment and the standard backward-looking alternative. Consequentialism, or the exclusively forward-looking method, attempts to determine what ought to be done at present by fixing attention entirely on future results. To be sure, any sensible consequentialist will consult the past for lessons and clues helpful in predicting future outcomes: e.g., recalling that you offended someone yesterday may enable you to predict that the person will be cool to you tomorrow unless you apologize. But beyond this, consequentialists have no concern with the past, for their "bottom line" is always "what happens from now on," evaluated independently of the earlier chapters of our lives and histories. For the consequentialist, assessing a life or history from a narrative perspective becomes impossible, or at least bizarre, as what must be evaluated at each shifting moment is "the story from now on" independently of what has already been written.[15]

---

14 G. E. Moore, *Principia Ethica* (Cambridge: Cambridge University Press, 1912), pp. 27f.

15 That is, the evaluation is independent of the past in the sense that the past makes no intrinsic difference to the final judgment and the future is not evaluated as a part of a temporal whole

The standard Rossian alternative to this exclusively forward-looking perspective is to introduce certain *(prima facie) duties* to respond to certain past events in specified ways, e.g., pay debts, keep promises, pay reparation for injuries. These duties are supposed to be self-evident and universal (though *prima facie*), and they do not hold because they tend to promote anything good or valuable. Apart from aspects of the acts mentioned in the principles (e.g., fulfilling a promise, returning favors, not injuring, etc.), details of historical and personal context are considered irrelevant.

By contrast, the narrative perspective sketched above considers the past as an integral part of the valued unities that we aim to bring about, not merely as a source of duties. If one has negligently wronged another, Ross regards this past event as generating a duty to pay reparations even if doing so will result in nothing good. But from the narrative perspective, the past becomes relevant in a further way. One may say, for example, that the *whole* consisting of your life and your relationship with that person from the time of the injury into the future will be a better thing if you acknowledge the wrong and make efforts to restore what you have damaged. For Ross, the duty is generated by the past and unrelated to bringing about anything good; from the narrative perspective, however, the requirement is just what is required to bring about a valuable connected whole with past, present, and future parts, the best way to complete a chapter, so to speak, in two intersecting life stories.

So far, neither the Rossian nor the narrative account has told us much about the ultimate reasons for their evaluations, but they reveal different ways to consider the matter. The Rossian asks us to judge particular cases in the light of "self-evident" general principles asserting that certain past events tend to generate present (or future) duties. The alternative perspective calls for examining lives and relationships, over time, in context, as organic unities evaluated (partly) in narrative terms.

To illustrate, consider two persons, John and Mary, who value being in a relationship of mutual trust and respect with one another. Each trusts and respects the other, but that is not all. Each also values having the trust and respect of the other; moreover, each values the fact that the other values having his trust and respect.[16] And they value the fact that this all is known and mutually acknowledged.

Now suppose that other people have been abusive and insulting to Mary, and that John is worried that Mary may take things he has said and done as similarly insulting, even though he does not think that he consciously meant them this

---

including the past. As noted, however, consequentialists will still look to the past for lessons and clues about how to bring about the best future.

16 For an interesting illustration of reciprocal desires (e.g., A wanting B, B wanting A, A wanting B to want A, B wanting A to want B, A wanting B to want A to want B, etc.), see Thomas Nagel, "Sexual Perversion," *The Journal of Philosophy*, 66 (1969): 5–17.

way. Although he is worried, Mary does not seem to suspect him; and he fears that if he raises the issue he may only make matters worse, creating suspicions she did not have or focusing on doubts that he cannot allay. Perhaps, he thinks, their future relationship would be better served if he just remained silent, hoping that the trouble, if any, will fade in time. If so, consequentialist thinking would recommend silence. Acknowledging this, he might nonetheless feel that duties of friendship and fidelity demand that he raise the issue, regardless of whether or not the result will be worse. Then he would be thinking as a Rossian.

But, instead, he might look at the problem from an alternative perspective, asking himself what response best affirms and contributes to the sort of ongoing relationship he has and wants to continue with Mary. Given their history together, it is important to him to do his part towards restoring the relationship if it indeed has been marred by perceived insults or suspicions. To be sure, he wants *future* relations of mutual trust and respect, but not at any price and not by just any means. Their history together is not irrelevant, for what he values is not merely a future of a certain kind but that their relationship over time be of the sort he values. He values an ongoing history of mutual trust and respect that *calls for* an explicit response in this current situation, not merely as a means to a brighter future but as a present affirmation of what they value together. Even if unsure which course will be best for the future, he may be reasonably confident that the act that best expresses his respect and trust (and his valuing hers, *etc.*) is to confront the problem, express his regrets, reaffirm his respect, ask for her trust, be patient with her doubts, and welcome an open dialogue. If the insults were deep and it is not entirely clear whether or not he really associated himself with them, then mere words may not be enough to convey the message or even to assure himself of his own sincerity. Positive efforts, even at considerable cost, may be needed to express appropriately and convincingly what needs to be said. How the next chapter unfolds is not entirely up to him, and he would not be respectful if he presumed otherwise by trying to manipulate the best future unilaterally.

The example concerns only two persons and their personal values, but it illustrates a perspective that one can also take regarding moral problems involving many persons.

V

Turning back to our main subject, I suggest that some of the values that give affirmative action its point are best seen as cross-time values that fall outside the exclusively forward-looking and backward-looking perspectives. They include having a history of racial and gender relations governed, so far as possible, by the ideals of mutual respect, trust, and fair opportunity for all.

Our national history provides a context of increasing recognition and broader interpretation of the democratic ideal of the equal dignity of all human beings, an ideal that has been flagrantly abused from the outset, partially affirmed in the bloody Civil War, and increasingly extended in the civil rights movement, but is still far from being fully respected. More specifically, blacks and women were systematically treated in an unfair and demeaning way by public institutions, including universities, until quite recently, and few could confidently claim to have rooted out racism and sexism even now.[17] The historical context is not what grounds or legitimates democratic values, but it is the background of the current problem, the sometimes admirable and often ugly way the chapters up until now have been written.

Consider first the social ideal of mutual respect and trust among citizens. The problem of implementing this in the current context is different from the problem in the two-person example previously discussed, for the history of our racial and gender relations is obviously not an idyllic story of mutual respect and trust momentarily interrupted by a crisis. Even so, the question to ask is not merely, "What will promote respectful and trusting racial and gender relations in future generations?" but rather, "Given our checkered past, how can we appropriately express the social value of mutual respect and trust that we want, so far as possible, to characterize our history?" We cannot change our racist and sexist past, but we also cannot express full respect for those present individuals who live in its aftermath if we ignore it. What is called for is not merely repayment of tangible debts incurred by past injuries, but also a message to counter the deep insult inherent in racism and sexism.

Recognizing that problems of this kind are not amenable to easy solutions deduced from self-evident moral generalizations, we may find it helpful instead to reflect on an analogy. Suppose you return to the hometown you left in childhood, remembering with pride its Fourth of July speeches about the values of community, equality, and fairness for all. You discover, however, that the community was never as perfect as you thought. In fact, for years – until quite recently – certain families, who had been disdainfully labeled "the Barefeet," had not only been shunned by most folk but had also been quietly terrorized by a few well-placed citizens. The Barefeet had been arrested on false charges, beaten, raped, and blackmailed into silent submission. The majority, perhaps, would never have done these things, but their contempt for the Barefeet was such that most would have regarded these crimes less important than if they had been done to insiders. Fortunately, the worst offenders have died, and so have the victims of the most outrageous crimes. Majority attitudes have changed somewhat, though often merely from open contempt to passive disregard. Some new citizens

---

17   Racism and sexism present significantly different problems, but I shall not try to analyze the differences here. For the most part, and especially in the analogy to follow, my primary focus is on racism, but the relevance of the general type of moral thinking considered here to the problems of sexism should nonetheless be evident.

have come to town, and a few of the Barefeet (now more politely called "Cross-towners") have managed to become successful. Nonetheless, the older Cross-towners are still fearful and resigned, and the younger generation is openly resentful and distrustful when officials proclaim a new commitment to democratic ideals. It is no surprise, then, that few Cross-towners take full advantage of available opportunities, and that the two groups tend to isolate themselves from each other.

Now suppose you, as one of the majority, could persuade the rest to give a message to the Cross-towners, a message appropriate to the majority's professed value of being a community committed to mutual respect and trust. What would you propose? And, assuming that doing so would violate no one's rights, what means would you think best to convey that message sincerely and effectively? Some would no doubt suggest simply forgetting about the past and hoping that time will heal the wounds. But, whether effective in the future or not, this plan fails to express full respect for the Cross-towners now. Others might suggest a more legalistic approach, trying to determine exactly who has been disadvantaged, the degree of loss, which citizens are most responsible, etc., in order to pay off the debt. But this, taken by itself, faces the sorts of disadvantages we have already considered. If, instead, the value of mutual respect and trust is the governing ideal, the appropriate message would be to acknowledge and deplore the past openly, to affirm a commitment to promote mutual respect and trust in the future, to welcome full interchange and participation with the Cross-towners, and to urge them to undertake the risks of overcoming their understandable suspicions by joining in a common effort to work towards fulfilling the ideal. This would address not merely the injury but also the insult implicit in the town's history.

The more difficult question, however, is how to express such a message effectively and with evident sincerity in an atmosphere already poisoned by the past. Mere words will be taken as mere words, and may in fact turn out to be just that. What is needed is more positive action – concrete steps to prove commitment, to resist backsliding, and to overcome reluctance on both sides. The sort of affirmative action taken in the U.C.L.A. program described in Section I seems especially appropriate for this purpose. Here the emphasis was on outreach, increasing awareness of opportunities, accountability and proof of fairness in procedures, and allocating resources (fellowships, release time, etc.) in a way that showed trust that, if given an adequate chance, those formerly excluded would enrich the university by fully appropriate standards. These seem the most natural way to give force to the message, though arguably other methods may serve the purpose as well.

There is another historical value that is also relevant and seems to favor even more radical steps in affirmative action. The issue is too complex to address adequately here, but it should at least be mentioned. What I have in mind might be called "fair opportunity." That is, implicit in our democratic ideals is the idea that our public institutions should be so arranged that they afford to individuals, over time, more or less equal opportunities to develop and make use of their natural talents and to participate and contribute to those institutions. The idea is hard to make precise, but it clearly does not mean that all should have equal chances to have a desirable position, regardless of effort and natural aptitude. The physically handicapped and the mentally retarded suffer from natural misfortunes, and, though society should not ignore them, they cannot expect standards to be rigged to ensure the former equal odds at making the basketball team or the latter equal odds of being appointed to the faculty. Similarly, those who choose not to make the effort to develop their capacities have no right to expect public institutions to include them in a pool from which candidates are selected by lot. But when persons have been disadvantaged by social injustice, having had their initial chances diminished by the network of public institutions themselves, then positive steps are needed to equalize their opportunities over time.

This ideal calls for something more than efforts to ensure that future generations do not suffer from the same disadvantage, for those efforts fail to respond to the unfairness to the present individuals. But, for obvious practical reasons, legal efforts to remedy precisely identifiable disadvantages incurred by individuals are bound to be quite inadequate to address the many subtle losses of opportunity caused by past institutional racism and sexism. Since no perfect solution is possible, we need to choose between this inadequate response and policies that address the problem in a less fine-grained way. Affirmative action programs that employ a working presumption that women and minorities generally have had their opportunities restricted to some degree by institutional racism and sexism will admittedly risk compensating a few who have actually had, on balance, as much opportunity as white males. But the practical alternatives, it seems, are to accept this risk or to refuse to respond at all to the innumerable ways that institutional racism and sexism have undermined opportunities too subtly for the courts to remedy.

Given these options, what would be the message of choosing to limit redress to precisely identifiable losses? This would say, in effect, to women and minorities, "We cannot find a way to ensure *precisely* that each talented and hard-working person has an equal opportunity over time; and, given our options, we count it more important to see that *none* of you women and minorities are overcompensated than to try to see that the *majority* of you have more nearly equal opportunities over your lifetime. Your grievances are too subtle and difficult to measure, and your group may be harboring some who were not disadvantaged. We would rather let the majority of white males enjoy the advantages of their unfair headstart than to risk compensating one of you who does not deserve it."

Now *if* it had been established on antecedent grounds that the affirmative action measures in question would violate the *rights* of white male applicants, then one could argue that these coarse-grained efforts to honor the ideal of fair opportunity are illegitimate. But that premise, I think, has not been established. Affirmative action programs would violate the rights of white males only if, all things considered, their guidelines temporarily favoring women and minorities were arbitrary, not serving the legitimate social role of universities or fulfilling the ideals of fairness and respect for all. The considerations offered here, however, point to the conclusion that some affirmative action programs, even those involving a degree of preferential treatment, are legitimated by ideals of mutual respect, trust, and fair opportunity.

All this, I know, is too brief, loose, and incomplete, but, I hope, it is worth considering nonetheless. The main suggestion is that, ideally, a central purpose of affirmative action would be to communicate a much needed message sincerely and effectively. The message is called for not just as a means to future good relations or a dutiful payment of a debt incurred by our past. It is called for by the ideal of being related to other human beings, over time, so that our histories and biographies reflect the responses of those who deeply care about fair opportunity, mutual trust, and respect for all.

If so, what should public universities try to say to those offered opportunities through affirmative action? Perhaps something like this: "Whether we individually are among the guilty or not, we acknowledge that you have been wronged – if not by specific injuries which could be named and repaid, at least by the humiliating and debilitating attitudes prevalent in our country and our institutions. We deplore and denounce these attitudes and the wrongs that spring from them. We acknowledge that, so far, most of you have had your opportunities in life diminished by the effects of these attitudes, and we want no one's prospects to be diminished by injustice. We recognize your understandable grounds for suspicion and mistrust when we express these high-minded sentiments, and we want not only to ask respectfully for your trust but also to give concrete evidence of our sincerity. We welcome you respectfully into the university community and ask you to take a full share of the responsibilities as well as the benefits. By creating special opportunities, we recognize the disadvantages you have probably suffered, but we show our respect for your talents and our commitment to ideals of the university by not faking grades and honors for you. Given current attitudes about affirmative action, accepting this position will probably have drawbacks as well as advantages.[18] It is an opportunity and a responsibility offered neither

---

18 How severe these drawbacks are will, of course, depend upon the particular means of affirmative action that is selected and how appropriate these are for the situation. For example, if, to meet mandated quotas, high-ranked colleges and universities offer special admission to students not expected to succeed, then they may well be misleading those students into a wasteful and humiliating experience when those students could have succeeded and thrived at lower-ranked

as charity nor as entitlement, but rather as part of a special effort to welcome and encourage minorities and women to participate more fully in the university at all levels. We believe that this program affirms some of the best ideals implicit in our history without violating the rights of any applicants. We hope that you will choose to accept the position in this spirit as well as for your own benefit."

The appropriate message is no doubt harder to communicate to those who stand to lose some traditional advantages under a legitimate affirmative action program. But if we set aside practical difficulties and suppose that the proper message could be sincerely given and accepted as such, what would it say? Ideally, it would convey an understanding of the moral reasoning for the program; perhaps, in summary, it would be something like the following.

"These are the concerns that we felt made necessary the policy under which the university is temporarily giving special attention to women and minorities. We respect your rights to formal justice and to a policy guided by the university's educational and research mission as well as its social responsibilities. Our policy in no way implies the view that your opportunities are less important than others', but we estimate (roughly, as we must) that as a white male you have probably had advantages and encouragement that for a long time have been systematically, unfairly, insultingly unavailable to most women and minorities. We deplore invidious race and gender distinctions; we hope that no misunderstanding of our program will prolong them. Unfortunately, nearly all blacks and women have been disadvantaged to some degree by bias against their groups, and it is impractical for universities to undertake the detailed investigations that would be needed to assess how much particular individuals have suffered or gained from racism and sexism. We appeal to you to share the historical values of fair opportunity and mutual respect that underlie this policy and hope that, even though its effects may be personally disappointing, you can see the policy as an appropriate response to the current situation."

Unfortunately, as interests conflict and tempers rise, it is difficult to convey

educational institutions. This practice was explicitly rejected in the policies at Pomona College and at U.C.L.A. described in section I, but William Allen suggested to me in discussion that in his opinion the practice is quite common. The practice, I think, is unconscionable, and my argument in no way supports it.

Geoffrey Miller described in discussion another possible affirmative action program that would be quite inappropriate to the circumstances but again is not supported by the line of argument I have suggested. He asks us to imagine a "permanent underclass" of immigrants who are "genetically or culturally deficient" and as a result fail to succeed. Because we do not share a common social/cultural history of injustice resulting in their condition, the historical dimension of my case for affirmative action is missing. And because they are a "permanent" underclass, and thus the "genetic or cultural deficiencies" that result in their failure cannot be altered, one cannot argue that universities can help them or can even sincerely give them an encouraging "message" by affirmative action. This does not mean, however, that there are not other reasons for society to extend appropriate help. Also any suggestion that certain urban populations now *called* "permanent underclass" are accurately and fairly described by the "fictional" example is politically charged and needs careful examination.

this idea without giving an unintended message as well. White males unhappy about the immediate effects of affirmative action may read the policy as saying that "justice" is the official word for giving preferential treatment to whatever group one happens to favor. Some may see a subtext insinuating that blacks and women are naturally inferior and "cannot make it on their own." Such cynical readings reveal either misunderstanding or the willful refusal to take the moral reasoning underlying affirmative action seriously. They pose serious obstacles to the success of affirmative action – practical problems that may be more intractable than respectful moral disagreement and counterargument. But some types of affirmative action invite misunderstanding and suspicion more than others. For this reason, anyone who accepts the general case for affirmative action suggested here would do well to reexamine in detail the means by which they hope to communicate its message.[19]

19 Although my aim in this paper has been to survey general types of argument for thinking that some sort of affirmative action is needed, rather than to argue for any particular program, one cannot reasonably implement the general idea without considering many contextual factors that I have set aside here. Thus, though the moral perspective suggested here seems to favor the second method described in section I (recruitment, special funds, accountability) over the first method (proportionality given a fixed lower standard), the need for more detailed discussion is obvious.

Index